Blink

Blink

A STORY ABOUT THE RAPTURE

A Novel

Angela L. Rodriguez

Copyright 2017 Angela L. Rodriguez

www.67owls.com

All rights reserved. No part of this book may be reproduced or transmitted in any form or by any means, electronic or mechanical, including photocopying, recording, or by any information storage and retrieval system without pre-written permission of the publisher except where permitted by law.

Some Scripture quotations are taken from the Holy Bible: King James Version. Cambridge Edition: 1769; King James Bible online, 2015. www.kingjamesbible-online.org

Some Scriptures taken from the Holy Bible, New International Version, NIV. Copyright 1973, 1978,1984, 2011, by Biblica, Inc. Used by permission of Zondervan. All rights reserved worldwide, www.zondervan.com. The NIV and New International Version are trademarks registered in the United States Patent and Trademark Office by Biblica, Inc.

This novel is a work of fiction. Names, characters, places and incidents are used fictitiously. Historical facts were researched in order to keep the story relevant and up to date with current events, as well as events from the past. Scientific facts were researched as well.

Book Cover: Inspiration for the cover design provided by Dylan Rogers

ISBN-13: 9780997075793
ISBN-10: 0997075791

67 Owls Publications
Orlando, Florida
This book is dedicated to Jesus Christ, King of Kings, Lord of Lords

Special Thanks To:
Karen Quiroz
Jennifer NeSmith
Barb Stukey
Tracy Mendoza
Tammie Bucher
Holly Shever
Natalie and Dylan Rogers
Catherine Simmons
Christine Jenkins
Vivian and Aida Katz
Linda Meredith "Mom"
Brenda McEwen, and Jennifer
Bruce and Julie Mayhew, Bethany, Abbey and Olivia
Hank and Tiffany Nielsen, Kayla and Mckenzie
Hector, Brandon and Jonah Rodriguez

Without the encouragement of my friends and family I would have stopped writing. Thank you for believing in me, and keeping me on track.

Those who hope in the Lord will renew their strength. They will soar on wings like eagles; they will run and not grow weary, they will walk and not be faint. Isaiah 40:31

Foreword

§

I DIDN'T PLAN ON WRITING this book. I had already written an 824 page book called *What are The Chances? The Uncanny Connections Between Titanic, 9-11, Israel and the United States*. Writing that colossal book took so much time and energy! After I was done with it, *I felt like I'd written the Titanic!*

But, about six months after I published the book something strange happened. It all began with a hawk. Yes, a hawk! Let me explain….

For years I had been studying birds of prey- also known as **raptors**. I was fascinated with how they catch their prey. Birds of prey (raptors) such as hawks, falcons, eagles and owls swoop down swiftly to catch their prey. Sometimes they grab their prey mid-air. The agility and accuracy of these birds is truly remarkable. The prey is snatched in the **blink of an eye**. Falcons can dive in a stoop and snatch their prey at speeds of over 200 miles per hour.

The more I thought about **raptors**, the more I thought of a spectacular event described in the Bible known as the **rapture**. 1 Corinthians 15:51,52 says, "Listen, I tell you a mystery: We will not all sleep, but we will all be changed-**in a flash, in the twinkling of an eye, at the last trumpet**. For the trumpet will sound, the dead will be raised imperishable, and we will be changed."

Matthew 24, 39-41 says, "That is how it will be at the coming of the Son of Man. Two men will be in the field; one **will be taken** and the other left. Two women will be grinding with a hand mill; one **will be taken** and the other left."

In 1 Thessalonians 4:15-17 it says, "According to the Lord's word, we tell you that we who are still alive, who are left until the coming of the Lord, will certainly not precede those who have fallen asleep. For the Lord himself will come down from heaven, with a loud command, with the voice of the archangel and with the trumpet call of God, and the dead in Christ will rise first. After that, we who are still alive and are left **will be caught up together** with them in the clouds to meet the Lord **in the air.** And so we will be with the Lord forever."

The amazing event being described in the verses above is known as the **RAPTURE**. The Bride of Christ (true followers of Jesus Christ) are snatched away, or taken in the blink of an eye. The Groom (Jesus Christ) comes to steal his Bride away at a time when most people are unaware. The Bible says he will come like a "thief in the night."

Though the Bible does not use the word rapture, it uses the word **harpazo**, which means **TO SEIZE, CATCH UP, SNATCH AWAY** (reference: Strong's Concordance). It can also mean **to take by force, or to steal or plunder.**

The word rapture is used to describe this event because this is what the word means. The word rapture is derived from a Latin word called *rapio*, which means to seize or snatch away.

Raptors are birds that seize or snatch their prey. The name is derived in this same way. It is taken from late Middle English (from Latin) and is translated as **plunderer.** Sounds a lot like a "thief in the night", right? Certainly when a raptor snatches its prey it is, in essence, *stealing it*.

Now, back to the hawk I mentioned earlier. One day I was walking with my friend (who already knew I was fascinated with raptors) and we had an encounter with a beautiful hawk (*a raptor*) eating a large squirrel. He was out in the open- literally a few feet in front of us. This experience amazed me because I was able to observe the raptor up close. Our eyes met and I instantly felt a strange connection. My friend and I snapped several photos. You will see one of the photos in the back of this book.

The next day I went back to the spot where I saw the raptor. I wanted to see if there were any bones left behind from the squirrel the hawk had eaten. It had just finished raining, but I wasn't concerned. The sky looked clear. So, I walked over to the spot where I saw the raptor and looked for any evidence of the squirrel carcass. To my shock, as I was observing the area where the raptor sighting took place, I heard a loud crack and boom, and then I saw sparks! I was almost struck by lightning as I stood there looking for the bones/carcass! The incident scared me to death, *but I knew it meant something.*

After the lightning strike, unusual things kept occurring. It was similar to what happened to me when I wrote the other book, *What Are the Chances?*

As time went on, I realized there was a message being formed from all the supernatural experiences. I could tell it was all about the rapture. It was about the Lord's Feasts, and the stories of the Bible pointing to the rapture. It was also about the "one new man" described in Ephesians. The Jew and Gentile are the "one new man". The connection of the two was essential to understanding the Lord's symbolism with the rapture.

Lots of things contained in this book really happened such as: the hawk and eagle sighting, the lightning strike, the verse sent after the lightning strike, my son becoming a glider pilot, and the details of some of the dreams described, *to name a few.*

One of my favorite "signs" was when the Lord placed it upon my heart to read *The Hiding Place*, by Corrie ten Boom. I was already familiar with the book so I couldn't figure out why I needed to read it. Still, I felt the "urging" so I went ahead and read it. During that same time I found out some amazing information about the Jewish holiday known as *Rosh Hashanah, or the Feast of Trumpets.* The same week I finished reading **The Hiding Place**, I found out Rosh Hashanah is also called **the Hidden Day**. You will have to read to book to find out why that's important!

Another strange occurrence happened after I finished reading *The Hiding Place.* I just happened to take my son to a brand new doctor to get his tonsils out after finishing the book. I was sitting in the waiting room and I looked over to my right. I saw a wall with a faux (fake) hole in it. It was situated behind the doctor's office, but you could see it easily through the window. *It looked a lot like the hole in the wall described in The Hiding Place. Corrie ten Boom's family used this hidden opening in the wall to hide the Jews from the Nazis.* **In fact, I'd just looked at the picture in the book that morning.** The wall behind the doctor's office was there for ornamental purposes, but it reminded me of the picture I'd *just seen* in the book. I thought maybe it was just a coincidence. But, then I met the doctor. **He just happened to be from Israel and was Jewish.** He told me he had lived all over Israel. At that point I figured there were too many coincidences to be coincidences. I was definitely meant to read that book again. A similar situation happened when I read **The Diary of Anne Frank**. I knew I was supposed to read it, and after I read it I felt certain about the message, and what I was supposed to write about it. You will have to read to find out.

Lots more happened than I have time to write about- LOTS MORE! But, let's just say everything I wrote in this book had inspiration from a situation, or was prompted by the Holy Spirit.

As usual, writing this kind of book took a lot of research and creativity. I try to teach you things I've learned through characters and events- some are fictional people and places, while others are real people I know, and places I went.

My goal with this book is not to pinpoint any dates for the rapture. No one knows that date except the Father in heaven. My goal is for you to see the powerful symbolism of the rapture that God has already used within the Bible, and his Holy Feasts. I am also trying to explain the way the Lord showed me. One thing I've learned about God is that he is mysterious and he doesn't think the way we think. He is very clever, and sometimes he doesn't lay it all out in black and white.

The Bible itself has many layers. As you peel each one back, you find more information. Mysteries are revealed in each layer. We only have to ask God to show us, and be available for him to use us. We don't have to be biblical scholars. We can be fisherman, teachers, housewives or even electricians (you'll understand that one later).

After you read this book you will probably take a second look at raptors. Since I began writing the book I see them every day! Perhaps the same thing will happen to you! Oh, and you might take a second look at lightning too!

Come take a journey with me to find out about a spectacular future event known as the rapture. But don't **BLINK,** or you could miss it.

*At the end of some chapters there are **Author's Notes**. These are special notes added by me to give you extra knowledge and insight. Sometimes it's too difficult to weave every detail into the story. This is my way of getting it all in so you have a full picture. They are mainly extra facts and ideas, but I suggest reading them because they provide important details.*

This book is inspired by BENJAMIN, the beautiful red tailed hawk in my neighborhood. Seeing him soar through the sky gives me great joy on my daily walks………………

Special thanks to all the residents of Lake Lagrange Heights! You never thought your neighborhood would be the subject of a book did you? Lagrange in French means Barn or Granary. In the Bible, the barn or granary is associated with the agricultural harvest. The agricultural harvest is used in the Bible to illustrate the harvest of God's people. One day God's people will be harvested from the earth at an event known as the Rapture. After the Rapture, other harvests will take place- each one with specific and symbolic timing. Which harvest will you be part of?

Table of Contents

	Foreword	vii
Chapter 1	The Hawk	1
Chapter 2	Jolted	4
Chapter 3	The Eagle	8
Chapter 4	The Book	14
Chapter 5	The Hiding Place	17
Chapter 6	Soaring	21
Chapter 7	The Hidden Day	26
Chapter 8	The Thief	33
Chapter 9	Alarm	38
Chapter 10	Appointments	42
Chapter 11	The Wedding	45
Chapter 12	Jericho	54
Chapter 13	Camping Out	60
Chapter 14	Dreaming	64
Chapter 15	Rahab	67
Chapter 16	The Mystery of the Shofar	75
Chapter 17	The Voice of the Trumpet	83
Chapter 18	The Potter's Field	89
Chapter 19	Lightning	94
Chapter 20	New York	103
Chapter 21	Trump Tower	113
Chapter 22	Grand Central Station	123
Chapter 23	Water Landing	129

Chapter 24	Wall Street	133
Chapter 25	Golden Eagle	138
Chapter 26	Raptors	145
Chapter 27	The Final Battle	150
Chapter 28	Flight 1549	155
Chapter 29	The Diary	173
Chapter 30	Grace	176
Chapter 31	PI	190
Chapter 32	Eclipse	194
Chapter 33	Civil War	210
Chapter 34	Connections	219
Chapter 35	The Field	226
Chapter 36	Harvest and Redemption	229
Chapter 37	Magnolia	245
Chapter 38	The Gate	249
Chapter 39	Western Wall	256
Chapter 40	Blink	262

The Pledge of Allegiance · 271
The Mystery of 13 · 275
Amazing Information about the 2017, 2024 Total
Solar Eclipses · 279
The Lord's Feast Known as Shavuot · · · · · · · · · · · · · 283
Revelation about Psalm 91 · 289
Notes about Trumpets · 295
Hebrew Months Corresponding with Western
(Gregorian) Calendar Months · · · · · · · · · · · · · · · · · · · 301
Dates for Rosh Hashanah (Feast of Trumpets) and
Yom Kippur (Day of Atonement) for the Next
Eight Years 2017- 2024 · 303
More Eclipse Facts · 307
Bibliography: · 309
Photos · 311

CHAPTER 1
The Hawk

IT WAS A BEAUTIFUL SUMMER evening. The sky resembled cotton candy with its swirly pink, orange and blue streaks. A breeze circulated with wispy bursts of air. It seemed like fall, not the middle of summer. Ruthie walked over to her neighbor's house, glad she was be able to take a long walk with her friend on an evening like this.

As soon as she stepped foot in the driveway, her neighbor Jennifer appeared. She was ready for a serious workout. Ruthie and Jennifer immediately started walking and chatting about the news, the weather and anything that popped into their minds. Before they knew it they were at the front of their neighborhood, right near the neighborhood entrance stone marker, which read *Lake Lagrange Heights*. As they continued talking, they barely noticed what was sitting on the entrance marker. It was large and fierce- its eyes glaring and staring straight ahead. Something red dripped from its beak, along with a white, stringy substance.

That's when Ruthie and Jennifer looked up. Startled out of conversation, they spied the mysterious bird.

"Whoa! Will you look at that!" whispered Jennifer, in a somewhat frantic tone.

"Whoa is right! It's a hawk! And he's right there on the neighborhood entrance sign, just out in the open!"

"Yeah, and he's tearing apart his evening meal!"

"Ugh gross, is that a squirrel?"

"Yes, and it's a fresh one! It looks like he just killed it," Jennifer observed.

At that point the hawk had stopped eating the fresh squirrel he'd caught. His eyes were glued on Ruthie and Jennifer. Did he perceive them as a threat? Would he attack? Just one look at his sharp talons made a person worry. If he could snatch a squirrel with those talons, could he do the same to a human? No, that's silly. He couldn't lift a human. But, he could use those sharp talons to attack. He could surely scratch out an eye!

As Ruthie stood pondering these things, Jennifer poked her in the rib and said, "We might want to move to the other side of the road. I think he's worried we're after his dinner."

"Uh, yeah, you're right," Ruthie stuttered. "Wait, we've got to get a picture. We can't let this moment slip by without documenting it."

"Well get the picture fast before **we** become his dinner!"

Ruthie could barely get her phone out to take the picture. Her hands were shaking with both fear and excitement. In the time it took her to grab the phone and snap one photo, Jennifer had already snapped at least six.

"Great, we've got pictures. Now let's get out of here," suggested Jennifer.

They made their way to the other side of the street, never taking their eyes off the hawk. It continued staring, a piece of squirrel flesh hanging from his sharp beak.

"That was amazing, but also kind of ominous," Jennifer stated.

"There's something more to this than meets the eye," answered Ruthie.

"What do you mean?"

"Just give me some time. Something else is going on here. I just have to think it through."

"What's there to think about? A large hawk killed its prey, and we witnessed it eating its meal."

"Yeah, that's what *we saw*. But I'm not so sure that's what it means," Ruthie insisted.

"Well, you let me know when you find out. As of now I'm remembering this moment as a *one of a kind* encounter with nature up close!"

Just then Ruthie and Jennifer heard a loud screeching sound. They looked in the sky and noticed a beautiful hawk circling overhead.

"Guess he's finished with his dinner," Jennifer said.

"Maybe he's finished, but somehow I think this is just the beginning."

CHAPTER 2
Jolted

THE NEXT DAY RUTHIE COULDN'T get the incident off her mind. She kept picturing the hawk. He really was a beautiful bird- so graceful, yet mysterious and stoic. Why did she think there was more to *seeing* this bird? What message did he bring? He was just a bird after all.

After scouring her brain for an answer, she decided to let well enough alone. Perhaps she was putting too much thinking into this. She had better things to do than letting her time be monopolized by a bird.

She decided to pull up the daily news on her phone. It was always important to keep up with world events. She was just reading through an article on the Syrian crisis when Michael walked into the kitchen.

"Mom, I'm starving. Can we go out for lunch today? I'm craving Mediterranean food."

"Didn't you just eat?"

"That was two hours ago," he retorted.

She started to argue, but remembered Michael would only be here a short time. Why not spoil him a little.

"Sure, that would be fine. Just give me a few minutes."

Michael was on leave from the Air Force Academy for a few more days. It was great to spend time with him again. Most of the year, he was away at school in Colorado. She missed having him at home, even if he was hungry every minute of the day. Feeding him every two hours was a small sacrifice.

Ruthie grabbed her purse and she and Michael were out the door. When they arrived at *Jerusalem Grille* they were happy to find they were the only ones in line. It was a quick and easy meal to grab. When they stepped out the door to leave, it was another story. Rain was pouring down.

"Where did the rain come from?" questioned Michael. "It was sunny and clear when we walked into *Jerusalem Grille*."

"You got me. Let's just make a run for it."

They both bolted to the car, getting completely drenched in the process.

"Ugh, I'm soaked," Michael complained.

Ruthie looked at her shoes. They were sopping wet. Nonetheless, at least their food was warm and they could just change when they got home.

Strangely enough, the rain stopped as abruptly as it began. No sooner had they driven out of the parking lot when the rain ceased.

"Weird. It starts in a flash, and stops in a flash," Michael said.

"You know Florida weather. It's bipolar."

As Ruthie drove into her neighborhood she couldn't help but notice the neighborhood entrance stone marker. That's where the hawk stared her down while eating its prey yesterday. Suddenly, she wondered if the hawk had left any bones behind from the squirrel it devoured. She felt the urge to look on top of the stone entrance sign. She parked the car on the other side of the street.

"Michael, I'm going to check something real quick. Just stay here for a second."

"Yeah, ok. I'll wait."

Out of the car she jumped, walking right over to the neighborhood entrance stone marker. She inspected the top of it carefully. The stone platform the hawk had stood upon yesterday was completely bare. No bones. Not even a clump of fur left behind. She inspected the crevices between the stones to make sure nothing fell between the cracks. Not a trace of the squirrel carcass was left. She turned to face Michael, who was waiting in the car. Within seconds of turning around she heard a loud boom, then a series of shrill, ear-blasting cracks. The next thing she knew, sparks were flying all around her. Stunned, she could barely move. Lightning had struck. Had she been hit? She glanced to her right, noticing the street sign, which stood near the neighborhood entrance stone marker. The metal street sign, which said **KINGFISHER DRIVE**, was moving back and forth, as if jolted by the lightning.

"Mom, get in the car!" Michael shouted.

She realized he was right. She needed to get out of there now! She bolted for the car, barely able to breathe.

"Did you see what happened?" asked Ruthie.

"I think you were almost struck by lightning!"

Ruthie was shaking. He was right. The lightning had been so close, possibly a few feet away.

"Actually, I think it struck somewhere between the neighborhood entrance stone marker and the Kingfisher street sign. I saw sparks around you, and around the sign and stone marker."

Ruthie could barely talk. What did it mean? The hawk had been on the neighborhood entrance stone marker the day before. Now lightning had struck in the same area.

That's when Ruthie noticed Michael's shirt. *It had a lightning bolt on it.*

"Michael, your shirt has a lightning bolt on it," she said.

"Yeah, it's my Air Force Academy T- shirt. Some of our shirts have lightning bolts on them because our mascot is the falcon. The falcon is the fastest animal in the world. Lightning and falcons are both super swift."

"The falcon is a **raptor** also," Ruthie added.

"Huh? What does that have to do with anything?"

She was going to explain about the hawk she saw the day before- *the raptor*. Both hawks and falcons were raptors, or birds of prey. They are known for snatching their prey at lightning speed. Raptors are fast and accurate. **Their prey is snatched in the blink of an eye, sometimes mid-air**. But, she didn't have time to explain all the details.

"What are the chances that you almost get hit by lightning, and I have a lightning bolt on my shirt?" asked Michael, laughing.

Ruthie thought it was odd to say the least. Yet, as she presumed the day before, there was more to this incident than the obvious. There was definitely a message here, *but what message?*

Author's Notes:

A bird of prey is also known as a **raptor.** Examples of birds of prey, or raptors, are hawks, eagles, osprey, vultures, owls, and falcons. Raptors snatch their prey from the air or the ground, and then eat it.

Lightning (*baraq*) is defined in Strong's Biblical Concordance as a bright, glittering sword, or a flashing sword.

CHAPTER 3
The Eagle

Ruthie walked in the door, drenched from the rain, and still shaken by the lightning incident. Michael grabbed his food and went off to watch T.V. She was hungry, but she couldn't settle into eating just yet. Her mind was spinning. The lightning strike was no accident. It was a message. But what did it mean?

Before she could ponder the answer, her phone started beeping. A text message. It was from her friend Esther. It said, ***"For as lightning cometh out of the east, and shineth even unto the west; so shall also the coming of the Son of man be." Matthew 24:27***

She was puzzled. What did that mean? She thought for a moment. "Let's see, lightning is very fast. It shines in the sky from one end to the other. It can come without warning, and with great power," she thought. She paused for a few moments.

"Oh, I got it! The Son of man is Jesus! When he returns it will be fast, just like lightning flashing quickly across the sky. And technically lightning happens when a cloud becomes electrically charged. When Jesus returns he will be riding on the clouds," she thought to herself.

But how did Esther know she was almost struck by lightning? Only Michael knew. What strange timing. Even stranger was that Michael had a lightning bolt on his shirt today.

"Why did you send this verse?" Ruthie texted Esther.

"Studying the book of Matthew today. It's about the return of Jesus. Thought it was a cool verse."

It was a cool verse, but how uncanny for Esther to pick that particular one. If the lightning strike hadn't *just happened*, maybe it wouldn't be a big deal. But, Ruthie knew *timing was everything with God*. There was more to this. She had to figure out what it was.

She decided to look it up the verse in the book of Matthew. She read all of Matthew 24 to get a full context of the verse. After reading, she was astonished.

The chapter begins with Jesus talking to the disciples about the destruction of the Temple. Shortly afterward, the disciples begin asking Jesus what things will happen at the "end of the Age", or when the world is nearing its end. They also ask Jesus about the signs of his imminent return to earth. Jesus explains that many things must happen before he returns. He warns about the coming of many false prophets and Anti Christs. He emphasizes the spread of war, and how nations will fight each other. He says there will be famines, earthquakes, and rampant diseases spreading all over the Earth. He says the people of God will be persecuted, killed and hated because of his name. Sadly, the love of most people will become cold and dark during this time. Jesus goes on to explain there will be great tribulation for all who dwell upon the Earth, and a great deception will take place that will fool even the elect. Next, it mentions the verse about lightning.

"For as lightning cometh out of the east, and shineth even unto the west; so shall the coming of the Son of man be."

Ruthie thought about the verses preceding the "lightning verse". They were all describing things she had seen in just the last few years. But, her generation wasn't the only ones to see things like this. The verse about wars stood out as something common to all generations. Wars had been going on since sin entered the world. Some were worse than others. What about the World War II generation? Surely they must have thought it was the "end of age" when Hitler was in power, and the world was in chaos. Yet, here we were, over 70 years later, and Jesus hadn't returned. War continued up to this very day, without a pause.

But what about the natural disasters Jesus mentioned? Every time she turned on the news there was a report about a tornado, hurricane, earthquake, or some sort of massive flooding. Natural disasters were on the rise. She had been documenting these events for the past few years. The United States alone had experienced record breaking hurricanes such as *Katrina* and *Sandy* in the last decade, not to mention some of the busiest hurricane seasons in history. Winter storms were at their maximum in 2014 and 2015, according to weather records. Droughts and fires plagued the west, while floods ravaged the South and Midwest. Earthquakes had devastated several countries such as Japan, Nepal and Italy, resulting in widespread death and injury. There were earthquakes happening in the United States as well. Is this what Jesus was warning about in Matthew 24?

What about when Jesus talked about diseases, or pestilences? Did he mean diseases like cancer, Zika or even autism and Alzheimer's? These diseases and conditions were now widespread. Everyone knew someone with one or more of these disorders. Those were only a few examples.

The part of Matthew 24 that stuck in her mind the most was when it said, "the love of most will grow cold." Truly this was becoming an epidemic. She saw so much loss and death in the world. Divorce, abuse, drug addiction, greed and overwhelming stress were just a few of the issues that plagued our society. Day by day Ruthie saw the flame of love dwindling in the eyes of those she loved. She could see many people had lost hope. The world was becoming darker, and love seemed harder to find.

In Matthew 24 Jesus said his followers would be persecuted and killed. Right now Christians around the world were being killed by terrorist groups like ISIS and Al Qaeda. Attacks and bombings were commonplace around the world, and even in the United States. A civil war was raging in Syria, destroying the lives of Christians and Muslims alike. Yes, Jesus' words were ringing true in this day and age. How close were we to his return?

She looked back at the lightning verse. Her eyes wandered to the verse listed *right after it*. It said, **"For wheresoever the carcass is, there will the eagles be gathered together."**

"What does that mean?" she thought. "Eagles gathering around a carcass?"

"Hey Mom, check this picture out on Facebook!" Michael interrupted. *Ruthie was startled out of thought.*

"Huh? What are you talking about? Facebook?" Michael rushed over with his phone. He shoved the phone in her face.

"Check out this eagle photo! He's sitting right on top of the electrical pole in our neighborhood!"

"What? Let me see!" She snatched the phone from Michael's hands.

She stared at the picture. She couldn't believe it. There was a photo of a beautiful eagle, with its wings outstretched, perched on an electrical pole.

"This picture was taken in *our neighborhood?* Where exactly?"

"It says it was taken in front our neighborhood entrance stone marker. You know, the one that says *Lake Lagrange Heights*. Our neighbor Shannon took the photo."

"Wait, isn't that where lightning almost struck me? I was right next to the *Lake Lagrange* neighborhood entrance marker, and near our street sign, *Kingfisher Drive*."

"This happened near the other *Lake Lagrange* neighborhood entrance marker- the one near Raeford and Dawley Street. Remember, we have <u>two</u> entrances to the neighborhood, and both have stone markers."

Michael was right. There were two neighborhood entrance stone markers. One was located on her street- *Kingfisher Drive*. The other was located on *Dawley and Raeford Street*, on the other side of the neighborhood. That was interesting. There were **two raptors** spotted on or near these markers in the last two days. The hawk (which is a raptor) was on the *Lake Lagrange* stone marker the day before. Today, there was an eagle (also a raptor) spotted by the other *Lake Lagrange* neighborhood stone marker. Lightning had almost hit Ruthie as she was standing near the *Lake Lagrange* neighborhood entrance marker on Kingfisher Drive. Now, here was this eagle sitting on an electrical pole by the other *Lake Lagrange* entrance marker at Dawley Street. Lightning is a form of electricity and this eagle was on an electrical pole…. so were these two sightings connected?

She looked back at the verse again. It said, **"Wheresoever the carcass is, there will the eagles be gathered together."**

What were the chances Michael pulled up the eagle photo at the same time she was reading the verse about the eagles? She closed her eyes. A thought crossed her mind.

In the verse it said ***there was a carcass***. A carcass! That's was it! Yesterday, when she and Jennifer spotted the hawk on the *Lagrange* neighborhood entrance marker, it had been eating **a carcass- a squirrel carcass**! That was strange. The verse mentioned an eagle and a carcass, *yet it was the hawk that had a carcass*. The eagle on the electrical pole *didn't have a carcass*. Still, they were **both raptors and they were both on, or near the *Lake Lagrange* neighborhood entrance markers**.

What did it mean? What kind of a riddle was this?

"Mom…….hey Mom! Hello? Is anyone there?"

"What? Can't you see I'm trying to think?" Ruthie grumbled.

"Think about what? Did that lightning strike go to your head?" Michael laughed.

She sighed. She couldn't explain if she tried.

"Yeah, you are probably right Michael. I think I need a nap."

"You didn't even eat your food."

"I know. I'm not in the mood."

"I can take it off your hands if you're not hungry."

"Be my guest."

Why couldn't the Lord just spell things out in plain English? Why all the puzzles? The only thing she could gather is that in the Bible **Jesus did talk in parables**. Perhaps this was the same sort of thing. A parable about raptors, lightning, street signs and neighborhood markers. Whatever it was, she would do her best to figure it out. For now, she needed to rest. That would clear her mind, or so she thought.

Author's Notes: To see the picture of the hawk and the neighborhood entrance stone marker, turn to the back of this book and look under PHOTOS. There is also a picture of the eagle.

CHAPTER 4
The Book

Ruthie felt exhausted mentally. She knew there was something the Lord was trying to tell her, yet she couldn't quite piece it all together. She only had a few pieces of the puzzle. She wasn't Einstein! She needed more clues. At this point in her life she had grown accustomed to the way God worked. He was quite an enigma. His ways were definitely not her ways. Revelations weren't as simple as one two three. They often involved some sort of wild goose chase, or a trek into the unknown. Sometimes she felt like she was in the movie *National Treasure*.

There was no sense in fighting it. She had to go with it. In time, she would figure it out. For now she needed to rest. Just a short nap is all she needed. She lay down on her bed and within seconds she fell asleep.

Immediately she found herself adorned in a beautiful wedding dress. Layers of lace covered the dress, with rows of tiny pearls. Specks of crystal-like glitter radiated from the dress and illuminated the room. Where did she get this beautiful dress? It didn't look like the one she'd wore on her wedding day. This one was more elegant. More regal. She had never seen one like it before. Why was she wearing it?

She looked to her right and she saw a lamp. The brightness of it enveloped her. She picked up the lamp and realized it was ancient- not a lamp of today's world. This one had a long wick, and was filled to the rim with oil. She carefully picked it up, so as not to spill the oil.

Suddenly she heard a loud, almost piercing shout. Her heart skipped a beat. Next, she heard the sound of a trumpet blasting. The walls around her shook. She knew something amazing was about to take place.

And that's when she saw him. He burst into the room, grabbed her by the arm, and off she went in the blink of an eye. It happened so quickly. All she could see and feel was light- pure, unhindered light.

She woke up with an amazing feeling of peace. What just happened in that dream? Who was she marrying? After all, she was already married! But, she had on a wedding dress. Someone came and took her away. She saw a flash of light….almost as if lightning had….

"Mom, are you awake?" Michael asked, gently knocking on the door.

"Yes, I'm up. What's going on?"

"Nothing. Just wanted to give you this package. It was on the front doorstep."

"Where did it come from?"

"I don't know. I just stepped outside to feed the cats and it was lying there on our doorstep."

Ruthie looked at the package. It was just a simple manila envelope with no markings on it. She opened it, curious about the contents.

It was a book called *The Hiding Place*, by Corrie ten Boom.

"I know this book," said Ruthie. In fact, she checked this book out last year. But, she returned it long ago. Yet, here it was again.

"Where did the book come from?" Michael asked.

"There's no return address, or any markings for that matter," Ruthie stated, puzzled.

"Well, that doesn't make any sense. Books don't just land on your doorstep."

Ruthie looked over the book. She had read it before. It was an amazing story. Corrie ten Boom and her family rescued hundreds of Jewish people during World War II. The family hid the Jews in a secret "hole" they made in the wall of their home. Why was she receiving this book again?

"Maybe someone wants you to read that book," Michael suggested.

"Yes, I think you're right. But who?"

Ruthie chuckled to herself. Did she really ask the question who? By now she knew things didn't just happen. The master of all puzzles and parables was sending her another message. She knew she better get to reading the book again. She must have missed something the first time. Chances are, she would find a *new piece* of the puzzle.

CHAPTER 5
The Hiding Place

§

Ruthie didn't waste any time starting the book. She dove right in, finishing it in a matter of hours. When she was done she sat there trying to figure out what she'd gleaned this time, versus the first time she had read it. Of course, it was just as good the second time as the first. But, there had to be a reason the Lord wanted her to read it again.

She decided to flip through the pages of the book. Actually, there were several pictures inside it. Maybe there was something about the pictures. She studied each one, looking for any hidden clues. She had just turned the page when she saw it. It was a picture of Corrie ten Boom standing by the hole in the wall where the Jews were hidden. This hole had been in Corrie's bedroom and was cleverly disguised to look like a regular wall. But behind the wall was a hiding place, with room for seven or more people. When the Nazis came to search the house, they never found the hiding place. *Hundreds of lives had been saved because of this hiding place.*

Ruthie stared at the picture. In the picture, Corrie ten Boom was older. She was standing by the hole in the wall. Behind the hole you could see bits and pieces of the hiding place that once saved so many lives. At the time of the picture, Corrie's bedroom and house had been turned into a museum. Thousands of visitors were able to pass through the museum each year, just to get a glimpse of the hiding place.

As she stared at the hiding place in the wall, two words resounded in her spirit. The words were **HIDING PLACE**. She thought this was strange. Why the words hiding place? Wasn't that obvious? That's what the book was called.

She thought about Corrie ten Boom's favorite verse- *Psalm 119:114* which says, **"You are my hiding place and my shield; I hope in your word."**

"Well, God is our hiding place because we can go to him anytime we have a problem," she said to herself. "And there's also Psalm 91 which says, 'He who dwells in the shelter of the Most High will dwell in the shadow of the Almighty. I will say of you Lord you are my refuge and fortress.' So, that verse is saying God is our refuge, or **our hiding place**."

She felt like she was on the right track. Yet, something was missing. Something big.

"Hey you!" said Ruthie's husband Thomas, as he peeked in the room. "Are you *hiding* from me? I've been calling you for the last three hours! Did you lose your phone? Jonah and I finished our zoo trip and wanted to take you and Michael to dinner."

"Oh, I'm sorry. I must have left my phone in the kitchen."

"Well, get up and let's go eat."

"Did someone say eat?" Michael interrupted.

Ruthie shook her head. What else was new? Did he ever get full?

Within a few minutes she was up and ready. They all started out the door when Thomas noticed Jonah was missing.

"Oh great, where is he? I'm starving! Now we gotta track him down," Michael complained.

"Jonah! Jonah!" screamed Thomas.

"I'll go find him," Ruthie said.

She searched all over the house, calling his name. Where could he be? She listened intently, hoping to hear something that would tip her off to his whereabouts.

She heard a scratching sound. It was coming from the den. She looked around. Where was he? She inched closer to the couch. It sounded like it was coming from the wall *behind the couch*. As she walked closer, she could see the back end of Jonah's body sticking out.

"What are you doing down there?" she asked, frustrated, but interested.

"Look, I found a secret passage. It's here in the wall," Jonah shrieked with excitement.

"Huh? We don't have any secret passages."

"Yes we do. Look Mom," he said, pointing to a large hole in the wall.

"What in the world?" Ruthie said. "Why is there a hole in the wall?"

"Are you guys coming or what?" complained Thomas as he entered the den.

"Thomas, how come you never told me about this hole in the wall? What's it doing here?"

"Oh that? I'm working on some electrical wiring for the Christmas lights, so I had to cut through the wall to…"

Ruthie cut him off. "I can't believe you cut a hole in the wall! I sure hope you plan on…" She stopped herself mid-sentence.

"I just needed to get through the wall to do some new wiring for the lights. There's no electrical panels on the right side of the house, so I have to run wires from the attic through this wall. I plan on fixing the hole in the wall after I get the wiring done. I started it yesterday and forgot to tell you," Thomas explained.

Suddenly Ruthie wasn't mad. She thought about the timing of this "hole in the wall." How could it be that Thomas just cut this hole in the wall the day before she received the *Hiding Place* book? How could it be Jonah *just happened* to be trying to hide in the wall the same day she read the book again? There was no overlooking this. It couldn't be a coincidence.

"What do you mean you're going to cover it up Dad? It's the perfect hiding place," whined Jonah. "That stinks!"

"Sorry buddy. We can't just leave a hole in the wall," Thomas explained.

"Well at least I found something cool before you closed the hole up."

"You found something?" Thomas asked.

"Yep," Jonah said, holding up a beautiful gold watch.

"Where in the world did you get that?"

"Inside the hole," Jonah insisted.

"What? That can't be. Why would a watch be inside the wall?" Thomas asked, looking the watch over. "This isn't just any watch either. It looks like an antique. I bet this watch is 50 years old."

Ruthie was intrigued. Of all things to find- *a watch*. At that moment she thought of something amazing. Corrie ten Boom was a **watchmaker**. In fact, she was the first female licensed watchmaker in Holland. She had just finished reading *The Hiding Place*, by Corrie ten Boom, and then Jonah finds this watch in the wall. What were the chances of that?

"Dad, why are you trying to do the wiring for the Christmas lights in the middle of summer? Christmas is four months away," Michael asked. "No offense, but you usually wait till the eleventh hour to get things done."

"Good question. I really don't know. I just woke up yesterday and the idea popped in my head. I figured it was better sooner than later. I promised your Mom I would get the lights up on time this year for once."

Ruthie thought it was odd that Thomas would start wiring the lights so early. As Michael stated, it wasn't his way to start anything early. This was all **timing**. Too many things were falling into place at the right time. She smiled as she looked at Jonah holding the watch. **TIMING**- isn't that what watches are for?

CHAPTER 6

Soaring

THE NEXT DAY WHEN RUTHIE awoke she felt uneasy. An unknown mystery lay before her. How could she not want to solve it? Yet, she had no idea where to begin.

"Mom, I really want some donuts this morning," said Jonah, looking hopeful.

"Oh, I don't know. It's not like I need a donut. You can burn one off in a matter of minutes. I have to run around the block 20 times."

"Oh Mom, one won't hurt."

"That's the problem. I'm gonna want more than one."

"Hey, if you're getting donuts I want three glazed and one Boston Crème," Michael chimed in.

"Oh great! Now I'm outnumbered. Fine. Let's go before I change my mind."

It was no use arguing with two boys over donuts. Really, could she blame them? Secretly she planned on eating three, and yes, the extra exercise would be worth it.

She drove a few miles down the street to their favorite donut shop, *Bakery Plus*. They ordered a box of 12, just to make sure there was enough for everyone, and maybe leftovers (though leftovers was pushing it).

She pulled out of the donut shop and headed home, only to notice there was a road block.

"Are you kidding me? Weren't we just driving down this road? There wasn't a road block before, so why now?"

"Who cares, just take a different way," mumbled Michael, his mouth full of donut.

"Fine, I guess I'll take the long way. At least we have donuts to eat," she said, picking one up.

They drove for a few minutes, but Ruthie wasn't really focusing on the route. She was eating donuts and laughing with the kids.

"Mom, where are you going? I don't recognize this road. I think you took a wrong turn," Michael stated.

"Oh, I think you're right. Pull up your phone's map ap, and see if you can reroute me."

"Mom, look! Look over there!" Jonah shrieked.

"What? Where?"

"Over there! Over there!" he yelled, pointing at the sky.

"Whoa, that is so cool," Michael said, also pointing.

Suddenly she saw it too. A beautiful, large eagle was gliding through the air. It was flying in circles, but every now and then it would swoop down, only to resume its circling pattern.

"It's circling over the top of the church," Michael observed.

"Yeah, but what kind of church is that?" Jonah asked. "I don't see a cross, but I see some kind of star on the building. I've seen that star somewhere before."

"Yes, you have seen that star Jonah. It's the Star of David. The church you see is a Jewish Synagogue. It's where the Jewish people go to worship God."

"Oh, I remember now. But why don't they have a cross?"

"Well Jonah, it's an Orthodox Jewish Church so that means they don't believe Messiah has come yet. They are still waiting for their Messiah."

"You mean they don't know Jesus?" Jonah asked.

"Well, they don't know Jesus is their Messiah. They don't realize he already came over two thousand years ago and died on the cross for them."

"How come they don't realize it? Why?"

"Well, it's a lot to explain Jonah. There are many details I'd have to explain."

"Jonah, what Mom is trying to say is that Jesus is **HIDDEN** to them."

"What do you mean **HIDDEN?**" asked Jonah. "You mean they have to go find him?"

Ruthie felt goosebumps on her skin. Did Michael just say that Jesus, the Messiah, was HIDDEN from the Jewish people?

"You see, when Jesus died on the cross many Jews did believe he was their Passover lamb, or their Messiah. But many did not. If fact, he was crucified because the Pharisees (Jewish authorities) wanted him to die. They said he was breaking the law, and leading people astray."

"That's not fair. Why would they do that?"

"Jonah, like Mom said, it can get complicated. But the interesting thing is that Jesus, who is Jewish, **knew** he was going to die on the cross. His father (God) sent him to Earth to be the sacrifice for our sins. God sent him to save the Jewish people, and us. Jesus was **willing** to die for us."

"I don't really understand why they didn't believe. Why did you say it is **hidden** from them?"

"Well, after Jesus was crucified, there were still many Jews who would not accept the truth that he was the Messiah. Even though they were told in advance by the prophets what their Savior would be like, they didn't believe. They didn't recognize him. Because of this, they were given 'eyes that could not see.' It says in Romans 11, verse 8 they were given a 'spirit of slumber, eyes that could not see, and ears that would not hear; unto this very day.' I guess you could call it a *spiritual blindness*."

"Huh? I don't understand. Are you saying they just can't see the truth?"

"I told you it was complicated," said Michael.

But Ruthie knew what Michael was talking about. She knew Romans 11 well. That same chapter also said that God **would not forsake his**

people. Even though many were blinded to the truth of who Jesus was, God would wake them up one day. The great thing is that thousands were already waking up. In Israel many Messianic churches had been planted. Messianic synagogues were filled with Jewish people who knew the truth about Jesus. They accepted him as their Savior. Their eyes had been opened. In the United States there were more than 200 Messianic Churches. The spiritual blindness was slowly being lifted. One day the spiritual blindness would disappear.

"Jonah, because Messiah (Jesus) is hidden to many Jews, it is our job to help them see. We need to share Christ's love with them, and pray," Ruthie added. "We pray for their eyes and ears to be open to the gospel. And if their eyes do not open right away, that's ok too. No matter what, we are to love God's chosen people. Jesus will not be hidden to them forever."

"Mom, can you go back to where the eagle was flying? I only got to watch him for a minute?" Jonah asked.

"I suppose so," Ruthie said, turning the car around to drive back.

As they neared the synagogue again, they noticed the eagle had something in its beak.

"Hey, I think he has a fish in his mouth. Wow! That was quick. Wonder where he caught it?"

"Look, there's a lake behind the synagogue. That must be where he caught it."

"He must have really good eyesight to pull a fish right out of the water," Jonah said.

"Yeah, I think eagles are also called **fish hawks**. They are very fast, and can see up to 5 kilometers away. Catching fish is quite difficult because the fish are camouflaged by the water."

"Did you say an eagle is also called a **fish hawk**?" Ruthie asked. Something just clicked when he said that. An image of her street sign, **Kingfisher Drive** flashed in her mind. Then, she saw an image of the **hawk on the Lake Lagrange neighborhood marker**. Next, she pictured the **eagle that was on the electrical pole.**

"That's it," she said.

"What's it?" Michael asked.

She was on to something but she couldn't explain it yet. She wasn't 100% sure of what it was. Still, it was something. Another piece of the puzzle. She already knew one piece. Jesus, the Messiah of both the Jews and Gentiles, was **still hidden** from a large majority of the Jews. Was this what God was trying to tell her? No, that couldn't be the whole message. She already knew this because she was familiar with Romans 11, and what it said about Israel's spiritual blindness. No, there was more. But at least she was getting closer.

"I just read a quick article on my phone and it said fish are an eagle's main source of food. They live by lakes so they can always have a fresh supply. But, they've also been known to **steal fish** from other birds if they have to," Michael explained.

"Steal fish? I didn't know that."

"Also, it says no other bird can soar as high as the eagle. And, they can fly through storms. They can even fly above the storm if they have to."

"Sounds to me like the eagle is an extraordinary raptor. No wonder it's our national bird," she responded.

The eagle disappeared from sight. It flew across the lake and into a tree, too high to see from their viewpoint.

"Ah man. Now the eagle is **hidden**," Jonah said.

"Interesting choice of words," Ruthie thought.

"You know Mom, I always liked the verse that says, "Those who trust in the Lord will soar high on the wings of eagles," Michael said.

"I like that one too." Truly, she would have to trust God with this. In her own strength, she could do nothing. But, in his, the possibilities were as vast as the sky.

CHAPTER 7
The Hidden Day

HIDDEN. SURELY, IT WAS THE word of the day. Could it point to hidden treasure? Maybe. Yet, what sort of treasure? Knowledge could be treasure. Most people pictured pirates when they thought of treasure. But Ruthie was more of a researcher. In the past she had often searched for the spot that marked X. Instead of using a map, she found things in unexpected ways. It's not like she could follow coordinates. Sometimes she simply searched using the Internet. Why not give it a try? No need to walk along sandy beaches and use treasure maps. Perhaps a computer would do.

She dashed to the computer and pulled up a search engine. What should she type? Hide? Hidden? No, that was way too broad. She thought for a few minutes and then something came to her. She saw an image of the eagle flying over the Jewish Synagogue. "I wonder," she thought.

Quickly she typed two words into the search engine: **HIDDEN JEWS**. "Let's just see what turns up," she thought.

The first heading that popped up was one that read, *The Hidden Day: Rosh Hashanah*. "What? Hidden Day? Rosh Hashanah?"

She decided to open the article and give it a read. Her eyes grew bigger and bigger as she read each paragraph. Surely she had stumbled onto a hidden treasure. How could she have missed this before in all her readings about the Jewish Feast of Rosh Hashanah?

She already knew the Feast of Rosh Hashanah ushered in the New Year for the Jewish people. Prior to Rosh Hashanah the Jewish people spend significant time asking God for forgiveness of past sins, or sins committed during the course of the year. Rosh Hashanah was a time when they "wake up their souls" so they can be aware of any sin in their lives and repent of it. During the month of Elul, which is the month preceding Rosh Hashanah, a shofar is blown every day. (*On our Gregorian calendar, Rosh Hashanah would occur in September or October, depending on the year*) The shofar blown each day is loud and piercing. It is meant to wake up every believer so they can be in tune with God. When Rosh Hashanah finally arrives, **the shofar is blown 100 times.** This is the day the Jewish people believe their names will be written in the *Book of Life* for one more year. *These were things she knew already, but the next part was new.*

She read, "Another name for Rosh Hashanah is the **HIDDEN DAY**". The Hebrew words for HIDDEN DAY are *Yom HaKeseh*. The word keseh comes from the word kacah, which means to **cover, conceal or HIDE.** There are several reasons why this special feast is called the Hidden Day. One reason comes from Jewish tradition. Prior to Rosh Hashanah, the shofar is blown every single day. But there is one day it is not blown. This is the day before Rosh Hashanah, or Elul 29. The shofar is not blown on this day because it is meant to conceal or hide the day from the evil one- Satan. Apparently Satan is familiar with the feast days since he is also familiar with the word of God. Satan also knows the shofar is sounded during this particular feast. Though Satan knows the feasts exist, he does not know exactly how Jesus will fulfill them. For instance, he knew the feast of Passover would happen, but he did not know Jesus would fulfill it himself by *becoming the Passover lamb*. In fact, Jesus was crucified at the precise time the Jews were slaughtering the lambs for the morning sacrifice on Passover. **Jesus died at the exact time of the evening sacrifice.** Did Satan know this would happen? No- That part was **hidden** to him. While he may be familiar with feast days, he doesn't know God's plan or timing.

But there was another reason. Rosh Hashanah (also called *The Feast of Trumpets*) was a feast that did not fall on a full moon. Many feasts of the Lord were easier to keep track of because they occur at full moon, or times when the moon is easily visible. **Not with Rosh Hashanah**. This feast falls at the beginning of the lunar month, on the first day. In order to know it has begun one must be able to see **THE NEW MOON**. This is very difficult because **a new moon is barely visible**. The new moon can be invisible, until the sun sets. Its appearance, if detected, will look like a very thin crescent shape, which would be visible at sunset. One would need very keen eyes to see it.

Back in biblical times there were special people appointed to see and document the new moon. Then, they were to notify the rabbinical council in Jerusalem of its presence. Usually, two witnesses were appointed to testify to the sighting. Once testified to the Council, a message would be sent by the use of a fire signal. The amount of time it took for the witnesses to get to the council to testify, and the amount of time it took for the council to send out the fire signals, could obviously vary, depending on the circumstances. So, the sighting and revealing of the new moon wasn't given at an exact time. It was somewhat **hidden** because no one knew if the news of the sighting would get to them at the right time.

When the Jews went into captivity in Babylon, finding out it was a new moon at Rosh Hashanah became even more difficult. Since the Jews were dispersed, it took much longer for news to reach them. Oftentimes, it could take up to two days. For this reason the feast was celebrated over the course of two days. Also, at other times in history, the Jews could be living in different communities that may be far apart, so it could take a while for the news of the new moon sighting to reach them. So, technically no one knew for sure when it actually started because it depended on when the two witnesses testified they'd seen it, and when the information was transmitted to the right people. In fact, if one takes into consideration that many factors can affect the sighting of a new moon such as temperature, fog, clouds, altitude, light pollution or humidity, it's easy to see how it could be hidden. Because of this, no one can really predict when the new moon will come into view, and since Rosh Hashanah starts at the sighting of the new moon, it is hidden. Thus, it was a hidden day.

Ruthie was intrigued by the fact that Rosh Hashanah was known as a **hidden feast.** No one really knew exactly when it would occur. She thought about this deeply. As she thought, an image popped in her mind- **JESUS.**

"Wait, there is a parallel here," she mumbled aloud. "We don't know when Jesus will return. The exact time is **hidden from us.**"

Suddenly she realized a huge connection was forming. Jesus was the connection. She had already read in the past about Rosh Hashanah foreshadowing the return of Jesus. In Matthew 24 it says, "but of the day and the hour no one knows," when referring to the return of Jesus. Yet, it also said there would be *signs before his return.*

She went back to the search engine on the computer. She typed in *Jesus and Rosh Hashanah.* Immediately she found at least 10 articles about this subject. She read through a few of them, just to brush up on the details. There were a few things that stood out to her.

The feast of Rosh Hashanah, also known as the Feast of Trumpets, is characterized by its use of the **shofar (the trumpet)**, or the Awakening blasts. In 1 Corinthians 15:52 it says, "In a moment, in the twinkling of an eye, **at the last trumpet; for the trumpet will sound,** and the dead will be raised imperishable, and we will be changed." This verse described the rapture, when Christ comes to fetch his Bride from Earth. It would be quick like lightning, and a trumpet blast would sound to signal his coming.

Ruthie thought about the wording- **"the last trump"**. Leading up to Rosh Hashanah, the trumpet would sound every day, and then on the actual feast day, it would be **sounded 100 times**. Could this be referring to "the last trump"?

In the month before Rosh Hashanah (known as Elul), the Jewish people repent of all sin so their names will be written into the Book of Life. Yet, *we who are in Christ* are forgiven because of the blood he shed on the cross. We repent and he forgives us. When he becomes our

Savior, our names are written in the Book of Life. Yet up to the very day he arrives on Earth again to fetch his Bride, we are to continue to repent of sin because he lives in us. The Holy Spirit searches our hearts daily and helps us identify those sins. On the day when he returns with the **sound of the trumpet** (shofar), our hearts will be ready because he is within us every single day.

She looked back at the reading on Rosh Hashanah. She was drawn to a sentence. It said, "Astronomical calculations alone could not predict a new moon. This is why it was imperative to ***have faithful witnesses to testify about seeing the new moon.*** These faithful witnesses were expected to reach Jerusalem in a timely manner and if necessary, use a mule or horse to get there."

She pictured Paul Revere, riding his horse in order to let the colonists know "the British were coming." Like Revere, these witnesses had a timely message. They had a duty to get the message out that Rosh Hashanah was here. This message was of upmost importance because God gives specific instructions for this feast in Leviticus 23, and specifically asks the Jewish people to keep it. Technically, God's feasts were "divine appointments." Who wanted to be late for an appointment with God?

Jesus rode on a humble donkey when he entered Jerusalem on the feast of Passover. He brought the message that the King was here. He was King of the Jews and King of the Gentiles. Certainly, if Jesus fulfilled the feast of Passover, as well as the three other Spring Feasts, he would fulfill Rosh Hashanah. This *Hidden Day* would be revealed some day at the right time and the right hour. Could Rosh Hashanah be the feast carrying the message that Jesus was returning for his Bride? All these years God's ancient people had been celebrating it. **Perhaps it was a "dress rehearsal" for the real thing**.

Well, this must be the reason God wanted her to read the *Hiding Place* again. Now, she knew all about Rosh Hashanah and how it was a Hidden Day to the Jews, and to Christians. Yes, this was the answer. Yet, something still seemed unsettled or unfinished.

"I hate it when this happens," she sighed. "Cheer up Ruthie," she told herself, "you should be honored the Lord would even bother with you. He doesn't have to reveal anything to you, or anyone. He could conceal or hide it. But he chooses to make it known. How he does it is up to him, not you."

Author's Note: Speaking of hidden............ I grew up on a street called **Calypso Drive.** As I was working on my first book I suddenly became interested in the word- **Calypso.** There was something I knew I needed to know, so I looked it up. Calypso is a Greek word that means, **"she who conceals, covers or hides."** The origin is from a Greek myth about a nymph named Calypso who fell in love with Odysseus after he became shipwrecked on the island she inhabited. She wanted Odysseus to stay with her, but he refused her invitation. She forces him to stay with her on the island by using enchanted singing. She keeps him on the island for **seven years.**

The root word of **APOCALYPSE is CALYPSO.** When the word is broken down we have **APO** which means off, or away from. Then we have the word kalyptein (Calypse) which means to cover, conceal or hide. In some translations it also means to save. **So, the two words together mean to REVEAL, UNCOVER AND DISCLOSE. (the opposite of hide, cover or conceal)**

When most people define the word APOCALYPSE they will say it means "the end of the world", or a cataclysmic event. Actually, this is one of the *modern* definitions of the word. Church going folks will say the **APOCALYPSE** is what's described in the book of Revelation. Well, Revelation means to reveal, or uncover something. But, here's what I'm thinking. The details of the Apocalypse, as well as some of the events leading to it, are still somewhat of a mystery to us- **they are hidden**. But, what if the Lord's Feasts (Rosh Hashanah, Day of Atonement, Feast of Tabernacles, Passover, Unleavened Bread, First Fruits, Pentecost….) are there to help us **UNCOVER** some of these mysteries? Rosh Hashanah is called the **Hidden Day,** but what if the details have been there all along? What if God is just waiting for us to uncover them? If we truly follow what the Bible says, and *become the olive branch*- Jew and Gentile on the same olive tree- won't we start to uncover these mysteries? God's end time plan is often called the APOCALYPSE- but remember, APOCALYPSE doesn't need to be a negative word- after all, it means to **REVEAL, UNCOVER AND DISCLOSE**. Don't you want to know what God is trying to DISCLOSE AND REVEAL? If you do, you need to look at his ancient people, the Jews, and their biblical traditions. Jesus, after all, is Jewish. The Bible calls for us to be the "one new man", where there is nothing separating the Gentiles from the Jews.

Two witnesses were needed to sight the new moon at Rosh Hashanah. There are also **two witnesses** mentioned in Revelation 11. These witnesses will prophesy for 42 months during the Tribulation. They will have the power to turn water into blood, and to destroy with fire. They will speak God's word to a world in turmoil. Many believe the two witnesses will be Moses and Elijah, while others say it is Moses and Enoch.

Keep in mind that Rosh Hashanah always occurs on Tishrei 1 on the Hebrew calendar. This feast will not occur on the same day each year on the Gregorian calendar (solar calendar most of the world follows). The Hebrew calendar follows the cycles of the moon and sun so the date of Rosh Hashanah will vary from year to year on the Gregorian/Western calendar- usually occurring in September or October each year. This is because the Gregorian calendar is strictly a solar calendar, not a lunar calendar. Most Jewish people have a Hebrew calendar so they can keep up with the dates each year. See chart in the back of this book for Rosh Hashanah/Yom Kippur dates from 2017 through 2024 on the Western Gregorian calendar.

CHAPTER 8
The Thief

Today was the neighborhood picnic and Ruthie was scrambling to get the dessert made. She was always the last one to arrive at these events. For once, she wanted to show up on time. She pushed herself harder, and to her astonishment, she was out the door on time, with a few minutes to spare.

"Wait, I left my watch," Jonah said.

"Are you kidding me? For once, I want to be…"

"Got it," he said, putting the watch on as he walked out the door.

"That watch doesn't really fit you," she said, observing how the watch drooped from his wrist. Ever since he found the watch inside the wall he couldn't seem to part with it.

"I don't care. It makes me look rich," he retorted.

"Rich? I don't know about that. Just don't lose it. It could be an antique."

They headed down the street to the neighbor's house. Ruthie's neighbor Shannon was hosting the picnic. Ruthie placed her dessert on the table and greeted everyone. "Wonder if they noticed I made it on time for once," she thought.

"Wow, that's some watch you got there," Shannon said, noticing Jonah's watch.

"Yeah, I found it in the wall," he said, a huge grin on his face.

Shannon gave Ruthie a confused look. "It's a long story," Ruthie laughed. "Actually Shannon, I wanted to ask you about that eagle picture you posted on Facebook."

"Oh, wasn't it unbelievable? I came out one morning and there it was on top of the electrical pole, spreading its wings for the world to see."

"Yes, the photos were beautiful. How long was it sitting up there?"

"I don't know -maybe an hour. It must live near the lake behind my house. You know, *Lake Lagrange*."

"True. That's why our neighborhood is called *Lake Lagrange Heights*."

"I've seen eagles by the lake from time to time. They swoop down and grab fish. Sometimes they steal them too."

"Yes, I've heard that before."

"After I took the picture of the eagle the other day, I looked up some information about them. Did you know they put thorns in their nests? And they have over one million sensory cells per square millimeter in their eyes. Also, they never look back before they grab their prey. They fly without hesitation and capture their prey, which is mainly fish."

"Fascinating birds aren't they?"

"Yes they are. Hey, you live on Kingfisher Drive so I'm surprised the eagle didn't perch itself near *your* street sign. After all, your street is Kingfisher and the eagle is King of catching fish."

Ruthie thought about this. The **eagle** is called a **fish hawk**. Interestingly enough, the Kingfisher Drive street sign was right next to the *Lake Lagrange* neighborhood stone marker, and there was a **HAWK** on that marker a few days ago. So you have the King **FISH**er sign next to the **HAWK**. Thus, fish hawk. She was almost struck by lightning between the *Lake Lagrang*e neighborhood marker, and the Kingfisher sign.

A verse came to mind as she thought about these things. It was Mark 1:17 which says, "Come ye after me, and I will make you fishers of men." She pictured the eagle, with its superior vision, diving down to grab a fish, never looking back, never losing sight of its mark.

"I get it now. Jesus, our King, says we are to be fishers of men. We should be fishing for people! We are to keep our eyes open and continually bringing others to Christ, even up until the day he returns like lightning," she thought to herself.

"Hey Ruthie. Are you ok? You look like you've zoned out," Shannon said.

"Oh sorry, I think I did for a minute. Guess I need some rest," she answered.

"Before I forget, I wanted to tell you about a break in that happened in the neighborhood."

"Oh no! When and where?"

"It was the new couple who just moved in at the end of your street."

"Really? They just moved in two weeks ago. What a horrible welcome."

"Tell me about it. Well, here's the lucky thing, depending on how you look at it. The woman was actually at home when the break in happened."

"How's that lucky? I'd be terrified."

"Well, listen to the story. You see, the woman was alone at home. It was midnight and she was in her bedroom."

"Why was she home alone?"

"Her husband was away on business. Anyway, it was midnight and…"

"Wow, she was up late. Most people would be asleep."

"Ruthie, not to be rude, but can I finish the story?" Shannon asked.

"Sorry."

"Like I was saying, she was awake and it was midnight when she heard a noise. She quietly left her room and snuck down the hallway. She peeked into the living room and do you know what she saw?"

"No idea."

"A man's head sticking through the living room window!"

"Ugh, I would faint."

"Anyway, she was pretty scared, but she just grabbed a lamp and threw it on the ground real hard to startle him."

"What did he do?"

"It must have scared him because he took off running without closing the window. But guess what she saw in his hands as he was running?"

"What?"

"A can of gasoline."

"Huh? Are you kidding? What was he going to do with that?"

"Maybe steal some stuff and then burn the house down. I don't know, but I'd say she dodged the bullet on that one!"

"That's horrible! Why on earth would you say she was lucky?"

"Well, she was awake! What if she had been asleep? Can you imagine? The thief would have stolen everything and burned down her house. But she was alert, even late at night."

"I see what you're saying. How many people would be awake at that time and know what to do when the time came?" Ruthie said.

"You're telling me. Though, if a thief were trying to break in my house I think my dog would let me know. The question is, would he actually attack the thief, or lick him to death?"

"I'm thinking I'll be staying up a little later from now on. You know, Thomas is gone every third night because he's on shift at the Fire Department. I'm alone with Jonah a couple nights a week."

"That's why I wanted to tell you. You need to be alert Ruthie. You don't even have an alarm system. Do you know how easy it would be for a thief to break in?"

Right then something resonated in her spirit. **A thief breaking in**. Where had she heard of that before?

"Ruthie, I'm not trying to scare you. I just wanted you to be aware," Shannon insisted.

"Don't worry. I know. I'll talk to Thomas about getting an alarm system," she said, walking toward the food table.

She stared at all the food. She wasn't hungry now. Shannon had said something important. The woman down the street had been alert and awake when the thief broke in. This saved her life and her home! This was somehow linked to all the other clues about the *Hiding Place*. She could sense the connection. Somehow she sensed this particular piece of the puzzle was more important than the rest. "Without this piece, there is no hiding place," she said under her breath. Why did she say that? Just then Jonah ran up to her, frantic and upset.

"Mom, my watch has been stolen!"

"Stolen? Are you sure? It probably just fell off your arm. I told you it was too big for your wrist."

"Is someone looking for their watch?" asked Mr. Reynolds, one of the neighbors at the picnic.

"Yes, that's mine. Oh, thank you, thank you," Jonah said, clutching the watch.

"I found the watch in the bowl of Goldfish crackers. It must have fallen off your wrist when you were grabbing a snack young man," Mr. Reynolds added.

"GoldFISH- get it Ruthie? The watch fell in the gold FISH," Shannon observed.

"Oh yeah, because of the eagle and the fish," Ruthie laughed.

She smiled to herself. The *watch, the eagle, the fish and now thieves*. It was a matter *of time* before she would figure it out.

CHAPTER 9

Alarm

After the picnic Jonah was tired and he lay down on the couch to sleep. "This is a rare moment," she thought. Thomas and Michael were fishing, and would probably be gone for another few hours. She chuckled to herself. They were out FISHING. What were the chances?

What should she do with a little time to herself? Actually she was tired, but she didn't want to sleep. For once she could watch T.V., uninterrupted. Now was her chance with everyone occupied. She turned to look for the remote and found it sitting on the side table. It was sitting right on top of her Bible. She reached for the remote, feeling slightly guilty. Was there something else she should be doing? No, it would be good to just unwind and watch T.V. She pushed the power button. A crackling noise came from the T.V., along with a blinding flash.

She covered her face, waiting for some sort of explosion. Slowly she lifted her face, only to see the blackness of the T.V. screen.

"Great, the T.V. is fried," she said to herself. "How did that happen? Must have been an electrical surge or something," she muttered. Thomas was not going to be happy when he came home. She better call him. Then again, why spoil his fishing trip with Michael. She could tell him when he got back.

She looked over at the side table. There was her Bible. "Might as well give it a read," she thought. "No T.V. for me today." She grabbed it quickly, and did something she normally would not do. Usually, when she opened the Bible, she would turn to a particular book or verse. But this time, she decided to let the Bible open randomly. She just let it fall open.

"Let's see what it says," she said, as she pointed to the text on the page. She read aloud, "But of the times and the seasons, brethren, ye have no need that I write to you. For you know that the day of the Lord so cometh like a **thief in the night**. For when they shall say, peace and safety; then sudden destruction cometh upon them, as travail upon a woman with child; and they shall not escape. But ye, brethren, are not in darkness, that the day should overtake you as a **thief**."

Ruthie was stunned. These verses talked about a **thief in the night**. Didn't Shannon just tell her about a thief breaking into her neighbor's house? The neighbor, however, had been awake and alert so when the thief came, she was ready. "She wasn't overtaken by the thief- just like the last part of the verse," Ruthie muttered aloud.

She put the Bible down for a moment. A few words were echoing in her thoughts. **The Day of the Lord.** "The Day of the Lord will come like a thief in the night," she said aloud. She knew some things about the Day of the Lord already. This day signaled the beginning of terrible tribulation, darkness and the wrath of God. It wasn't a day to be hanging out at Disney, or having a picnic in the park. The Day of the Lord was about judgement. For those who do not know Christ it will be a day (time) of punishing human sin. The prophet Isaiah describes the Day of the Lord as a cruel time of wrath and fierce anger, and a time when the land would become desolate. **He said the sun shall be darkened and the moon will not shine.** The proud and haughty people will be put in their place, and the wicked will be punished.

The prophet Zephaniah echoes the words of Isaiah by saying the Day of the Lord will be a day of distress, and a day of clouds and thick darkness. **It will be a day of the trumpet.**

Suddenly she realized something. **It was a day of the trumpet!** Hadn't she just read about Rosh Hashanah, also called the Feast of Trumpets? A month prior to this feast a shofar (trumpet) is sounded each day, and then on the day of the feast the shofar sounds 100 times. But how could Rosh Hashanah be tied to the Day of the Lord? Somehow she didn't picture Rosh Hashanah as a day of gloominess and distress. In fact, Rosh Hashanah was considered a good day because if you repented before it arrived, your name would be written in the Book of Life (at least for another year). Then again, though the feast of Rosh Hashanah was still being celebrated, *it had not yet been fulfilled*. Would the day of the Lord ***fulfill the feast***?

She grabbed her Bible and opened up to the book of Zephaniah, chapter 1. She read verses 14-16 aloud. "The great day of the Lord is near, it is near, and hasteth greatly, even the voice of the day of the Lord: the mighty man shall cry there bitterly. That day is a day of wrath, a day of trouble and distress, a day of wasteness and desolation, a day of darkness and gloominess, a day of clouds and thick darkness, **A day of the trumpet and alarm** against the fenced cities, and against the high towers."

As she pondered the verses, she heard a shrill, piercing noise. It sounded like her phone's alarm. But she hadn't set an alarm on it. It was still day time, and she only set her alarm at night.

Then she thought about the Day of the Lord- it was **a day of the alarm**. Was her phone's alarm going off coincidence or divine timing? She didn't know, but she knew she had to figure it out.

Author's Note: In the Bible Jesus says he will return like a **thief in the night**. For that reason he says we are to always be on the alert, and we shouldn't "fall asleep." If we go back to ancient Jewish traditions we will find some amazing parallels. Firstly, back in the ancient days of the Temple, the High Priest put other priests in charge of tending the temple fire, and guarding the temple property. These guards were not allowed to fall asleep on the job. They had to stay awake and alert all night.

The High Priest was known to check up on the guards, though they never knew when he would come. In fact, he was referred to as a thief in the night. He would usually come when they least expected it.

If he found a guard asleep on the job, ***particularly the one tending the fire,*** he would take an ember from the fire and set the guard's robe on fire! How's that for falling asleep on the job!

Now, think about this- when Jesus died on the cross he became our High Priest. We then became holy priests under his authority. When Jesus, our High Priest, returns, he expects us to be "on duty" and not asleep. **We are to have the fire of Jesus in our hearts, burning fully when he returns**. If not, the door will be shut in our face. Just read the parable of the Ten Virgins at midnight in Matthew. We are to be ready for the sound of the last trump. If we "fall asleep" and become consumed with the world, we will not be ready when he returns for the Bride. We will miss the open door.

From the Ten Virgins:

"The virgins who were ready went in with him to the wedding banquet. And the door was shut. Later the others also came. 'Lord, Lord,' they said, 'Open the door for us!' But he replied, 'Truly I tell you, I don't know you.' Therefore, keep watch, because you do not know the day or the hour." Matthew 25, 10-13

CHAPTER 10
Appointments

Ruthie knew there must be tie between Rosh Hashanah and the Day of the Lord. She would need to do more research on this mysterious feast. There had to be more to learn. But today wasn't the day. She had an appointment to keep. Unfortunately, this involved getting some cavities filled. She dreaded these things. The shot, the grinding, the sound of the drill- these were all unpleasant things. Still, off she went. The consequences of unfilled cavities were not worth the risk.

She arrived at the dental office on time. For once, they took her right back, where she quickly sat in the dentist's chair. "We've got two cavities to fill today so it may take a while," the dentist warned.

Ruthie shook her head in agreement, though not with enthusiasm.

"I'm going to give you a shot to numb the area," the dentist stated. Ruthie braced herself as the needle plunged in. Luckily, it was over in a few seconds. "I'm going to give the numbing medicine time to work. I'll see you again in a few minutes." Ruthie nodded as the dentist exited the room.

She sat there for a few seconds, already starting to feel numb. She closed her eyes for just a few moments. Too bad she couldn't just take a nap through the fillings. She kept her eyes closed, trying to relax. She felt herself drifting off. Was she sleeping? No, this was something else. Her eyes were closed, but she could see something.

It was a beautiful lush garden, adorned with every kind of plant and flower imaginable. Spectacular to behold, with colors unrecognizable on Earth. Had she ever seen colors like this before? If so, she couldn't describe or name them. Streams of flowing water mingled in with the landscape, showcasing water the color of clear crystal.

Among the rows of flowers, and amidst the lush greenery, she noticed a door. It was tall and white, with light bouncing off its surface. Where did the door lead? What was behind it? She couldn't fathom the answer. As she stared at the door, a set of figures appeared from behind a tall tree. She couldn't see their faces, but she could tell it was a man and woman. A white wedding dress adorned the woman, and the man wore a dark suit. It was definitely a bride and groom. The woman was carrying a small oil lamp, while the man carried what looked like a horn. Was it a ram's horn? A shofar?

The couple proceeded toward the door. The man opened the door for the woman and invited her in. Within seconds they both disappeared behind the door.

"So, how's your mouth feeling? Everything all numb?" the dentist asked, upon entering the room. Ruthie opened her eyes, and the vision disappeared.

She nodded her head in disappointment. She wanted to see more of the vision. Is that what it was? A vision?

She tried to picture the vision in her mind again. But the sound of the dentist's drill stifled her thoughts. She suddenly wished she were home, lying in her bed. Surely, she would have seen the entire vision if she were there, with no distractions.

The dentist finished filling the cavities in under two hours, and sent her to the front check out. As she glanced at the receptionist, she could see the frustration on her face.

"Everything ok?" Ruthie asked.

"Oh, it's just……well, *patients are not keeping their appointments.*"

"I'm sorry, what do you mean?"

"We have a lot of patients who *miss appointments*. Then they expect us to find them a new appointment at the drop of a hat. I try to reschedule people, but sometimes it's almost impossible."

Ruthie heard what she said, but her mind wandered to something else- **the Lord's appointments**. The Feasts of the Lord were appointments with God. That meant Rosh Hashanah was an appointment with God. How many people were missing the appointment every year? She had been missing them herself.

"Don't worry Ruthie. You are not one of people I'm talking about," the receptionist added.

"Maybe not at the dentist office, but in God's office I'd say I've missed more than a few," she thought to herself.

CHAPTER 11
The Wedding

Ruthie drove home, still thinking about the vision at the dentist's office. What was that vision all about? The beautiful piece of property, a bride and groom, and a door. They stepped *behind a door*. A big, white door. She wished she could go back to that place in her mind.

She kept driving, trying to focus on the road. She drove for a few minutes, taking in the view just a little. She noticed a quaint park to her left. Why hadn't she stopped there before? It looked so peaceful and serene. "Well, that settles it. I'm stopping. A little time at the park is just what I need," she said to herself. "Maybe I can reimagine the vision."

She parked and walked over to a bench. It sure was lovely. Not quite as lovely as her vision, but it would do. She hadn't sat down more than a few minutes when she heard a woman's voice.

"This is such a beautiful place. I come here once a day. I call it my **hidden place**," she said.

"Your hidden place?" Ruthie asked.

"Yes, because most people don't even notice it's here. Yet, it's been here all along."

"You must be right because I've lived in this area all my life and I'm just now finding it."

"You know what else is hidden?" the woman asked.

"You mean besides socks that keep getting lost in the laundry?" she laughed.

"Well, let's just say this is way more important than a sock. It could be a matter of life and death."

"Oh, then I don't know what you mean," she admitted.

"For in the time of trouble he shall hide me in his pavilion: in the secret of his tabernacle shall he hide me: he shall set me up upon a rock," the woman stated.

"Are you quoting a verse?"

"Yes, I am. That was Psalm 27:5. It is talking about a day when the Lord will hide us from the terror and judgment coming upon the earth."

"What do you mean *hide us?*" Ruthie inquired.

"On the Day of the Lord, the whole earth will be judged for sin. The Lord's wrath will be poured out. But his wrath will not be poured out on the Bride. The Bride of Jesus will be taken to a place of refuge- a place of safety. It will be *a hidden place.*"

"What do you mean? Where is the Bride of Jesus taken?"

"To heaven of course," the woman answered matter of factly.

"Do you mean when the Day of the Lord comes, the Bride of Jesus, his true followers, will be taken to heaven?"

"Exactly."

"So, are you talking about the rapture? That's when the Bride of Jesus is snatched away in the blink of an eye."

"Yes, that is what I'm saying. The Bride will be raptured, much like when a hawk grabs his prey mid-air. It will be quick, and take many by surprise. The ram's horn (shofar/trumpet) will sound, and the Bride will be taken to the **hidden place- God's property in heaven.**"

"Wait, I think I know the verse that describes this. I believe it's from John 14, verses one through three. "In my Father's house there are many mansions: if it were not so, I would have told you. I go there *to prepare a place for you.* And if I go there to prepare a place for you, I will come again, and receive you unto myself; that where I am, there ye may be also."

"That verse is describing a Jewish wedding. But remember a Jewish wedding is symbolic of the rapture. Jesus is Jewish, so when he comes for his Bride one day (the Church), he will do this as a Jewish groom, following ancient wedding customs," the woman said.

"Oh yes, I've heard about the ancient Jewish wedding. The Jewish wedding started with a legal contract. When a man was interested in marrying a woman, he would bring a contract to the Bride's father. The contract would include the price to pay for the Bride. Back then you had to pay for your Bride to make up for the fact that the family was losing a daughter. Oftentimes, the price would be high. Next, the groom had to pay the price for the Bride. Once the contract was agreed upon and the price paid, the groom would leave. Then he would go back to his <u>Father's property</u>. The Father would now ***prepare a place on his property*** for the Bride and Groom. The Father would build a beautiful bridal chamber on his property and fill the room with food, and all the things they would need for seven days. That's how long the Bride and Groom would be inside. It was their special place for that time, kind of like a sanctuary just for them."

"My, oh my. **That sounds a lot like a hiding place** now doesn't it?" the woman said.

"You're right. The Father was building a special place on his property just for them."

Ruthie remembered her vision earlier at the dentist's office. There was a Bride and Groom, and they were on a beautiful piece of property. They entered through a white door.

"Tell me about the rest of the Jewish wedding," the woman urged.

"Oh yes, let me see ….where was I? Oh yes, the Father was busy building the bridal chamber on his property. In the meantime, **the Bride had to wait**. Sometimes she had to wait a very long time. It could take up to a year for the father to build the special chamber. The Bride wasn't even allowed to see the Groom and she had to wear a veil wherever she went. This way, anyone who saw her knew she was promised to the Groom. She must have missed her groom, but she knew he would come back for her at the right time. She had an oil lamp with her at night, just in case the Groom came in the evening, or middle of the night." Just then Ruthie remembered her vision again. In the vision, the Bride carried an oil lamp. She smiled at the thought.

"Go on with the rest," the woman said.

"Well, at some point the father would finish the chamber. As soon as he was done he would tell his son 'Go Fetch Your Bride'. Immediately the Groom would set off to the Bride's house, followed by his wedding party. Oftentimes this would occur at midnight. It is possible the Bride would be asleep. Then again, since she knows her groom could come at any time, she may have laid down with her wedding dress on, just in case the Groom showed up. The groom did give the Bride a little warning before he made it to her house. One person in the wedding party would give a loud SHOUT. A shofar would be sounded as they approached her house as well. As soon as the Bride heard the shout and shofar she would grab her oil lamp and wait for the Groom to arrive. In a few moments the Groom would burst into her home and steal her away. It was like lightning! It all happened so quickly, but she was ready."

Ruthie paused for a moment. There was something very familiar about what she just said. The hidden bridal chamber on the Father's property…. the shout and the shofar………..the part about being stolen……. the lightning.

"So the Bride was stolen from her home in the blink of any eye, with the sound of the trumpet," the woman stated.

"Yes. It sounds like…….."

"Rosh Hashanah?" the woman asked.

"Yes, exactly like Rosh Hashanah. A shofar is played on Rosh Hashanah and it is called the **Hidden Day**. In the ancient Jewish wedding the Bride is stolen from her home and it happens with the sound of the shofar, and with a shout."

"Here's a verse for you about the coming of Jesus. 'For the Lord himself shall descend from heaven with a shout, with the voice of the archangel, and with the trump of God: and the dead in Christ shall rise first: Then we which are alive and remain shall be caught up together with them in the clouds, to meet the Lord in the air: and so shall we ever be with the Lord.'"

"Oh my goodness. There's the shout and the trumpet- *the shofar*. Jesus will come back like a Jewish Groom won't he? In the verses it mentions the clouds. I remember reading that Rosh Hashanah is called the Hidden Day, but it is also called **The Day of Dark Clouds**." Suddenly Ruthie remembered in her vision the Groom had a shofar, or ram's horn. It all reminded her of the verses.

"I do believe Jesus will follow the customs of a Jewish wedding when he returns. And there's something else."

"What?"

"Did you know another name for Rosh Hashanah is Ha' Kiddushin?"

"What does that mean?"

"Ha Kiddushin means **wedding of Messiah**."

"Whoa! I didn't know that!"

"Listen carefully to these next verses from 1 Thessalonians 5", the woman said.

"*Now, brothers and sisters, about times and dates we do not need to write to you, for you know very well that the day of the Lord will come like a **thief in the night**. While people are saying 'Peace and safety', destruction will come on them suddenly, as labor pains on a pregnant woman, and they will not escape. But you, brothers and sisters, are not in darkness so that this day should surprise you like a thief. You are children of the light and children of the day. We do not belong to the night or to the darkness. So then, let us not be like others, who are asleep, but let us be awake and sober. For those who sleep, sleep at night, and those who get drunk, get drunk at night. But we belong to the day, let us be sober, putting on faith and love as a breastplate, and the hope of salvation as a helmet. For God did not appoint us to suffer wrath but to receive salvation through our Lord Jesus Christ.*"

"Oh wow! There's the thief part again. The other day my neighbor was talking about a thief breaking into a house, but *the owner was awake*. It was very late at night, but she was awake."

"The owner of the house was ready for the thief. How late was it?"

"Midnight."

"Sounds like a Jewish wedding to me, at least the thief part. You see, when Jesus comes for his Bride **she will be stolen**. It will be quick, and the shofar will sound. She will be ready with her oil lamp, which is symbolic for the Holy Spirit. But many others will be found asleep spiritually. *The time of Jesus' return will be hidden to them.* They will be caught off guard. They will sleep through the wedding."

"You know what? That reminds me of the Ten Virgins story from the book of Matthew. There are ten virgins who are waiting for the Groom to come. Five of the virgins had their oil lamps ready, but the other five did not. The wise virgins already had oil in their lamps in case the Groom showed up at any moment. The other five were foolish, and did not put any oil in their lamps. The Groom was taking too long to come so they fell asleep. When midnight came a cry rang out saying 'Here's the Bridegroom.' The wise virgins were ready with their oil, but the foolish ones didn't have any. They asked the wise ones for some oil, but it was too late. The wise virgins told them they needed to get their own oil. So, while the foolish virgins were out buying oil, the Bridegroom came. He took the five wise virgins and then he shut the door behind him. Later, the foolish virgins came to the door and asked for the door to be opened. But it was too late. The Lord said to them, 'Truly, I tell you, I don't know you'.'"

"The Bridegroom came like a thief and the ones who were asleep missed the wedding supper. The **door was shut**. Ruthie, did you know that another name for Rosh Hashanah is **the Day of Opening the Gates and Doors**? It is called this because on Rosh Hashanah the gates/doors of heaven are opened. Prior to Rosh Hashanah people have repented of their sins. When the day finally arrives, they should be cleansed. According to Jewish tradition, their names are written in the Book of Life and a new year begins. As Christians we know as soon as we ask Jesus to come into our hearts the gate/door is open for us. Remember, Jesus says in Revelation, 'Behold, I stand at the door and knock: if any man hear my voice and open the door, I will come in to him, and will sup with him, and he with me.' Yet this verse also foreshadows the rapture, which could happen someday on Rosh Hashanah. On this feast day, the doors/gates of heaven are open for the Bride and the Groom. Their names are in the Book of Life and Christ is the Groom. Of course, we don't know what exact year or hour the Lord will return. Will he fulfill the rest of the feasts? Will he fulfill Rosh Hashanah? I believe so. Since Rosh Hashanah is celebrated **every year** at the appointed time, we do not know the exact year. Also, it is a two day feast, so we don't know the exact day or hour. But, it is possible Rosh Hashanah is a dress rehearsal for the real thing- the day he returns for his Bride at the trumpet call! Jesus fulfilled the Spring feasts of Passover, Unleavened Bread, First Fruits and Pentecost to the day and the hour. It makes sense he would fulfill all the others. But we have to stay alert, just like the Bride. Even though it is night here on Earth, we are to stay awake spiritually. We are children of the day. Ruthie, what happens after the Groom **steals** the Bride away?"

"That's the best part. The Groom takes the Bride to his Father's property. And then they go into a special Bridal chamber, where they stay for seven days. It's like they are hidden from everyone. It's just the Groom and the Bride in their very own special place."

"Do you mean a hidden place?" the woman asked.

"I see now. **The Hiding Place**. Heaven is the hiding place for Jesus' Bride. When the rapture happens, the shofar will sound and Jesus will take his Bride to heaven **to be hidden**."

"And what is the Bride hidden from?"

"The Day of the Lord."

"It's just as Psalm 27:5 says, 'For in the time of trouble he shall hide me in his pavilion: **in the secret of his tabernacle shall he hide me**; he shall set me upon a rock'."

"Just so I'm crystal clear, you are saying when the day of the Lord comes, the Lord will hide his people- his Bride?"

"Yes. The tabernacle represents the Lord dwelling with us. We will be hidden in his tabernacle- his dwelling in heaven. He will set us on a rock. And do you know what creature nests on the highest rock?"

"No, what is it?"

"An eagle."

Ruthie was stunned. An eagle? Hadn't she just seen a picture of an eagle on the electrical pole in her neighborhood? What about the long conversation with her neighbor about eagles? What about the eagle circling the Jewish Synagogue?

"Eagles represent God's people. One day we will all be **gathered together** when Jesus comes for his Bride. **And the Bride is STOLEN- just like when the eagles (raptors) steal fish.** "

"Wheresoever the carcass is, there will the eagles be gathered together," Ruthie said.

"I see you have read Matthew 24. That whole chapter describes the signs that will happen before the return of Christ."

"Yes, I've read it. I feel like my eyes are being opened a little more each day."

"Well, keep looking because this is only the beginning. You've got a lot more to learn. Go home and look up these two things: **mercy and the shofar.** Trust me, your eyes will open even more." With that the woman walked away.

"Wait, I never even asked your name," Ruthie said.

"It's Lucia."

"Is that the Spanish word for light?"

"Yes, it means light. Now go home and look up what I told you."

"I will," Ruthie promised.

As she walked back to her car there was one thing she forgot to ask. How did the woman know her name? Oh well, she was used to that sort of thing. God's ways are often hidden, but amazing.

Author's Notes:

The book, *The Hiding Place*, by Corrie ten Boom, tells the story of how Corrie and her family hid the Jewish people in a hiding place in the wall of her house. Every single Jewish person she hid survived. None were captured or found by the Nazis. Though Corrie herself endured the horrors of a concentration camp, she lived to tell her story in *The Hiding Place*. Here's something fascinating! Corrie was born on April 15, 1892, and she died on April 15, 1983. She died when she was **EXACTLY 91** YEARS OLD. Now, here's what's amazing- **PSALM 91** is perhaps the most famous Psalm in the Bible with regards to protection. It describes a **hiding place** with God! The psalm specifically says, "He that dwelleth in the **SECRET PLACE** of the most high shall abide in the **shadow (safety)** of the Almighty….. there shall be no evil befall thee, neither shall any plague come near my **dwelling**….Because he hath set his love upon me, therefore will **I deliver him: I will set him on high,** because he hath known my name."

Corrie ten Boom, a woman who **HID** God's chosen people, is a symbol for what God will do for his children who have Christ as their Savior. **He will HIDE them from the evil of the world in his SECRET PLACE.** Corrie was born and died on the same date- APRIL 15. *Titanic* sank on April 15 in 1912. It is perhaps the most well-known disaster in history! Some were spared, while others were not. There weren't enough lifeboats to save everyone. That is how it will be at the rapture. Some will be spared, while others will face the chilling waters. Personally, I'd rather be in the *Hiding Place*, than in the frigid water. How about you?

CHAPTER 12
Jericho

Ruthie drove home, anxious to look up what the woman suggested. She knew she had to research "mercy and the shofar." She wondered how to go about looking it up and exactly where to start. Just as she pulled into the driveway she saw her son Jonah, running out of the house with something in his hands. As she looked closer she realized it was a trumpet.

"Mom, look what I found in Michael's room! A trumpet! Why didn't you tell me he had a trumpet?" Jonah proceeded to blow a series of loud, off pitch blasts.

"Jonah, don't play the trumpet outside. It will disturb the neighbors."

"Maybe it will **wake them up** from their naps," he laughed.

Ruthie watched Jonah with interest. He waltzed around the yard, blowing the trumpet. How strange that he would find the trumpet today of all days.

"Jonah, go inside with the trumpet please. "

"Ahh, do I have to? I'm having fun!"

"Now Jonah!" she insisted.

"Fine," he stated, walking inside with the trumpet.

Ruthie followed him inside. She ignored the scowl on his face as she passed him in the kitchen.

"Look, if you really want to play the trumpet we can get you some lessons. But you can't just go outside blaring it all over the neighborhood. Michael took lessons and that's how he learned to play."

"Yeah, I guess. Hey, did you notice I was marching in circles with the trumpet?" Jonah asked.

"No, I guess I didn't pay attention. Why were you doing that?"

"Come on Mom. You know…."

"No, I don't."

"Jericho!"

"Jericho?"

"Yeah Mom. Don't you remember the story of Jericho? The Israelites marched around the city, blew the trumpets and the walls fell down!"

"Yes, you are right. That's what you were doing?"

"Well, I was just acting it out, but it was fun."

"That's pretty neat Jonah."

"I wonder why God made them blow all those trumpets?" Jonah inquired.

"Yes, they had to blow trumpets and give a shout too…." Ruthie stopped mid-sentence.

What was it? She closed her eyes for a moment. She repeated herself. "They had to blow trumpets and give a shout."

"You just said that Mom," Jonah laughed.

There was something familiar about what she just said. An image of the woman from the park popped into her head.

"That's it!" she exclaimed. "At the park I described a Jewish wedding to the woman. When the Groom came for the Bride **there was a shout, and the shofar or trumpet was sounded**. That's how the Bride knew the Groom had come."

"Mom, are you ok? What wedding? Who are you talking about?" Jonah asked.

"Sorry Jonah. Don't worry about it. But thank you for reminding me of Jericho. I needed to know that!"

Jonah shrugged his shoulders and carried the trumpet into his room. Ruthie knew Jericho held a clue about the trumpet (shofar), and perhaps even mercy. These were the two things she was supposed to research. She dashed off to the den, and turned on the computer. Into the search engine she typed **Jericho and the trumpets.** Immediately a cascade of articles popped up on the screen. She browsed through a few, then stopped on an article called, "**The Trump of Jericho**". She read the first few paragraphs aloud:

"The Israelites were given specific instructions on what to do before they reached Jericho. They had to follow these instructions perfectly in order for God's plan to be successful. Before they could even approach the land God promised them, they had to cross an important and symbolic river called the Jordan. This river held great significance to God and represented crossing over into their new lives. Once they crossed this river, they would be in the land God promised them. It was a land where God would protect them, and make them victorious over all their enemies.

God had an order for how they should cross. He commanded the Israelite priests to carry the Ark of the Covenant into the waters of the Jordan first. They were to go ahead of everyone else while carrying the presence of God in the Ark. This was a rather difficult feat because the waters of the Jordan were very high, as it was the flood stage during the harvest season. None the less, the priests did as they were told and stepped into the high waters. Immediately when their feet touched the water's edge, the water ceased flowing, piling up **into a wall** on both sides. This created an area of dry ground for the Israelites to cross though."

Ruthie thought about the faith it must have taken to step foot in the Jordan. They could have been swept away by the rushing waters. But, they knew God was with them. They knew something better lay beyond the river. So, they went forward, one step at a time, until every last Israelite had passed through the river.

Ruthie read on. "Once the Israelites made their way across the Jordan, the Lord spoke to Joshua. He instructed Joshua to choose twelve men from among the Israelites- one from each tribe. These men were to pick up twelve stones from the middle of the Jordan River, right where the priests were standing. In other words, they were to take the stones from the place where the priests' feet stood firm. This, of course, would be right near the Ark of the Covenant, which held God's presence. Next, they were to carry the stones on their shoulder and place them in the very spot where they would lodge that night. The stones would be placed at their campsite, in the new Promised land. In addition, Joshua also set up twelve more stones in the middle of the Jordan, where the feet of the priests stood, and in the presence of the Ark of the Covenant."

There were several details that struck Ruthie as she read about the crossing of the Jordan. She immediately thought about the stones. The twelve Israelites had to each pick up a stone and *carry it upon their shoulder.* An image rushed through her mind as she pictured this act. It was the image of Jesus. She pictured Jesus carrying the cross *upon his shoulder.* A verse resonated in her mind. "For to us a child is born, to us a son is given, and *the government shall be on his shoulders.* And he will be called Wonderful Counselor, Mighty God, Everlasting Father and Prince of Peace." She realized something very important. There was a reason God commanded the Israelites to pick up twelve stones. Perhaps God was foreshadowing Jesus himself, who would literally take the world upon his shoulders. He would carry the cross and be crucified for our sins on it. The government would treat him like a criminal, yet he was dying for everyone on the planet. She couldn't get over the symbolism. Even the number of stones was symbolic. In the Bible, the number twelve symbolized God's power and authority. But, it also symbolized a perfect foundation- a perfect foundation of government. Jesus, of course, is the perfect foundation for mankind. He is the only one who is perfectly just, and has authority over all the Earth. He is the perfect government. In the Bible Jesus is called **THE FIRM ROCK** on which we stand. A foundation without Christ is sinking sand.

Yet, there was something else. There wasn't just one stone monument to be set up. There were two. One was placed in the new land, at the specific spot where the Israelites would lodge. The other would be in the middle of the Jordan, in the very spot where the priests stood.

"Why two?" thought Ruthie. She closed her eyes. She saw a beautiful river. She saw Jesus. He was being baptized in the river. "That's it," she said aloud. "The two stone monuments represent our lives before and after Christ. The stones in the middle of the Jordan are our lives before we accept Christ. The stones in the Promised land represent our new lives in Christ. We essentially inherit the Promised Land once we accept Christ. We inherit eternal life. Crossing the Jordan is like crossing over into our new lives, and that life promises eternity in heaven with Jesus."

At that moment Ruthie heard a loud zapping noise. Next, all the power in the house went out. An eerie quiet permeated the air, with darkness in toe.

"Mom, all the power's out! Did you hear the zapping sound?"

"Yes Jonah, I heard it." He ran to the window.

"Whoa, there's a huge storm outside. Where did it come from?"

"I don't know. I thought sunshine was the forecast for today."

"Oh wow! Look!" shrieked Jonah.

"What is it?"

"Your computer Mom. It's blinking. How is your computer on if all the power is out?"

Ruthie looked at the computer, blinking on and off. It wasn't a laptop. It was plugged into the wall, dependent on power. Why was it on at all? Shouldn't it be completely shut off just like everything else? As she stood there, trying to figure it out, she wondered about the timing of the zapping sound, and the power going out. It must have been lightning, or some sort of power surge from the storm. She could hear thunder outside. She peeked out the window and saw streaks of bright lightning. A still small voice spoke to her in the midst of the storm. ***"As lightning cometh out of the east and shineth even unto the west, so shall also the coming of the Son of Man be."*** This verse was about the rapture.

"Does the rapture have something to do with Jericho?" she whispered under her breath. Suddenly, she heard a loud crack just outside her door. Thunder shook the house.

"Mom, it sounds like the lightning and thunder is right at our front door," Jonah cried.

Ruthie couldn't argue with him. That's exactly what it sounded like. She looked out the window. Dozens of jagged lightning bolts pierced the sky like sharp swords.

"The house feels like it's shaking! Can thunder and lightning knock a house down?" Jonah asked.

She started to say no, but in her mind she saw a giant, stone wall. It towered high above her head, with unfathomable strength. The stones of the wall were massive, piled high in the sky. But, then it fell. It collapsed without warning. It was as if an invisible force had shoved it over with one fell swoop.

"Jericho," Ruthie said aloud.

More lightning crackled outside. She knew she'd found a connection. **The rapture. Lightning. Stones. Jericho.** Now she needed to figure out how they were related.

CHAPTER 13
Camping Out

Ruthie's power was out for the rest of the night. The sudden, raging storm had knocked out power in all the surrounding neighborhoods. The power company assured everyone it would be restored by the next day.

"Isn't the power coming on soon?" Jonah asked, disappointed.

"It won't be back on until tomorrow. There are a lot of power lines to fix."

"Well, what are we supposed to do now?" asked Jonah. "It's too early for bed. I usually watch my favorite shows and……"

"I've got an idea," Ruthie suggested. "Why don't I read the story of Jericho to you?"

"There aren't any lights to see."

"I'll just grab a few candles. We can read by candlelight. It will be fun- Sort of like camping out."

"Camping out? I can grab my pop-up tent and we can put it in the living room. Then it will really be like camping out," Jonah suggested.

Ruthie started to object but then she saw the excited look in Jonah's eyes. "Go ahead and get your little tent. I'll get the candles."

Jonah grabbed the tent and set it up in a matter of minutes. Ruthie lit candles and grabbed a flashlight. Inside the tent they went, Bible in hand.

"Hey Mom, we are doing what the Israelites did right now because they had to camp before they went into Jericho," Jonah said.

"You're right! You know a lot about the story already."

"We learned about it at Vacation Bible School last year. I have a great memory."

"Tell me what else you know about Jericho."

"Well, let's see. After the Israelites crossed the Jordan, they camped not far from Jericho. They had to wait for Joshua to tell them what to do. Joshua had to ask God for the instructions."

"What were God's instructions?"

"The instructions were weird."

"How so?"

"Well, in most movies I've seen an army will just charge into a city and attack it. But, Jericho had big, gigantic walls. My Sunday School teacher said the first stone wall around Jericho was around 12 feet high and 14 feet wide. On top of this wall was *another wall* made of mud-bricks. That one was about 20 feet high."

"Wow, it sounds gigantic."

"I'm not done telling you about the walls Mom. There's more. There was another wall that was higher than the first wall. It was at the top of the hill and it was over 40 feet high. That means it was like looking at a gigantic hill, with two walls towering over it. My teacher said the Israelites looked like measly ants compared to the walls."

"It's amazing how many details you remember Jonah."

"Here's where things get weird Mom. Like I said before, the walls were very, very high. Usually an army would try to damage the walls by burning them. Or, maybe they could build their own ramp and climb their way in. If that didn't work they could dig a tunnel underground and get in that way. If none of those ideas worked, they could just surround the city and wait for the people inside to starve. If the Israelites waited long enough, the people would run out of food and then they would have to come outside the walls to fight. But all those things would take a lot of time. I guess God didn't want the Israelites to waste time. So, he gave them these weird instructions."

"Go on. But let's not call them weird instructions. How about we say they are supernatural instructions?" she suggested.

"Ok… God gave Joshua these **supernatural instructions**. He told Joshua and the Israelites to march around Jericho one time for six days, and then on the seventh day they had to march around the city seven times."

"How about I read the instructions aloud," Ruthie suggested.

"Sure."

"This is written in Joshua 6. It says, 'March around the city once with all the armed men. Do this for six days. Have seven priests carry trumpets of rams' horns in front of the Ark. On the seventh day, march around the city seven times, with the priests blowing the trumpets. When you hear them sound a long blast on the trumpets, have the whole army give a loud shout; then the wall of the city will collapse and the army will go up, everyone straight in,'" Ruthie read from the Bible.

Jonah nodded his head in agreement and said, "Each day after they were finished, they had to go back to their camp to stay the night. Then, they would get back up the next day and do the same thing again. But, the seventh day would be their shining moment. They marched around the city seven times and then the priests sounded *the last trump*, and immediately Joshua gave the command to Shout! The Army shouted and the wall collapsed. The Israelites ***went up into the city*** and took it."

Ruthie heard all that Jonah described, but one part stood out. It was the part when Jonah said the priests sounded ***the last trump.*** She quickly looked in her Bible at Joshua 6. She read through the whole chapter, looking for where it said THE LAST TRUMP. She couldn't find those exact words. She did see where it said in verse 5, "when you hear them sound **a long blast on the trumpets**, have the whole army give a loud shout; and then the wall of the city will collapse."

"Jonah, why did you say the last trump?"

"Well, isn't the long blast on the trumpet the last one to be played?" Jonah answered matter of factly.

"Yes, I suppose you are right." But Ruthie felt there was more to it. It was something more detailed, and even mysterious.

"I think you're right Mom. The instructions weren't really weird because God isn't weird. He is supernatural. He does things differently, but he always does it in a way that no one would expect."

"His ways are not our ways. That's for sure," she answered. In her own mind she wondered where God was going with all this. **The Last Trump. Gigantic walls collapsing. Jericho.**

Suddenly the power came back on.

"I thought it wouldn't be on until tomorrow," Jonah remarked.

"It's not what I expected, but then again, life is often full of surprises," she answered.

"Hey Mom. Can we just sleep in this tent tonight?"

"Ugh, it's not very comfortable."

"Pleeeese," he begged.

"Oh, all right. But, only if we can go to bed now. I'm tired."

"You're the best!"

Ruthie lay in the tent, thinking about Jericho. She could hear the trumpets in her mind. She closed her eyes, drifting off to sleep, the sound of the imaginary trumpets in the background. Maybe this is why she had such a strange, supernatural dream.

CHAPTER 14

Dreaming

RUTHIE WAS IN THE MIDST of a deep sleep. Nothing short of a blow horn could wake her up.

A vivid dream began. She found herself in what looked like a house, though it looked nothing like the houses of her time. The reddish, tan walls were rustic and simple. The furniture, if it could be called that, was disheveled and scant at best. There were no TVs, ovens, microwaves, or modern conveniences. The dwelling screamed ancient in more ways than one. Where was she?

She noticed a window as she turned around to face the back of the dwelling. She raced over, peering out the window. As she stuck her head out, she spied a glint of red from below the window. She moved closer, realizing it was a long scarlet-colored cord. She stood there, lost in the moment, mesmerized by the brightness of the cord. As she ran her fingers across the fibers, she heard shouting and screaming. Sheer terror reverberated from the shouts. Something horrible was happening outside.

She dashed to the door, unsure if she should open it. One second. Two seconds. Three seconds- It opened on its own.

She peered around. Bricks piled on top of bricks. Smoke billowing, fires blazing. Every inch around her was on fire. Everything except her dwelling. To her left were heaps of brick as far as the eye could see. To her right, even larger piles of smoldering rubble. Every direction she looked was heap upon heap of charred brick and clay. Yet, her home was strangely untouched. It was standing on its own in the midst of chaos, terror and destruction. She turned around, wanting to forget the destruction all around her. That's when she saw her family. They were in the dwelling with her. Despite the madness outside, they were safe and sound. She wondered how this could be.

She noticed her father. He was carrying something. It looked like a large clay jar. As she walked toward him, he handed her the jar. It felt heavy. It was filled to the brim with grain. How odd it was to be holding a jar of grain, while the outside world churned in chaos.

Just then she remembered the scarlet cord, still hanging from the window. She walked over and grabbed the cord with one hand, while holding the jar in the other. It seemed to fade into her hands, almost becoming part of her body. The vibrant red color of the cord seeped into her skin, as if it were the blood in her veins. What a strange feeling.

She looked beyond the window, her eyes widening. She could see the back wall of her dwelling, standing upright amongst heaps of reddish bricks. Her dwelling wall was the only one left in what looked like an entire city. How could it be?

As she stood pondering, she heard an unusual sound. It was loud and almost like a shriek. She looked into the distance, trying to figure out the origin of the piercing sound.

Finally, she saw it. It was wide-eyed and alert, full of vigor, yet stoic and still. Perched on a pile of rubble, with steam rising from the ashes around it, **a large hawk** sat. Oddly enough, it was similar to the hawk she'd seen not long ago in her own neighborhood. That hawk had perched on the neighborhood stone marker, with a carcass under its foot. This hawk could have passed for its twin.

In the blink of an eye, the hawk flew to her window. She stepped back, alarmed by its approach. With one fell swoop it snatched the scarlet cord with its feet. That's when she noticed the lightning in the sky. It flashed and crackled. And she heard something else. It was a series of trumpet blasts. The staccato-like rhythm pierced her ears. Just as she started to cover them, she heard a long, drawn out blast.

Next thing she knew, she was awake. She was inside the tent in her living room.

"Did you sleep well Mom?" Jonah asked.

"I think so," she answered.

"You think so?" he laughed.

The dream seemed so real. She knew it meant something. **It had to be tied to Jericho somehow**. Just one puzzle piece after another. She felt motivated by each piece of the puzzle. Because it would all lead somewhere only God knew.

CHAPTER 15
Rahab

RUTHIE KNEW THE DREAM CARRIED layers of meaning within. Jericho was more than a story about a wall falling down. It had to be allegory, or a story within a story. She could still hear the shriek of the hawk, and the blast of the trumpets. TRUMPETS! That's right- there were certainly trumpets present when the walls of Jericho came down.

Last night she and Jonah only read part of the story. She felt certain she needed to read the rest. She grabbed her Bible and started to read the part where the wall fell down.

"The seventh time around, when the priests sounded the trumpet blast, Joshua commanded the army, 'Shout! For the LORD has given you the city! The city and all that is in it are to be devoted to the Lord. **Only Rahab the prostitute and all who are in her house shall be spared***, because she hid the spies we sent.'"*

"That's it! RAHAB! Why didn't I think of her before?" Ruthie said aloud.

"Who's Rahab?" asked Thomas, walking in the door from work. He had just finished his shift at the fire department.

"Oh, Hi Thomas! How was your shift?"

"Not so good. I had zero hours of sleep. I was on the rescue engine all night, and we had a fire at 3 a.m."

"Ugh. I don't like it when you have to go to a fire," she said, cringing.

"You know, I am a FIREfighter! You can expect that."

"I know, but that doesn't mean I like it. What kind of fire was it?"

"This one was a little unusual."

"How so?"

"Well, it was at a music store so there were all sorts of instruments inside. When I walked in I could see half-melted saxophones, tubas, drums, flutes, and guitars. Everything was either burning, or charred to a crisp. Except for…..," Thomas paused.

"Except for what?"

"The trumpets."

"Did you just say trumpets?" she asked with a lump in her throat.

"Yeah, trumpets. It was strange because they were close to the other instruments that were damaged. But the trumpets were like new- no charring or anything. After we finished putting out the fire, I went ahead and grabbed the trumpets and brought them out. I couldn't salvage anything else, but at least seven trumpets were spared."

"Did you say **seven trumpets**?" Ruthie asked.

"Yes, there were seven. Anyway, I figured I could at least grab the trumpets and give them to the owner of the store. I'm glad there was something left after all the destruction. I don't really get it though. Doesn't make sense. Why weren't the trumpets damaged like everything else?" Thomas pulled out his phone and showed a picture of the trumpets to Ruthie.

The trumpets were shiny and new, just like Thomas described. "Now, **this** is the inside of the store," he said, showing her another photo.

As Ruthie looked at the photo she could only see complete devastation. Black ash covered everything.

"I guess this is one of God's little mysteries," Thomas stated, shaking his head.

Thomas was right, though perhaps it was more of a miracle. The timing of this couldn't be chance. She had just read about Jericho and trumpets. Strangely enough, the Israelites marched around Jericho **seven times on the seventh day** in order to claim victory over the land. Not only that, **seven priests carried seven trumpets** in front of the ark of God as the Israelites marched around the city of Jericho. She must be on the right track. After all, what were the chances of Thomas salvaging exactly seven trumpets from the fire! In her dream, only her house was spared after the trumpet blasts. In fact, fire destroyed everything at Jericho, just like the fire Thomas described.

"I'm going to take a shower. Maybe we can go somewhere and grab breakfast when I'm done," Thomas suggested. She nodded her head.

She kept thinking about the seven trumpets of Jericho. But, wasn't there some other place in the Bible that mentioned seven trumpets?

She dashed to the computer and searched, "seven trumpets in the Bible." Within seconds she had her answer. There are seven trumpets mentioned in the Book of Revelation. Beginning in Revelation 8, verse 6, seven angels holding seven trumpets **prepare to sound the alarm**. Ruthie read the verses aloud:

"The first angel sounded, and there followed hail and **fire** mingled with blood, and they were cast upon the earth: and a third part of trees was **burnt up,** and all green grass was **burnt up**. And the second angel sounded, and as it were a great mountain burning with **fire** was cast into the sea: and a third part of the sea became blood. And a third part of the creatures which were in the sea, and had life, died; and the third part of the ships were destroyed. And the third angel sounded, and there fell a great star from heaven, **burning** as it were a lamp, and it fell upon the third part of the rivers, and upon the fountains of waters; And the name of the star is Wormwood; and the third part of the waters became wormwood; and many died of the waters, because they were made bitter. And the fourth angel sounded, and the third part of the sun was smitten, and the third part of the moon, and the third part of the stars; so as the third part of them was darkened, and the day shone not for a third part of it, and the night likewise…..And the fifth angel sounded, and I saw a star fall from heaven unto the earth: and to him was given the key to a bottomless pit. And he opened the bottomless pit; and there arose a smoke out of the pit, as the smoke of a **great furnace**; and the sun and air were darkened by reason of the smoke of the pit. And there came out smoke locusts upon the earth; and unto them was given power, as the scorpions of the earth have power………….. And the sixth angel sounded, and I heard a voice from the four horns of the golden altar which is before God, Saying to sixth angel which had the trumpet, Loose the four angels which are bound in the great river Euphrates, And the four angels were loosed, which were prepared for an hour, and a day, and a month, and a year, for to slay the third part of men.….. And the seventh angel sounded; and there were great voices in heaven saying, 'The kingdoms of this world become the kingdoms of our Lord, and of his Christ; and he shall reign forever and ever.'"

The destruction described in Revelation 8 was specific and thorough. There was great loss of life among both humans and nature. There was **fire**, war and death. Ruthie could see parallels to Jericho. When Jericho's wall fell down, the city was attacked. The Israelites destroyed everything in the city, including animals, people and dwellings. They **set fire to everything**, except the gold, silver, brass and iron. They destroyed everything except……………**RAHAB and her family**.

She grabbed her Bible again and went back to the passage about Rahab in Joshua chapter 6. She skipped down to verse 22 and read through verse 25. She read the verses aloud. "Joshua said to the two men who had spied out the land, 'Go into the prostitute's house and bring her out and all who belong to her, in accordance with your oath to her.' So the young men who had done the spying went in and brought out Rahab, her father and mother, her brothers and sisters and all who belonged to her. They brought out her entire family and put them in *a place outside the camp of Israel.* Then they burned the whole city and everything ……. But, *Joshua spared Rahab the prostitute, with her family and all who belonged to her.*…and she lives among the Israelites to this day."

"Only Rahab and her family were spared. Everyone else was killed, and everything was burned to the ground," Ruthie said aloud.

She thought about her dream. Bricks and ash were strewn everywhere. Fire had consumed the area and all the dwellings…… except for one. Her house was spared. Why? Not only that, she remembered her family stood **inside her dwelling, safe from the chaos outside.** Everything was destroyed, except for her home and family.

She closed her eyes to see if she could picture the other details of the dream. The first thing she saw was the **scarlet cord.** It was hanging outside her window in the dream. Quickly she looked in her Bible to see if she could find anything about a scarlet cord. She had to go all the way back to Joshua, chapter two, but she found it.

After reading chapter 2 she understood Rahab had hidden the spies who came into Jericho. Though Rahab was a citizen of the pagan city of Jericho, she knew the spies served the *one true holy God*. She had respect for the spies and their God, so she risked her own life by hiding the spies under some flax on her rooftop. Had she not done this, the spies would have been captured and killed. In return for the favor, the spies promised to **spare her entire household**. They didn't just tell her this- **they pledged an oath that she would be protected.** As a sign, Rahab would leave a scarlet cord dangling from her window. This cord would be her protection. When the walls came down and the Israelites invaded Jericho, they would burn and destroy the entire city, minus the gold, silver, bronze and iron. This also included the people living within the city walls. Every living and non-living thing would be destroyed. **But, when the army saw the scarlet cord on the window, they would know not to touch that dwelling. The dwelling with the scarlet cord would be spared from the disaster.**

In Ruthie's dream the scarlet cord was so bright and beautiful. She knew there was a reason it was in the window. And her house was spared, just like Rahab's.

She closed her eyes once more. This time she saw her father. In the dream he was carrying a large clay jar of grain. He'd handed it to her. Why?

She examined the rest of the Jericho story, but she couldn't find anything about jars of grain. The one thing she did know is the invasion must have taken place **during the harvest.** She knew this because when the Israelites crossed over the Jordan into the Promised Land, *the waters were at flood levels*, which indicated it was **harvest time**.

Quickly she grabbed her phone so she could search the Internet. She typed in the words **Jericho and grain**. To her amazement she found an article from *Answers in Genesis* which explained something fascinating. It said the whole area of Jericho had been excavated by archaeologists and one of the things found at the ruins were **full jars of grain**. The grain had been charred, indicating a fire had taken place. Also, the fact that the jars were full meant the harvest had been just taken in from the fields. It also indicated the invasion was swift. If the invasion had taken a long time there would not have been full jars of grain. The people living inside of Jericho would have been forced to eat their stored grain. As the Bible described, the siege and invasion of Jericho only took seven days. Short and swift indeed.

And what about the flax on her roof? She had hidden the spies underneath it. Ruthie knew flax was used to make fine linen. In fact, when Jesus was born, it is likely he was wrapped in linen, as it describes him being wrapped in swaddling cloths. Many scholars also believe Jesus was buried in linen. In the Bible it mentions David dancing in a garment of linen (made from flax) when the Ark of the Covenant was brought to Jerusalem. During the time of the Exodus, the Israelites left Egypt, to escape the evil Pharaoh. During the Ten Plagues the flax and barley were destroyed. But, the Israelites made their great escape with the help of an Almighty God. In each instance of flax being mentioned, a great miracle took place. When it came to Rahab, she hid the spies under the flax, and in return a great miracle took place for her.

"So it was harvest time and the Israelites crossed over into their Promised Land. The Israelites broke down the walls through God's power, with the sound of the trumpets blasting, and a loud shout. The walls collapsed, allowing for a swift and brutal attack on Jericho. Everyone and everything was burned and destroyed, except for a prostitute and her family. The scarlet cord was a sign they would be spared, as it was a reminder of the oath," Ruthie said to herself. She took a few moments to think this over. Suddenly she burst out and said, "Rahab was a prostitute! She was a huge sinner…… a foreigner in God's kingdom….. she wasn't even an Israelite. She was a Gentile."

It was then she knew. She understood why. She realized what it meant. **Jericho was a foreshadowing of the rapture.** At the rapture, the Bride of Christ would be "snatched away" in the blink of an eye. It reminded Ruthie of a when a hawk seized its prey. Just as Rahab and her family were spared the wrath falling upon Jericho, the Bride of Christ would be spared God's wrath falling upon the earth. Jesus Christ swore an oath with his blood. This oath meant he would save his Bride. Those who accepted Christ were saved through his blood, which was a symbol of the oath he took. The cord hanging from Rahab's window was scarlet- the color of blood.

She thought about Revelation 8 and the seven trumpets being sounded. Destruction, death and chaos would commence at the sounds of these trumpets. There were more details to uncover, but she was almost certain of it. The last trump sounded before the walls fell down, and Rahab was spared. Jesus would return at the last trump, and the Bride would be spared the horror of the Tribulation.

"Ready for breakfast?" asked Thomas as he walked into the kitchen. Ruthie was still thinking about Rahab and barely heard his voice.

"Ready for breakfast?" he repeated.

"Oh…..yeah…of course," she answered.

"Deep in thought I see," Thomas stated.

"Yes, you could say I was. We better get going. Where's Jonah?"

"He was outside when I came home. Maybe he's still out there," Thomas suggested.

They walked outdoors and found him staring at the sky.

"Whatcha staring at buddy?" Thomas asked.

"You missed it! A giant hawk just grabbed a huge snake from the grass. I could see the snake dangling from his talons. The hawk flew up in our tree with the snake," he said, pointing to the tree.

"Wow! I wish we had seen it!"

"One minute the hawk was sitting on the electrical pole and the next he just snatched the snake from the grass. He was faster than lightning!"

As Jonah described what happened, Ruthie formed a mental image in her head. She could see the hawk grabbing the snake with its sharp talons. The snake had no chance. It had been defeated. Several verses were playing in her head…… Ephesians 1:22, "Everything has been placed under Jesus' feet." And Luke 10:19, "I have given you authority to trample on snakes and scorpions, and to overcome the power of the enemy."

She knew Jesus defeated Satan (the snake) at the cross. For now, however, the world was still influenced by Satan. But there would come a day when Jesus would step foot on the Mount of Olives and officially take the Earth back. Satan would be bound, and eventually thrown into the lake of fire. But before Jesus stepped foot on Earth again, he would also come to snatch his Bride, and whisk her off to heaven. This event, known as the Rapture, would occur in the blink of an eye. Much like electricity or lightning, it would be powerful, quick and dramatic. The hawk snatching the snake reminded her Jesus would set things straight one day. The Bride would be removed from Earth and taken to heaven as quick as lightning. Later Satan (the snake), would be removed from Earth and thrown into a pit.

"Well, looks like the hawk had his meal, so what do you say we get ours," Thomas exclaimed.

"Ok Dad, let's go."

CHAPTER 16
The Mystery of the Shofar

THEY WENT TO ONE OF Thomas' favorite breakfast eateries called *Early Bird*. Unfortunately, it was very busy so the chances of eating anytime soon were slim to none.

"I'm going to put our name on the waiting list," Thomas stated, much to Ruthie's dismay.

"I guess," she sighed.

In the meantime, they sat on a bench, passing the time. Thomas checked his email while Jonah played with her phone. Ruthie just sat there feeling hungry, and a little bored. "Oh well, it could be worse," she thought. She decided to pass the time by people watching. She scanned the restaurant, looking for people of interest. Everyone was either eating or talking. Nothing out of the ordinary. Feeling more bored than ever she turned her head. She noticed a man sitting to her immediate left. He had a kippah on his head, as well as a Bible in hand. "He could be interesting," she thought. After all, she loved learning about the Jewish people and their customs. But, what would she say to him? Perhaps something like, "Hi, I'm Ruthie and I love Jewish people. Can you tell me all about yourself and your lifestyle?" She laughed to herself. How silly she would sound.

"Are you a Christian?" said a voice.

She looked around, stunned at the question. It was the man with the kippah on his head.

"Me?" she asked.

"Yes, I'm talking to you," the man smiled.

"Uh, well, uh yes," she stumbled.

"I saw the cross around your neck," he stated.

"Oh yes, my mother gave me this after I was baptized."

"I'm a Christian too," the man stated.

She must have had a surprised look on her face because the man quickly said, "I know what you are thinking. I'm Jewish so I don't believe Jesus is the Messiah. But, let me assure you my eyes are wide open and I know who he is, and what he did."

"That's wonderful. I'll bet there are things you understand with your Jewish background that many non-Jewish people do not. You know how everything ties together."

"Well, there are many mysteries contained in the Bible, and **it is important for all eyes to see them**, both Jew and Gentile. Perhaps one of the greatest mysteries of the Bible surrounds the shofar, or as some call it, the trumpet."

Ruthie raised an eyebrow. Did he just say trumpet? She just read about Jericho and the trumpets, and there was Thomas' story about trumpets, and her dream.

"Do you know anything about the *Feast of Trumpets?*" the man asked.

"I do actually. I've been studying it. I know it's one of the Lord's Feasts and it's a day when the shofar is blown. Of all the feasts, it is one of the most mysterious because it comes each year at the New Moon on the first day of the Hebrew month Tishrei. The New Moon is very difficult to spot so The Feast of Trumpets is also called **The Hidden Day.** Back in ancient times there had to be two witnesses to spot the new moon, and then they had to testify they had seen it. Depending on the amount of clouds or the weather conditions, the witnesses may not see the New Moon right away. Once they spotted the moon, it could also take a while for this information to get back to all the communities. The Feast of Trumpets could not officially begin until the information was relayed to the people. So, the start of the feast was somewhat of a mystery."

"I am impressed. Most people are not familiar with any of the things you said. And you are right. The Feast of Trumpets is shrouded in mystery. Many feast days such as Passover, Tabernacles and Yom Kippur occur on a full moon, or when the moon is partially visible, which is much easier to spot. And, in the cases of Yom Kippur and Tabernacles, the ***days can be counted after Rosh Hashanah occurs.*** Yom Kippur occurs ten days after Rosh Hashanah, and Tabernacles arrives on the fifth day after Yom Kippur. The Feast of Trumpets, also called Rosh Hashanah, was not as obvious. Yet, there's something even more mysterious about this special feast."

"I would love to know," Ruthie said.

"It's the trumpets of course. That's the theme of the feast after all," the man laughed. "So, let's get right into it. You have to know the reasons **why the trumpet (shofar) is blown.**"

"Isn't it used to sound an alarm?" she asked.

"Yes, that is true, but there are other reasons as well. First, it is a call to worship God. The trumpet is used to initiate the biblical feasts where the Lord is worshipped, and to usher in the Sabbath, which is the Lord's day of rest. The Bible says to **praise God with the playing of the shofar.** It was used for praise and worship during ceremonies in the Temple. Interestingly enough, in Exodus 19 **the voice of God is described as being like a loud trumpet,** and he blew it before he gave the Israelites the Torah, which is also known as the LAW."

"**God's voice is like a trumpet**? That's fascinating to me."

"Of course, you have to remember the shofar (trumpet) is made of a ram's horn. Think about the story of Abraham and Isaac. Abraham was going to sacrifice his son Isaac to God and then at the last minute God provided a ram to be sacrificed instead. Abraham was fully prepared to sacrifice his son and God saw he was obedient. In his mercy, God provided a ram. **Thus, the ram's horn, or shofar, is a reminder of God's mercy.**"

"The whole story of Abraham and Isaac foreshadowed what would happen to Jesus. God would send his only son to be sacrificed for the world. He had mercy on humanity just as he had mercy on Abraham. He was willing to have his own son take the punishment for humanity," Ruthie added.

"That is correct, which leads me to another reason the shofar/trumpet is blown. **It is a call to repent.** In Isaiah 53, verse 1, it says to, 'cry aloud, spare not, **lift up they voice like a trumpet**, and shew my people their transgression, and the house of Jacob their sins.' Also, during the month of Elul, which occurs right before the Feast of Trumpets, the Jewish people are to spend their time repenting of sins as they prepare for this important feast day. They are to search themselves for any sins and seek to purify themselves before the Lord. The shofar is blown every day during the month of Elul to remind them of this need to repent."

"Can I guess the next reason? I think I might know one," Ruthie asked.

"Of course you can," the man answered.

"Is the next reason warfare?"

"Yes, how did you know?"

"Well, I just read about the Battle of Jericho, and before the Israelites took the city there were seven shofars blown. The walls came tumbling down when the trumpets were sounded, accompanied by a loud shout."

"You are exactly right. That's just one example though. How about the story of Gideon? He was outnumbered by the Midianites, but he was able to conquer the whole army with a meager 300 men. But, there were also 300 shofars sounded when the army ambushed the Midianites. The sound of the shofars confused the Midianites and Gideon secured a victory. **Shofars were often blown as signals during wars.** In Nehemiah 4:20, it says, 'When you hear the sound of the trumpet, join us there. Our God will fight for us.'"

"It seems to me like wherever the shofar goes, so does the Lord," Ruthie added.

"Yes, and sometimes **the Lord will even use the shofar as a warning.** In Ezekiel 33, verses 3-5, this is what it says,

'And he sees the sword coming against the land and **blows the trumpet to warn the people**, then if anyone hears the trumpet but does not heed the warning and the sword comes and takes their life, their blood will be on their own head. **Since they heard the sound of the trumpet but did not heed the warning, their blood will be on their own head.** If they had heeded the warning, they would have saved themselves.'

"As you can tell from the verses, the trumpet, or shofar, is a warning call," the man stated. "Here is another example from Numbers 10, verse 9," he added.

"And if ye go to war in your land against the enemy that oppresseth you, then **ye shall blow an alarm with the trumpets; and ye shall be remembered before the L**ORD **your God, and ye shall be saved from your enemies."**

"It's very clear in those verses the trumpet is used to warn God's people. It even says God will remember those who sound the trumpet," Ruthie added.

"That is very true. In fact, one of the purposes of the shofar is for *remembrance and mercy*. It reminds God to have mercy as he did with Abraham and Isaac. He has mercy on those who are obedient as Abraham was. But, I want to be clear with you about the warnings. The shofar is not only a warning call, it may very well usher in the Day of the Lord."

"The Day of the Lord? Isn't that when chaos and judgment fall upon the Earth?"

"Yes, it is a day of darkness and despair. Listen to these verses from Joel 2," the man declared.

'**Blow ye the trumpet in Zion, and sound an alarm in my holy mountain**: let all the inhabitants of the land tremble: for the day of the LORD cometh, for it is nigh at hand. A day of darkness and of gloominess; a day of clouds and thick darkness, as the morning spread upon the mountains; a great people and a strong army; there hath not been ever the like, neither shall any more after it, even to the years of many generations. A fire devoureth before them; and behind them a flame burneth; the land is as the garden of Eden before them, and behind them a desolate wilderness; yea, and nothing shall escape them….. before their face the people shall be much pained: all faces shall gather blackness…..the earth shall quake before them; the heavens shall tremble; **the sun and the moon shall be dark**, and the stars shall withdraw their shining.'

"That's just a taste of the Day of the Lord, but you get the picture. The trumpet is blown on that day and it will usher in a terrible time for the inhabitants of Earth."

"The shofar has so many uses. From worship and mercy, to warning and judgment," Ruthie said.

"You are correct. Yet, the most important use is still to come."

"Do you mean the return of Jesus?" asked Ruthie.

"That's exactly what I mean," the man emphatically stated. "And the Lord shall be seen over them, and his arrow shall go forth as the lightning: **and the Lord God shall blow the trumpet**, and shall go with whirlwinds of the south."

"What verse did you just quote?"

"That was Zechariah 9:14. Listen to verse 16," suggested the man.

"And the Lord their God shall **save them** in that day as the flock of his people: for they shall be as the stones of a crown, lifted up as an ensign (banner) upon his land."

"So, are you saying the shofar will play when Jesus returns for his Bride?"

"Of course that's what I'm saying. And I can assure you, it will be quick- just like the lightning that almost struck you Ruthie."

She looked at the man inquisitively. How did he know about the lightning strike?

"As lightning cometh out of the east, and shineth even unto the west, so shall the coming of the Son of Man be," the man quoted.

Ruthie could see the lightning from her dream. The dream showed destruction around her, but she and her family were spared. Lightning flashed in the sky, dark clouds filled the air and the scarlet cord hung by the window. A verse filled her spirit so she spoke it aloud.

"For the Lord himself will come down from heaven, with a loud command, with the voice of the archangel and with the trumpet call of God, and the dead in Christ will rise first. After that, we who are still alive and are left will be caught up together with them in the clouds to meet the Lord in the air. And so we will be with the Lord forever," she quoted back.

"I see you memorized 1 Thessalonians 4. **The rapture of the church**. Christ, the groom, returns for his Bride at the sound of the trumpet. Christ has shed his blood for the Bride, and the Bride has accepted his free gift of salvation. The Bride is spared doom and gloom. Instead, she is taken to the wedding supper in heaven. Let's finish it off with this last verse from 1 Corinthians 15:52," the man enthusiastically stated.

"In a flash, in the twinkling of an eye, **at the last trumpet**. For the trumpet will sound, the dead will be raised imperishable, and we will be changed." He stopped for a moment and stared at Ruthie. "Did you notice it said in the **twinkling of an eye**? It will be quick like lightning. And it will happen at the last trump."

"**The last trump-** I've heard that before. Let me think," Ruthie said. She closed her eyes. She searched her brain. It was on the tip of her tongue. "I got it! It's Jericho. In the story they blew a long trumpet blast right before they gave the shout. This happened right before the wall fell down. That must be the last trump."

"You have part of the answer Ruthie. Now, you must find out the rest. But don't expect God to speak with thunder and lightning like he usually does. That's how he spoke to the Israelites and to Moses when he gave them the Law. It is written in Exodus 19, verse 16, 'On the morning of the third day there was thunder and lightning, with a thick cloud over the mountain, and a very loud trumpet blast.' Ruthie, this is a description of God's voice, right before the Ten Commandments were revealed," the man declared. "God's voice is the trumpet. His language is the trumpet. His mystery is in the trumpet."

"What's the rest? How do I?"

"Ruthie, our table is ready," Thomas said.

"Our table? What?"

"Our table. Don't you remember? We came here to eat," Thomas reiterated.

"Ok, but just let me ask the gentleman next to me one more thing." She turned to her left. No one was there. "That's odd. He was sitting right next to me."

"I never saw you sitting next to anyone. What are you talking about?"

"That's because you were on your phone the whole time. He was right next to me…."

"Maybe you're just hungry," said Thomas. "Food will do you some good."

She searched the restaurant. No sign of the man. *He vanished in the blink of an eye.* But, he did leave something behind. It had fallen under the bench. She picked it up. It was a small booklet titled, **The Shofar's Voice.** Perhaps the answers she needed would be inside that little book.

Author's Note:

"Sing for joy to God our strength: shout aloud to the God of Jacob! Begin the music, strike the timbrel, play the melodious harp and lyre. **Sound the ram's horn at the New Moon, and when the moon is full, on the day of our festival**; this is a decree for Israel, an ordinance of the God of Jacob." Psalm 81, 1-4

CHAPTER 17
The Voice of the Trumpet

❧

After breakfast Ruthie was anxious to read the booklet left behind by the man. What was his name? He knew hers somehow. Why did strangers, or as some would call them, "foreigners" know her name? Very odd indeed.

"Jonah and I are going to fish at the lake," Thomas said as he walked past with a few poles.

"Oh, that's great. I think I'll just catch up on some things around here," she answered.

This would be the perfect time to read the booklet. There would be peace and quiet, with no distractions.

"See you later Mom," said Jonah, as he walked out the door with Thomas. "I wish we weren't *leaving you behind*."

"Just go have fun," she laughed.

Quickly she grabbed the booklet and began with the first chapter. It was called *Yom Teruah*. "I've heard those words before," she thought. She read the chapter out loud. It's not like anyone was home to listen. Plus, reading it aloud seemed to cement the information.

"Yom Teruah is also known as the Feast of Trumpets, or Rosh Hashanah. This means 'the Day of Blowing'. **Yom Teruah is the only Feast Day when the trumpet is blown 100 times during the service.** The trumpet is blown using a specific pattern of sounds. The first sound used is called TE'KI'AH. This includes a long blast, with one or two notes. Next is the SH'VA'RIM. This consists of three medium length blasts with two tones each. This represents the act of repenting, and the brokenness of the soul. After this comes the TE'RU'AH (as in Yom Teruah). This includes nine short, staccato blasts. These represent alarm, war and victory. Finally, the series ends with what is often called the **last great trumpet sound, or the last trump**. It is called TE'KI'AH GE'DO'LAH. This is played as a very long, drawn out single blast. **This note is played for an extended period of time, or as long as the trumpeter can blow it. This represents God's mercy, grace and redemption."**

Ruthie stopped reading for a moment. There was something about the pattern. The number of blasts within the pattern seemed familiar and symbolic. She read over the information again. The numbers that stood out were the **three and the nine.**

She started with the three. Why were there three medium length blasts with the sound known as SH'VA'RIM? Of course, **three represented the Trinity**- God the father, the Son and the Holy Spirit. When we receive Christ as Savior we have access to all three. That was surely the most well-known three in the Bible. But, what about the others? There were **three patriarchs** known as Abraham, Isaac and Jacob. Mankind descended from the **three sons** of Noah- Shem, Ham and Japeth. Abraham was commanded to sacrifice Isaac after he went on **a three day journey** to Mt. Moriah. Jonah spent **three days** in the belly of a whale. Moses and Elijah appeared with Jesus at the Transfiguration –three again. These were just a few examples of the number three being used in the Bible. In fact, there were hundreds of examples of how God used three in the Bible. Which one was significant here? It had to be something that lined up with the meaning behind the shofar sounds.

She looked back at the booklet and reread this sentence: The *SH'VA'RIM, which is <u>sounded in **threes**</u>, represents repentance and brokenness.* She couldn't picture anything but the cross. Jesus, our Savior, died on the cross for our sins. His body was broken for us, so we could repent and receive forgiveness of sins. She wondered what time Jesus hung on the cross. She quickly looked it up on her phone. ***"And it was the third hour, and they crucified him,"*** she read, quoting Mark 15:25. "There's the three," she said to herself.

Certainly, Jesus being crucified at the third hour reminded her of brokenness and repentance. If there ever was a time to play the shofar, it would have been then. Amazingly enough, Jesus rose on the **third day** and conquered death and sin, making the way for repentance. If that weren't enough, Jesus received **39 lashes** before going to the cross. Thirty-nine stripes on his back to pay for the sin of the world. Even the number **nine pointed to three because it is made up of three threes!** Jesus began his ministry at **30** (10x3), and died at age **33. Surely, the pattern of the shofar pointed to this marvelous event, with its pattern of threes.**

She looked at the booklet again. She read aloud, "The TE'RU'AH sound includes nine short, staccato blasts. These represent alarm, war and victory." She looked at the information about Jesus' death on her phone. In Matthew 27 it said, "And at the **ninth hour** Jesus cried with a loud voice, saying, 'Eli, Eli, lama sabachthani?', that is to say, 'My God, my God, why hast thou forsaken me?' ……Jesus, when he had cried again with a loud voice, yielded up the ghost." She realized **Jesus died at the ninth hour. He gave up his spirit at the ninth hour. He overcame death and Satan's plan at the ninth hour. The nine staccato blasts of the shofar pointed to victory. What a victory Jesus had on the cross!**

As she pondered the nine staccato blasts, another thought entered her mind. **There were 39 books in the Old Testament. There was the nine, and the three**! Jesus fulfilled the Law of the Old Testament when he came to Earth as God's son. In Matthew 5:17 Jesus says, "Do not think that I have come to abolish the Law or the Prophets; I have not come to abolish them, but fulfill them." Remembering this verse came from the New Testament, another thought occurred to her. **The New Testament has 27 books. Nine times three equals 27!** There was the nine and the three again! Of course, the New Testament tells the story of Jesus birth, life, ministry, death and victory. But, the nine blasts of the shofar also represented alarm and war. However, the Old Testament's 39 books were full of stories that included the wars Israel fought where the shofar was sounded as an alarm. The Battle of Jericho is told in the Old Testament, and the shofar was one of the keys to victory in that war.

Ruthie knew the number patterns couldn't be a coincidence. God was the author of numbers after all, and his ways are precise. **The voice of God is compared to a shofar in the Bible. Certainly God's son, his Word and his plan for redemption were embedded in the sounds of the shofar.**

There was still another shofar sound to investigate. Ruthie read aloud from the booklet. "The TE'KI'AH includes a **long blast**, with one or two notes." A long blast was mentioned in Jericho. **The long blast was played before the walls fell down**. It was the last blast to be played before they fell down! Where else in the Bible is a long blast played on the shofar?

She thought for several minutes. One verse seemed to repeat in her mind. "In a flash, in the twinkling of an eye, **at the last trumpet**. For the trumpet will sound, the dead will be raised imperishable, and we will be changed."

"The last trumpet. That must be it. The last trumpet must be the long blast," she exclaimed. She read aloud from the booklet. "The series of shofar blasts ends with what is often called the **last great trumpet sound, or the last trump. It is called TE'KI'AH GE'DO'LAH**. This is played as a very long, drawn out single blast. This note is played for an extended period of time, or as long as the trumpeter can blow it. This represents God's mercy, grace and redemption."

Ruthie felt stunned. There it was. **The final sound/blast of the shofar is called THE LAST TRUMP. Jesus returns for his Bride at the sound of the last trump**! Not only that, the arrival of the ancient Jewish groom was announced by a trumpet blast. This meant the Bride would be snatched away and taken to the "hiding place" of the Groom. A great wedding would take place in the near future. Ruthie could see it now. Jesus would return like a Jewish Groom for his Bride. The long blast of the last trump would sound, and the Bride would be snatched away. Like the meaning of the last trump, TE'KI'AH GE'DO'LAH, this would be the ultimate act of mercy, grace and redemption. The Bride would be spared from the coming judgment of the world.

Ruthie opened the booklet once more. She noticed a verse from Revelation 1:10. "On the Lord's Day I was in the Spirit, and I heard behind me **a loud voice like a trumpet.**" She knew who the verse was describing. It was the voice of Jesus. This part of Revelation described the experience of John, who heard the voice of Jesus, telling him what would happen in the last days on Earth. Now, she realized not only was God's voice like a trumpet, but so was **the voice of Jesus. The trumpet blast of the ancient Jewish Groom foreshadowed the voice of Jesus himself, returning for his Bride.**

Who was the Bride? Jesus' followers of course. But, **did they all really hear the shofar these days?** Symbolically it represented Jesus' sacrifice on the cross and even the word of God. But, it was also his voice. Was anyone listening? **The shofar sounded 100 times on Rosh Hashanah. The 100th trump, or the last trump, meant mercy for those who knew the voice of Jesus.**

A still small voice resounded in her heart and mind. "Rahab will hear it." Yes, she was a foreigner, but her heart belonged to God.

Author's Note about TRUMPS:

There are three types of TRUMPS

The FIRST TRUMP is associated with Mount Sinai when God revealed himself to the Israelites (under the leadership of Moses). This would have occurred on Shuavuot (or Pentecost). The Exodus had occurred and it was now time to give the Israelites God's laws- the Ten Commandments. Moses met with God, and then God revealed himself to the people in this way:

Exodus 19: verses 16, 19- "And it came to pass on the third day in the morning, that there were thunders and **lightnings,** and a thick cloud upon the mount, and the voice of a **trumpet exceeding loud**; so that all the people that were in the camp trembled…….And when the **voice of the trumpet sounded long, and waxed louder and louder,** Moses spake, and God answered him by a voice."

After the "law" was given to the people, it says this in Exodus 20: "And all the people saw thunderings, and the **lightnings**, and the **noise of the trumpet**, and the mountain smoking."

The LAST TRUMP is associated with the return of Jesus for his Bride, also known as the Rapture. It is associated with the Feast of Trumpets, or Rosh Hashanah.

The GREAT TRUMP is associated with Yom Kippur, or the Day of Atonement- In biblical days this is when the high priest went into the Holy of Holies to make atonement for the sins of the entire nation of Israel. After the Temple was destroyed this could no longer be done- but even today Jewish people will fast on Yom Kippur in order to receive forgiveness and atonement for sin. Another name for Yom Kippur is Shofar HaGadol, or the Great Shofar. Fasting for Yom Kippur is over in the evening, and at that time the shofar is blown to signal the end of the fast. It is only blown once and it is called the Great Trump. This Trump may be tied to the day when Israel as a nation recognizes Messiah Jesus as "the one who was pierced". Christ himself would make the atonement for the nation of Israel. This would take place during the end days of the Tribulation.

Isaiah 27:13 – "And it shall come to pass in that day, that the **GREAT TRUMPET** shall be blown, and they shall come which were ready to perish in the land of Assyria, and the outcasts in the land of Egypt, **and shall worship the Lord in the holy mount at Jerusalem.**"

Fascinating Fact: According to National Geographic, **cloud to ground lightning strikes the Earth 100 times per second.** When God appears before man in the Bible, the presence of **clouds and lightning** follow. The **100th TRUMP**, or the last trump, is sounded on Rosh Hashanah (Feast of Trumpets). This feast is also named The Day of Dark Clouds -The Day of the Lord. This feast foreshadows the coming of Christ. He will return like lightning on the clouds.

CHAPTER 18
The Potter's Field

※

Ruthie needed to understand more about Rahab. She knew many things already. Rahab hid the spies of Jericho on the roof of her house and by doing so, she saved their lives. In return, she and her entire family were spared when Jericho was burned and destroyed. The scarlet cord hanging outside her window reminded the spies to keep their oath to her, and not allow her home or family to be harmed. But why spare Rahab the prostitute? A pagan woman from a pagan land? Why even honor the oath to an outsider?

"Hey babe! Can you come out here? I need your help," Thomas yelled.

She quickly walked outside, wondering what he needed.

"Come over to the truck bed. I need some help getting these pots out," he said.

She walked over to the truck, where she saw three large clay pots.

"Do you like them? The man who owns the Music Store sent them over to the Fire Station today. He said they were a gift to the firemen for helping salvage the trumpets from his store. He sent seven in all, and I took three home. Apparently music isn't his only passion. He also makes his own pottery."

"Kind of an odd gift, don't you think," she answered, studying the pots carefully.

"I suppose, but they are handmade. I figured you could use them outside- maybe put a few plants inside them."

"That's true. For now let's just put them near the back porch."

"Whatever you say dear."

Ruthie grabbed a pot, immediately overwhelmed by how heavy it was. As she carried it, she couldn't help but think of Jesus, as he carried the heavy cross on his back. This pot was nothing compared to that. As she carried the large clay pot, three words entered her mind. **THE POTTER'S FIELD.**

Strange. In the past she had read those words in the Bible, but she couldn't place the meaning. What was the Potter's Field? She laid the heavy pot down on the grass. Thomas brought the other two pots one by one, setting them next to the first one.

She knew what she needed to do. She had to read about the Potter's Field. She ran inside and grabbed her Bible. She looked at the index.

"Let's see. Potter's Field. Matthew 27:7." She turned to the book of Matthew and read the verse. "So they decided to use the money to buy the potter's field as a burial place for foreigners." The money being referred to in the verse was the money used to betray Jesus. Judas, one of Jesus' disciples, agreed to hand over Jesus to the Temple Priests and guards for 30 pieces of silver. This led to the arrest, and eventual crucifixion of Jesus. Judas eventually realizes his huge, earth-shattering mistake and regrets his decision to betray Jesus. He returns the thirty pieces of silver to the chief priests and even says, "I have betrayed innocent blood." They reply, "What is that to us? That's your responsibility." So, Judas throws the money into the temple and leaves. Then, he hangs himself. When the priests find the coins they say, "It is against the law to put this into the treasury, since it is blood money." So, instead they buy a potter's field. **This field would be used as a burial place for foreigners**. It would later be known as the Field of Blood.

Something symbolic echoed from the story of potter's field. Something deep. **It was a burial place for <u>foreigners</u>, bought with the money that led to Jesus' crucifixion and death.** Jesus' death led to the redemption of the world- the redemption of all those who would accept him as Savior, even the foreigners. Those who were redeemed would be his holy Bride.

"Rahab!" she exclaimed. She knew she was on to something. **Rahab was a foreigner.** She wasn't an Israelite. She was a citizen of Jericho, and certainly not worthy of being in the company of God's chosen people. **But, she was spared on the day of alarm, the day of destruction.** The spies of Jericho swore an oath to protect her on the day of destruction. The scarlet cord would be the sign.

"The scarlet cord! I've got it! The blood of Jesus saves the Bride. The scarlet cord represents the blood of Jesus. It's what saves. Rahab was a foreigner and even worse, a harlot. Nonetheless, she is spared. The price Jesus paid on the cross was his very own blood- the blood that would save. But before this, another price was paid for him- the 30 pieces of silver. *Technically this could be considered the price of the Bride.* The thirty pieces of silver led to Jesus' arrest, and his death on the cross. This death spares the Bride.

Ruthie felt there was more about Rahab she needed to understand. She ran to the computer and typed in *Rahab and Jesus*. To her shock, she found out **Rahab married one of the spies she hid. Rahab, a foreigner and non-Jew, married a Jewish man. The man she married was named Salmon, who was from the tribe of Judah. By marrying Salmon, she became the mother of Boaz, who married Ruth. Ruth bore a son named Obed. Obed had a son named Jesse. King David is the son of Jesse. The line of Jesus came from the line of King David. Thus, by marrying Salmon, Rahab became part of the lineage of Jesus. A foreigner, grafted into God's family.**

Ruthie understood Rahab symbolized the Gentile Bride, **or the <u>foreign Bride of Christ</u>.** When Christ came to Earth, he didn't just come for the Jewish people. **He came for all people, even the foreigners.** When he returned for his Bride one day, he would be coming for "foreigners and Jews" who knew him as Savior- he swore an oath through his blood. This Bride would know his voice, and be shown mercy for only one reason- they knew Jesus as Savior, and his blood saved them.

The Potter's Field, also known as the Field of Blood, bought with 30 silver coins, would symbolize the grace of Jesus, who came to save foreigners like Rahab, as well as the Jewish people who believed he was Messiah.

Ruthie remembered something else! The clay jars found at Jericho! There were jars of grain found at Jericho. Archaeologists were amazed when they found **jars full of charred grain** at the ruins. This meant Jericho was seized quickly, during the **harvest season.** The attack had been just like the Bible described.

Now Ruthie knew. She could see it. At the rapture, the Bride of Jesus would be spared. It would be harvest time, and the trumpet would sound. The Jew and Gentile Bride would be taken in the blink of an eye to "the hidden place." Would it be on Rosh Hashanah? After all, this feast occurred right after the month of Elul (September or October, depending on the year), and the word ***Elul meant harvest.*** On Rosh Hashanah the trumpet sounded 100 times. The last trump signified mercy.

Jesus would pursue his Bride with great veracity. If there were 99 sheep safe and sound, but the 100th sheep wandered off, Jesus would pursue it. That's the kind of mercy Jesus had for his Bride. He didn't want anyone to stay lost. One day the Lord would return after the 100th sheep had been found. Abraham was 100 years old when his son Isaac was born. He waited a long time, believing in God's promises. Later, Abraham almost sacrificed his son, but God's mercy prevailed. A ram was provided in Isaac's place at the last minute. This ram foreshadowed the sounding of the shofar, which is made of a ram's horn. The shofar would sound at the return of our Savior, Jesus Christ. Like Isaac, the Bride would be spared and God's mercy would sound with the trumpet.

Ruthie shook her head as she thought about the irony of the situation. The owner of a music store loses all of his instruments, except for the trumpets. Everything burned to a crisp, except for the trumpets. As a gift, the owner of the music store sends several clay pots. All of these things were symbolic of Jericho- *the trumpets, the fire and even the clay pots.* There were far too many coincidences to be coincidence.

Author's Note: 30 pieces of silver is what Judas was paid to betray Jesus. This is considered the cost for the Bride because once Jesus was betrayed and arrested, he went to the cross to pay the penalty for our sins- the Bride's sins. Interestingly enough, Jesus began his earthly ministry at age 30. John the Baptist also began to preach at the age of 30. King David was 30 when he became the King of Israel. Joseph was 30 years old when he became second in command to Pharaoh. Levite priests officially entered into their service/duties at age 30. The prophet Ezekiel was 30 years old when he was called by God. The Jewish people mourn for 30 days.

It is clear the number 30 is very significant to the Lord.

CHAPTER 19

Lightning

A FEW DAYS HAD PASSED since Thomas brought the clay pots home. As usual, Ruthie felt like there were pieces still missing to the puzzle. She had part of the picture, but there were more details to uncover. She had the sudden urge to walk to the spot where she was nearly electrocuted a few months ago. Was there a clue she'd missed the first time?

She walked to the neighborhood entrance stone marker, located near her street, *Kingfisher Drive*. As she walked closer, something caught her attention. She realized the *Lake Lagrange* neighborhood entrance marker was **made of stones**. The stones were of all shapes and sizes, placed together in a rugged pattern. Come to think of it, *they reminded her of an ancient wall*. Yes, that's what it was! The neighborhood entrance stone marker resembled a wall! Wow! What a revelation. She had just learned about the walls of Jericho falling down, and about the life of Rahab, the woman who literally lived in the wall. Now here, at the spot where lightning almost struck her, and where the hawk stood with its prey, was *a stone entrance marker that looked like a wall*.

When the rapture occurred, Jesus would snatch his Bride, much like a hawk grabs its prey (but in a much gentler way of course). It would be quick as lightning, *but the Bride would be spared like Rahab*. The walls between heaven and earth would come tumbling down, but the Bride would be swept into the air. Instead of flying to a tree like a hawk, Jesus would fly us to heaven to be hidden from the time of trouble. Even the name on the neighborhood entrance marker pointed to the rapture.

Lake Lagrange Heights was written on the stone markers and **Lagrange** in French meant barn or granary. In the Bible, a granary (barn) refers to the harvest. The rapture would be the **harvest** of Jesus' Bride. Lake Lagrange **Heights** was a reminder the Bride would be harvested and flown to new **heights** in heaven. Not only that, when the Israelites took Jericho, they had to walk **upward** to get into the city!

As Ruthie pondered all these things she noticed something strange on the ground, sitting right next to the *Lagrange* neighborhood entrance marker. It looked like a piece of petrified wood. She picked it up, investigating every inch of the find. As she studied it, she realized it wasn't a piece of wood. The surface was rough, but contained small, crystalized pieces of what looked like glass. She rubbed her finger over the object, and it felt like tiny pieces of sand, sort of glued together. She had never seen anything like this before.

"Whatcha got there?" a man's voice said.

Startled, Ruthie almost dropped the mystery object.

"Sorry, I didn't mean to scare you," the man apologized.

"Oh, it's ok. I just found this um, well it's a…………….I don't really know what it is," she stammered.

"Do you mind if I take a look?"

"Sure. I'm clueless about what it is."

The man studied the object thoroughly, shaking his head and crinkling his forehead. "What you've got here is **fulgurite**," he finally said.

"Fulgur what?"

"Fulgurite. It's petrified lightning."

"What? Petrified lightning?"

"A fulgurite, or petrified lightning, is formed when lightning strikes sand, soil or rocks. The sand, soil or rock is hit by the lightning at extreme temperatures. The sand or soil fuses together and forms what you see here. Glass is made in a similar way."

"Wow! That's amazing. I noticed tiny pieces of glass inside."

"It looks like this one was formed when lightning struck a rock."

"How can you tell?"

"If you look closely, there are little vein patterns inside." He handed the fulgurite to Ruthie and pointed to the veins. "You see, it looks like a tiny tree in there- like little branches."

"Oh, you're right. How strange."

"Well, the amazing thing is that the branching patterns you see in this rock can happen in other materials, and even people."

"What do you mean people?"

"If a person survives a lightning strike, it is possible there will be some unusual marks left on the person's body." The man pulled out his phone and showed Ruthie a picture of a man who had been struck by lightning. His left arm was covered with what looked like tree branches. They were red, and raised slightly above the skin. He showed her another picture of a man who had marks on his back. Again, it looked like branches of a tree covering his back.

"That's crazy. The scarring looks just like tree branches."

"Lightning is caused by the massive discharge of static electricity from clouds, and it can eventually transfer to the ground, a tree, or a person. When the electricity flows through a person's body, it can branch out, causing the rupture of the capillaries beneath the skin. Then, you can easily see the pattern and path of the electricity. Only not everyone is so lucky. Many people die immediately from the sheer power of the lightning. But, the ones left with these scars give us a glimpse of our eternal father."

"Our eternal father? Do you mean God?"

"Yes, and I am also referring to his son Jesus. Think about what the Bible says in Isaiah 11:1. "There shall come forth a rod from the stem of Jesse, **and a Branch shall grow out of his roots**." This verse is referring to the lineage of Jesus. Jesse was the father of King David. But if we go back further we will see something extraordinary. If we look at Ruth, there's a special union that happens through God's mercy. Ruth, a foreigner and non-Jew, marries a Jewish man named Boaz. Together, they have a son named Obed. Later, Obed has a son and guess who it is?"

"Jesse!" exclaimed Ruthie.

"You are correct! **So that means a Jew and a Gentile form a special <u>branch</u> of the olive tree.** The natural branch of the olive tree is the Jew (Boaz), while the wild branch is the Gentile (Ruth). Through this marriage God reveals his future plan for salvation. **Jesus, the <u>BRANCH</u> of Jesse, would come to save both Jew and Gentile."**

"That's fascinating!"

"But there's more. Listen to this verse from Isaiah 11:10," the man stated. "There shall be a root of Jesse; and He who shall rise to reign over the Gentiles, in Him the Gentiles shall hope." This is the key Ruthie! Jesus is the Branch who brought hope **to everyone, even foreigners and outcasts**. Remember, in those days, Gentiles were considered foreigners in the kingdom of God. They were pagans, and considered unclean. However, amazingly enough, Jesus' female ancestors actually include more than one Gentile. They include Tamar, Ruth and Rahab."

"Did you say Rahab?"

"Yes, I said Tamar, Ruth and Rahab. Paul said in Romans 15:9, that Jesus became a servant so 'the Gentiles might glorify God for his mercy.'"

"Mercy? Did you say mercy?"

"Yes, that's what I said. Are you ok?" the man asked, noticing the perplexed look on her face.

She couldn't believe all the coincidences. The lightning just happens to strike near the neighborhood entrance marker that looks like a wall. She finds a piece of petrified lightning near the area, and then sees the pattern of a branch on it. Jesus just happens to be called **The Branch**, who descended from Rahab of Jericho. Just the fact that Rahab, Ruth and Tamar are descendants proves the mercy of God in saving foreigners. One day **the Branch** will return and pull out his Bride as an act of true mercy.

"Behold, the days are coming, says the Lord, that I will raise to David a **Branch of righteousness** in the Earth," quoted the man.

"That verse is about Jesus, the Branch who came to Earth to save us. Ever wonder why Jesus prayed in an **olive tree** grove before he was crucified? It's because he knew he was the Branch who would graft us all in, both Jews and Gentiles. How about the golden lampstand, or the menorah? It always contained only the purest olive oil, and the menorah has branches. The wick would be lit and the oil would make the lamp burn bright. That olive oil represents Jesus, the light. And one day he's going to return to the Mount of Olives in Jerusalem, where the world will be saved."

"I guess you could say lightning is the most powerful example of light we have on Earth," Ruthie added.

"Lightning is an extreme form of light and energy. Ever notice how it branches out when its strikes? It's like God is putting his signature in the sky," the man insisted.

"I never thought of it like that, but lightning does have a lot of power, so it makes sense."

"In Psalm 18 it says God shoots arrows, and sends great bolts of lightning to scatter enemies. It describes God's presence as being bright, surrounded by clouds, hailstones and lightning. Psalm 97 says God's lightning is so bright and amazing, the whole earth sees and trembles. It even says the hills melt like wax at the presence of the Lord."

"So essentially, lightning is a manifestation of God's power."

"Oh, it's even more than that Ruthie! Just listen to this verse from Matthew 28, describing an angel's appearance after Jesus rose from the dead," the man emphasized.

"And, behold, there was a great earthquake; for the angel of the Lord descended from heaven, and came and rolled back the stone from the door, and sat upon it. **His countenance (face) was like lightning**, and his raiment white as snow."

The man continued, "In Daniel chapter 10, an angel visits Daniel and this is how he is described. Listen carefully.

'His body also was like the beryl, and his face as the **appearance of lightning**, and his eyes as lamps of fire,'" the man quoted.

"It sounds like lightning shows God's power, but it also comes with a message. One angel carried the message Jesus had risen. The other angel brought a message about the future for mankind. Angels are God's messengers," Ruthie said.

"There's a message you've been learning about lately, and it's a very important one," the man stated.

"What's that?"

"The rapture!"

Just then she heard the rumbling of thunder. The timing was uncanny. She could feel the hair on the back of her neck stand up.

"Then the Lord will appear over them, **his arrow will flash like lightning**. The Sovereign Lord will **sound the trumpet**; he will march in the storms of the south," the man said, quoting Zechariah 9:14.

"The trumpet. The lightning. Jesus is going to return with the sound of the shofar," Ruthie said.

The man nodded his head. "The lightning is a key piece of the verse. Luke 17, verse 24 says when he returns he will appear like lightning, which lights up the entire sky. But after this the chapter goes on to say that most people won't be paying attention when the time comes. They will be eating, drinking and getting married up to that very day. As you read the rest of Luke 17, it becomes very clear. It says this,

'I tell you, in that night there shall be two people in one bed; **the one shall be taken, and the other shall be left. Two women shall be grinding together, the one shall be taken, and the other left**.'

"That's the rapture. Some are taken, while others are left. It will be quick, but once it happens, it will be obvious to everyone. Lightning is easily seen by everyone. Of course, not everyone will know people were taken into heaven. **Many will be deceived.** Some may even think it's an alien abduction! But ultimately, over time, everyone will know the truth," the man declared.

Another shudder of thunder roared from the sky. In that moment Ruthie pictured the charred grain left behind in Jericho. The walls fell down. The city was burned. Charred grain remained in clay pots. When the rapture happened the Bible verse said there would be two women grinding together. One would be taken and the other left. What would the women be grinding? It would be grain of course! **In the Bible, grain represented the harvest of God's people. When the rapture occurred, God's people would be harvested and taken to heaven.** All the pieces were falling into place and Ruthie understood.

"Did you notice in the verse I quoted it said there will be two people in the bed? One is taken and the other left?" asked the man.

Ruthie snapped out of her thoughts and replied, "Yes."

"Well, think of the symbolism of this. When the rapture happens, we know half of the world will be asleep while the other half is awake because of how the Earth rotates. Some people will be sleeping in their beds, while others, like the women grinding grain, will be awake. But did you realize this also refers to those who are spiritually awake and spiritually asleep? Just like the days of Noah, many people knew not the flood was coming. They were spiritually asleep. It will be the same way when the rapture comes. Many people just won't be ready."

A loud boom sounded, and a flash of lightning lit up the sky.

"Do you see the branching pattern of the lightning in the sky?" the man asked.

"Yes, it's so bright and beautiful."

"When **the Branch** returns for his Bride at the harvest, that will be a beautiful day," the man said. "I think we'd better get going though. Looks like the storm is already here."

"I'm just curious about something. How do you know all this information about lightning?"

"Well, I am an electrician by trade."

"Oh, so you know a lot about electricity, and lightning is electricity. That makes sense."

"I've got one more verse to share with you before we go on our way."

"What's that?"

"Job 36:30 says, 'He fills his hands with lightning and commands it to strike its mark.'"

"Are you saying God commands the lightning where to go?"

"Yes, that's exactly what I'm saying. You saw the lightning Ruthie. You know where it went. You know the message. You know you have to share it."

She stared at the man in bewilderment. How did he know she was almost struck by lightning? How did he know her name for that matter? She never gave him her name. Before she had a chance to ask him he was gone. How did he leave so quickly and without a trace?

"Just like lightning," she thought.

Rain began to pour down. Lightning flashed in the distance. She ran toward her house, all the while knowing *none of this could be chance*.

Author's Notes:

In this chapter the electrician talks about what happens to a person's skin when they survive a lightning strike. He said the capillaries beneath the skin will burst, forming a "tree/branch-like pattern." Think about this: Blood carries oxygen to every part of our body. How is it carried? Through veins. Trees have leaves, and leaves have veins. These veins carry food and water through the leaf, much like blood in our body carries nutrients.

Jesus spilled his **blood** on the cross so that we could LIVE in heaven, and have eternal life. In the Bible Jesus is called **THE BRANCH**. We (his followers) are part of the olive **TREE**. We are also told to BEAR GOOD FRUIT, like a **TREE**.

Isn't amazing how God confirms his word in NATURE, and even in our bodies!!!!!

Strong's concordance lists lightning (baraq) as entry number **1300**. Remember the **13** from Jericho? (6 days they marched around once, and the 7th day they marched around 7 times- **6 plus 7 equals 13**) The Israelites marched around Jericho a total of 13 times. Jericho is an allegory of the rapture. The whole city was destroyed except for Rahab.

She represents the Bride at the rapture. "For as **lightning** that comes from the east is visible even in the west, so will be the coming of the Son of Man." This verse describes the rapture.

On the set of *Passion of the Christ*, Jim Caviezel, the actor who played Christ, **was struck by lightning.** Luckily, he survived!!! Another person on the set was hit by lightning twice. I believe God was showing his awesome power on the set of that movie. Lightning is a fierce form of light! God is light.

CHAPTER 20
New York

Ruthie rushed to the front door, water dripping from her clothes. In just the short distance from the neighborhood entrance marker to her house, she had been drenched.

"What happened to you?" Thomas asked, cringing at the water now dripping on the kitchen floor.

"What does it look like?" she answered sarcastically.

"Well, as soon as you change out of those wet clothes, I've got some good news for you."

"I can't wait," she said with a tone of indifference. Thomas really had no idea about her strange and often uncanny experiences. Sometimes she wanted to explain, but she knew he would give her one of those puzzled looks. Or, he would try to explain it all in some rational way. Yes, it was better if she kept it to herself.

She changed into dry clothes, which quickly brightened her mood. Feeling refreshed, she walked to the kitchen. "Wonder what the good news is?" she thought to herself.

"Great! You're all changed. Now, for the good news."

"Hit me with it!"

"We're going to New York City!"

"New York? Why? When?"

"Why? Because it's the best city in the country! When? Tomorrow morning. You better start packing now."

She stood there a moment, thinking about the prospect of New York City. She'd been there before, but it had been a while. New York

City was so different from Orlando. The lights, sounds and people were in a class of their own. Yet, something stirred inside of her. She felt herself yearning to go.

"Well, are you going to go pack?" Thomas insisted.

A loud snap, crackle and boom echoed from outside.

"I hope the weather clears by tomorrow for our flight," Thomas said.

Ruthie hoped so. She really wanted to go, but who wants to fly through a storm? She packed her bag, as well as Jonah's and went to bed. Time moved quickly and before she knew it the alarm rang.

It rang at precisely 4:00 a.m.

"Is it already time to get up?" she mumbled.

"Not the alarm. I would kill for one more hour," Thomas groaned.

"You picked the early flight babe. Now get up, or we are going to miss it."

Early flights were always difficult because everyone seemed to move like molasses. Even Thomas slugged around, throwing his clothes into a suitcase at the last minute.

"You told me to pack last night and you haven't even packed," Ruthie complained.

"Yeah, yeah, I know. Chill out. I'm almost done."

Miraculously, they were all ready to go within the hour and off to the airport. Luckily, the lines for TSA were short, and they were at their gate in twenty minutes.

"That's the fastest time so far," Thomas bragged.

"So far so good. Now, we just wait to get our seats."

"Thomas Rodriguez, please come to the counter," a voice over the intercom said.

"Why are they calling you?" she asked.

"I don't know. I'll be back in a minute." Ruthie watched as Thomas spoke with the airline attendant at the counter. By the expression on his face, she could tell he was a little annoyed. He shook his head and walked back to the waiting area.

"What happened? They didn't cancel the flight did they?"

"No, they just had to move our seats around. Now, all three of us will be sitting in different seats."

"That's a pain. Why did they change our seat assignment at the last minute?"

"Well, we did book our flight at the last minute," Thomas answered.

"I guess you're right. I hope I sit by someone nice, or someone who sleeps through the flight."

"Yeah, I know what you mean. The last time this happened I had to listen to a screaming baby during the whole flight. We'll just hope for the best."

The time came to board the flight and Ruthie, Thomas and Jonah walked to their seats. Thomas sat in the front of the plane, while Jonah ended up in the middle. Ruthie ended up in the very last row, which only had two seats. When she sat down, there was no passenger in the seat next to her. "Wouldn't it be great if I had the whole row to myself?" she thought. No sooner had the thought entered her mind when a tall man, wearing a pilot's uniform, sat down in the empty seat. She did a double take when she saw him. *After all, why was a pilot sitting in the very last seat? Shouldn't he be in the cockpit!*

"Hello," he said warmly.

"Hi," she said, with a slight hesitation.

"I know what you're thinking. I should be in the cockpit right?" She shook her head.

"I actually just got off shift and I'm flying to New York to visit a friend. There just happened to be one open seat left on this flight, so I was able to hitch a ride," he laughed.

"Oh, I see. Well, I guess pilots have to fly just like the rest of us."

"Are you flying to New York for business or pleasure?" he asked.

"Pleasure. Just going to see the sights."

"New York is certainly the place for sights. You could stay a month and still never see everything."

"Please everyone, make sure your seatbelts are securely fastened as we will be taking off in a moment," the flight attendant stated.

"Guess we are off," the pilot said.

Within a few minutes the plane began taxiing down the runway. As it sped up to make its ascent, Ruthie had an uneasy feeling in her spirit. Something wasn't right. She looked out the window. Nothing unusual caught her attention. But, she couldn't shake the feeling. She decided to close her eyes and pray. The pilot sitting next to her noticed this and said, "Don't worry, we are in God's hands." This made her feel better for the time being.

Much to her relief, the first hour of the flight was quite smooth. It was hard to tell the plane was even moving.

"I wish all flights were this smooth," the pilot said.

"Yes, I can't stand turbulence. It makes me nervous."

"Turbulence is normal. Think of it like bumps on a road. Some are bigger and bumpier than others. Occasionally, you hit a pothole. Those are the ones that make people nervous."

Suddenly, as if on cue, a wave of turbulence began. It felt like a series of jolts, or jerking motions.

"Looks like we are heading into a thunderstorm," the pilot said calmly.

"A thunderstorm? The weather looked clear when we left."

"Thunderstorms can come out of nowhere sometimes. It's part of flying."

The plane pitched back and forth as if it were a toy in the wind. Ruthie had never experienced turbulence like this before. She felt terrified, and the pilot knew it.

"I know this seems scary and all, but you have to understand a few things," he stressed.

Just then the lights in the plane began blinking on and off. Ruthie peered outside her window and noticed jagged bolts of lightning all around the plane.

"There's lightning everywhere," she shrieked. At this point most people on the plane were noticeably alarmed. Some were whimpering, while others were praying.

"Things are not as bad as they seem," the pilot said calmly. Ruthie knew he was a pilot, but at the same time the weather outside was just plain chaotic. Shouldn't he be alarmed?

"We're safer inside this plane than we are in a house," the pilot stated, with no fluctuation in his tone.

"But we're flying right through the lightning. How can that be possible?"

"This plane is made of a very conductive metal- probably aluminum. That means an electrical charge of any type would flow freely across the plane."

"That doesn't sound safe to me!"

"That's the irony though. If lightning were to strike this plane, it would first hit an extremity, such as the wing or the nose. But, since the plane itself is an excellent conductor of electricity, the current would simply pass along the outside of the plane, and likely leave from the tail. The path would be unhindered for the electricity to flow. So, it would literally pass from the wing to the tail, or the nose to the tail, without doing any damage to the plane itself."

"You mean the plane wouldn't explode? It wouldn't burst into flames from the lightning?"

"No, even though lightning bolts can carry temperatures of over 50,000 degrees Fahrenheit, the inside of the plane and *the passengers would be **hidden** from the heat*, and the devastating effects of the charge."

"Did you say hidden? That's a strange word to use. I mean, why not use the word protected? The passengers would be protected from the heat and devastating effects."

"Sometimes when something is hidden, it is protected from devastating consequences, or circumstances," the pilot said.

A sudden crash of thunder echoed from outside the plane. Several passengers gasped.

"What are you trying to say?" Ruthie asked.

"I'm saying that God can choose to hide his people from even the worst of circumstances. See how we are flying up here in the clouds, surrounded by lightning, and the crashes of thunder? But, in the midst of it all, we are safe. There will come a day when the entire world is in chaos. The storms will come, the thunder will roar, and the Son of man will return like lightning."

Just then she heard a loud Boom. She stared outside the window in awe. A bright flash lit up the plane's wing. In a split second, she saw it travel down the wing and along the outside fuselage of the plane.

"The plane was just struck by lightning, wasn't it?"

"Yes, it was. Here we are, still flying to great heights. Didn't you say you live in *Lake Lagrange Heights?*"

"No, I never said that."

"My mistake, I thought you did."

"Hello everyone. We are sorry for all the turbulence. As you probably guessed, we flew through a very intense thunderstorm. But, the worst of it is over. We will be making our descent into New York City shortly. Please make sure your seatbelts are fastened for the remainder of the flight," the stewardess announced.

"I agree with her," the pilot said with a smile.

The plane landed smoothly in New York's *La Guardia* Airport. Ruthie felt a sigh of relief as it landed.

"Oh, I meant to tell you one more thing," the pilot said.

"What's that?"

"Don't forget to check out Trump Tower, located at Columbus Circle."

Ruthie was puzzled. Why was he telling her to visit Trump Tower? Was it because the current President of the United States, Donald Trump, owned the building?

"Ok," she answered with some hesitation.

"Just do it. You'll understand why after you see it." With that, the pilot grabbed his bag from the overhead bin. "Oh, I left my other carry on under my seat. Would you mind grabbing it?" he asked.

"Sure." She reached for his carry on item from under the seat. As she pulled it out she was astounded. "Excuse me, but is this a trumpet case?"

"Yes it is. I play the trumpet in my spare time. In fact, the friend I'm visiting plays as well."

Ruthie couldn't believe it. Of all things, **a trumpet.**

"Keep your ears open Ruthie. You'll know the sound when you hear it," he said with a wink. Then, he casually walked down the aisle. She grabbed her carry on and slowly walked off the plane, still thinking about what the pilot said. Thomas and Jonah were waiting for her at the exit.

"So, how was your flight?" Thomas asked.

"Really? How do you think it was?"

"I don't know. I was sleeping." Thomas laughed.

"Are you kidding me? You slept through the entire storm and turbulence and,"

"Yeah Dad, that means you even slept through the lightning strike," Jonah said.

"What? A lightning strike? When?" he asked.

"Never mind Thomas. Only *you* could sleep through that madness!"

"We'd better get a move on. We want to make the most of our day. Our first stop is going to be the Empire State Building."

"Yay," said Jonah. "The Empire State Building was in the movie *Elf*. Remember, that's where Buddy's Dad worked."

"Yes, that's right Jonah. It's been in a couple other movies also. It used to be New York's tallest skyscraper. In 1970 it was surpassed by the World Trade Center Twin Towers."

"Didn't those towers blow up?" Jonah asked.

"They didn't blow up. In 2001, two planes flew into them and they collapsed. It was a terrorist attack."

"Well, in the pictures it looked like they blew up. The buildings were on fire. Are you worried another terrorist attack will happen Dad? Could it happen again?" Jonah asked.

"Why don't we talk about the Empire State Building?" Thomas suggested, wanting to steer away from the subject of terrorist attacks.

"Actually, the Empire State Building became the tallest building in New York *again* after the Twin Towers collapsed in 2001. But then, they built *One World Trade Center* to replace the Twin Towers. It became the tallest building as of April 30, 2012. In fact, the tower is completely finished now. Are we going to see that?" Ruthie asked.

Thomas flashed Ruthie a look that said, "Drop the subject for now." She took the hint and decided to make conversation about something else until they got to the building.

After taking the subway, they reached their destination. Upon walking up to the building, Jonah's mouth dropped open. "Whoa. It's really tall. Look at the design on the front."

"Yeah, this building houses so many businesses it has its own zip code," Thomas added. "And do you know how it got its name?"

"Is it because New York is called the Empire state?" Ruthie answered.

"Yes, but did you know that name comes from the fact that New York was considered the seat of the American Empire, according to George Washington? It was the center of commerce and wealth, as well as power. New York City was our nation's first capital, not Washington D.C. New York has always been seen as the apple of America's eye. Some say our financial success began here. Just think about Wall Street."

"Well, I'd say success begins with God," Ruthie argued.

"Actually, George Washington was inaugurated in New York City, and he prayed for our nation that very day. He even said if our country ever forgot God, we wouldn't be blessed anymore. Well, I'm talking too much. We need to actually *see* the building! Let's go inside and make our way to the observation deck. I'm sure the view is going to be fantastic."

They took the elevator to the 86th floor. She was surprised to find that it was an open-air deck.

"I didn't know we would be viewing all of New York in the open like this," she commented.

"What do you mean? Don't you remember the scenes from *Sleepless in Seattle* where the two star crossed lovers kiss each other on the observation deck of the Empire State Building? They are out in the open, with their hair blowing in the breeze. You're the romantic. You should know this."

"I guess I forgot," Ruthie admitted.

"Hey, look over there. You can see Central Park. And over there you can see the Brooklyn Bridge, Times Square, and even the Statue of Liberty."

Ruthie found herself overwhelmed with the amount of landmarks she could see from this one location. As she stood there viewing all of New York City, she wondered how many people knew the Lord the way she did. Millions and millions of people were down there conducting business, sightseeing or perhaps just hanging out with friends. But how many of them would be "asleep" when the Lord returned? Suddenly, she felt the hair on the back of her neck stand up. A cool wind rushed across the deck.

"Ooh, did you feel that?" Thomas asked. "A storm is coming."

"Not again. I've had enough of storms."

"Never fear Ruthie because did you know this building has been struck hundreds of times! I think I read somewhere that it's struck around 23 times a year on average."

"That's comforting!"

"The building has a lightning rod so I wouldn't worry about it."

"Actually, in 2016 two lightning bolts struck the side of the building at the same time," a man nearby chimed in.

"Really? Well, the building is still standing so that means lightning is no match for the Empire State Building," Thomas said. Just then a loud crack of thunder sounded. Thomas flinched slightly, but kept talking. "You know what. I read somewhere during storms the Empire State Building produces a lot of static electricity. Because of that, couples come up here just to get an *electric kiss*. When you kiss, it could literally give off an electric shock." Thomas leaned in to kiss Ruthie. To her surprise, he was right.

"Ouch! You shocked me!"

"See, I told you. Talk about chemistry," he laughed.

"Why are you guys kissing?" Jonah asked, looking embarrassed.

"Excuse me, but we will need everyone to leave the observation deck temporarily, until after the storm is over," a worker communicated over a loudspeaker.

"Ahh, bummer," said Jonah.

Just as everyone began filing out of the observation deck a loud snap, pop and boom roared through the area. Ruthie turned to see a bright, almost blinding zig zag streak along the edge of the building. It moved quickly, as if it were following a path. She immediately thought about the lightning strike on the plane, and what the pilot had said. Perhaps the electrical current from the bolt simply flowed across the building's metal sheeting, and then off the building itself. She could still feel the static electricity on her neck, and even in her lips.

"Let's view what we can inside, and afterward we can check out Trump Tower. Hopefully, the weather will clear up," Thomas said. "Technically we will be visiting two of Trump's buildings today."

"Two? What do you mean?"

"Trump Empire State Partners, along with another business associate, owned the Empire State Building from 1994 to 2002."

"Really? I knew Trump owned a lot of buildings, but I didn't know about the Empire State Building."

It was strange for Thomas to mention Trump's buildings, especially Trump Tower. Hadn't the pilot said to visit Trump Tower? How odd. Or was it odd? Perhaps it was divine. There had to be a reason why the pilot told her to visit it, and she was intrigued to find out.

CHAPTER 21
Trump Tower

§

Getting to Trump Tower didn't take very long. It was only a 1.5 mile walk from the Empire State Building. When Ruthie arrived, she couldn't help but notice the brilliance of the building. The entire building was covered in dark, reflective glass. The sunlight bounced off various parts of it, creating an elegant sheen she hadn't seen in other buildings. The zig zag pattern of the building gave it an air of uniqueness by drawing your eyes to what looked like steps cascading up and down.

"I think this building used to be the only one in New York made entirely of glass."

Ruthie studied the glass façade of the building. There was something about it. Yes, it was beautiful, but that wasn't it. She couldn't put her finger on it.

"TRUMP TOWER," read Jonah, looking at the gold colored letters on the building. "I guess this must be the entrance."

"You're right buddy. This is where we go in." Thomas said, studying the entrance carefully.

"This entrance makes me feel like I've been dipped in gold with all the gold trim everywhere," Ruthie laughed.

"Well, I imagine it's supposed to exude wealth, and that's what gold does."

"Ooh, and look at the clock tower!" squealed Jonah as he ran over to it. "The top of the clock says *Trump Tower* on it, like the entrance."

As Ruthie watched Jonah in front of the clock tower, she suddenly became aware of the time. It was **9:11 exactly**. She immediately thought of the 9-11 terror attacks that happened 16 years ago. She felt a twinge of fear in her heart as she wondered about the future of New York City. Was it just a matter of time before another attack, worse than the first, took place?

"Hey Mom! Remember, in the movie *Back to the Future*, when the Hill Valley Clock Tower gets struck by lightning?" Jonah said, looking at the Trump Clock Tower. Ruthie didn't answer. She did remember that part in the movie. **A large lightning bolt struck the tower**, rendering it useless. Why would Jonah bring that up now?

"Why don't we all go in the building now?" Thomas suggested.

"I'm ready if you are," she answered.

They walked to the entrance doors, only to be stopped by a guard.

"Sorry, no visitors are allowed, unless you are on the registered list," the guard stated.

"You mean we can't go inside to have a look around?" Thomas gently asked.

"Sir, the President of the United States owns this building, and his family lives here. We can't just let *anyone* into the building anymore. No offense, but security has to be air tight."

"Of course. I'm surprised that didn't occur to me," Thomas answered, disappointed.

"It's ok babe. We don't have to go in. We saw the outside, and that's pretty spectacular."

"Yes, but I've heard the inside is amazing. It's decorated in brass and marble, with one of a kind stores and restaurants."

"It's not like we could afford to buy anything inside anyway," Ruthie laughed.

"I know. I just wanted to see it."

"I have an idea. Why don't we get something to eat? I'm starving. I'll bet you could find a great bagel or donut shop nearby. We could eat at Columbus Circle, right across from Trump Tower."

"I am pretty hungry," Thomas agreed.

"Me too! I want donuts," Jonah chimed in.

"Ok, we are on the hunt for a donut shop."

"If it's ok with you, I think I'll sit on one of the benches in Columbus Circle and wait. I'm feeling kind of tired."

"Sure. We'll be back in no time."

Ruthie found a bench in Columbus Circle, facing Trump Tower. She sat there silently, staring at the tower. She started thinking about the man who owned the tower- Donald Trump, the 45th President of the United States. "The 45th President," she said to herself in a low voice.

"He is the 45th President," a voice said. Ruthie turned her head and saw a tall man with olive skin. He must have overheard her. Why was this kind of thing happening all the time? It seemed everywhere she went there was someone who just had to share information with her. Most of the time, it was interesting and even fun, but for some reason, she didn't want to hear it right now. She really just wanted to rest and wait for her donut.

"Look, I know you're tired, but there are some things you should know," the man said.

Ruthie looked right at the man. He had bright green eyes and jet black hair. His voice and demeanor were gentle, and she knew she needed to listen.

"Ok, my ears are open."

"First, I want you to look up Isaiah 62 and read it to yourself," the man said. Ruthie did what the man asked.

"Ok, I'm finished. Now what?"

"Tell me what it's about."

"It is about the redemption of Israel. It's actually one of my favorite chapters in Isaiah. It reminds me that one day the land of Israel will be redeemed by their Messiah, Jesus."

"You are correct. Now I want you to read Isaiah 45." Ruthie did what the man said and then looked at the man with a puzzled expression.

"Why did you want me to read this chapter? Is it because Donald Trump is the 45th President and this is Isaiah 45?"

"Read the first two verses aloud."

"Thus saith the Lord to his anointed, *to Cyrus*, whose right hand I have holden, *to subdue nations before him*; and I will loose the loins of kings, to open before him the two leaved gates; and gates shall not be shut; I will go before thee, and make the crooked places straight: I will break in pieces the gates of brass, and cut sunder the bars of iron."

"What does it mean?" the man asked.

"Well, I know these verses are talking about King Cyrus, who ruled Persia during the time when the Jews were in captivity, and their Temple had been destroyed by the Babylonians. And I do know King Cyrus was a pagan, but he still allowed the Jewish people to go back to Jerusalem to begin rebuilding their homeland and Temple."

"You are correct. Now read verses 4 and 5."

"For Jacob my servant's sake, and Israel mine elect, I have even called thee by thy name: I have surnamed thee, though thou hast not known me. I am the Lord, and there is no God besides me: I girded thee, though thou hast not known me."

"And the meaning?" the man asked.

"I believe this part is alluding to the fact that King Cyrus, even though he is a pagan and doesn't know the one true God, is being called forth by God to do something great for Israel."

"Correct again. Now read verses 13 and 14."

"'I have raised him up in righteousness, and *I will direct all his ways*: he shall build my city, and he shall let go my captives, not for price nor reward,' saith the Lord of hosts... 'The labour of Egypt, and the merchandise of Ethiopia and of the Sabeans, men of stature, shall come over unto thee, and they shall be thine: they shall come after thee; in chains they shall come over, and they shall fall down unto thee; they shall make supplication unto thee, saying, Surely God is in thee.'"

"Before you ask," said Ruthie, "I think this part means God has set apart King Cyrus to release the Jews who are in captivity, and let them go back to their city Jerusalem, and rebuild the Temple. But King Cyrus will be given power over many nations by God, and many nations will be under Cyrus' rule. *It is all orchestrated by God* because he will use Cyrus to accomplish his plan for Jerusalem and his people, the Jews," Ruthie said.

"Correct once more. Now please read verse 17 and verse 25."

"But Israel shall be saved in the Lord with an everlasting salvation: ye shall not be ashamed nor confounded world without end. In the Lord shall all the seed of Israel be justified, and shall glory," Ruthie read.

"The rulers of this earth are under the authority of the Almighty. He chooses who he wishes. He can use them, or dispose them. In the case of Israel, the Lord can use any King or President to do his work," the man stated.

"Are you saying God is using Donald Trump, our President, to do something for Israel?"

"That is not for me to reveal or decide. The ways of our Lord are mysterious, but perfect. He only reveals bits and pieces. Regardless of who he allows to be in power, he expects us to do our jobs here on Earth. We are to be witnesses of the truth, and disciples of Jesus."

Ruthie looked up at Trump Tower. She wondered what God's plan was for President Trump. Whatever it was, the job was going to be difficult. The opposition at this time was fierce, and at times frightening.

"The thing most people don't understand is that God can use **all types of rulers**, both good and bad. Think about King Nebuchadnezzar. He destroyed the Jewish Temple and sent the people into exile. But God used Nebuchadnezzar as a punishment for the disobedience of his people. Yet **seventy** years later, he used King Cyrus, who wasn't even Jewish, to free the Jewish people and allow them to rebuild the Temple."

"Isn't President Trump **seventy** years old?" Ruthie asked. "You said the Jews were released from captivity after **70 years**."

"Yes, that is true. In fact, did you know on the day of his inauguration Trump was exactly 70 years, 7 months and 7 days old? Not only that, did you know it is currently the year 5777 on the Biblical Hebrew calendar? The Hebrew year began on Rosh Hashanah 2016 (October 3), and runs all the way through Rosh Hashanah 2017 (September 20). That means the election occurred right after the new year (5777) began. You probably know the number 7 represents completion and perfection."

"Whoa! That's prophetic. Based on the seventy and the sevens, it seems like the Lord has some big plans for the President, and for Israel."

"Here's something else to think about with regards to the seventy. The Second Temple was destroyed in **70 A.D.** The Temple King Cyrus had allowed the Jews to rebuild, was eventually destroyed by the Romans in 70 A.D."

"Seventy seems to be related to Jerusalem and the Temple, based on the information," Ruthie said.

"Yes, and you know who else is tied to the Temple don't you?"

"Jesus?" Ruthie asked.

"Of course! In fact, he predicted the destruction of the Temple in Matthew 24."

Ruthie pulled up the chapter on her phone and read it aloud.

"And Jesus went out, and departed from the Temple: and his disciples came to him for to shew him the buildings of the Temple. And Jesus said unto them, See ye not all these things? Verily I say unto you, there shall not be left here one stone upon another, that shall not be thrown down," she quoted.

"As you can see, Jesus predicted the destruction of the Temple that would occur in 70 A.D. But, he also declared that he would become the Temple. In John 2, verse 19 Jesus says 'Destroy this Temple and I will raise it again in three days.'"

"Jesus was talking about himself! He was saying he would be crucified and raised in three days. His body, the Temple, would be destroyed, but then raised up in glory. He would be the sacrifice. No longer would they need lambs for sacrifices, or even the Temple veil. It was torn in two."

"Here's another detail to think about. The golden lampstand, or menorah, had to be in the Temple at all times. It represented the light of God. In John, chapter 8, Jesus declares he is the light of the world, while at the Temple during the Feast of Tabernacles. Jesus fulfilled all aspects of the Temple, even though the Temple was destroyed in 70 A.D. Do you want to know something even more amazing?"

"Of course!" Ruthie exclaimed.

"After Jesus predicts the destruction of the Temple in Matthew 24, he starts talking about the end times, which will precede his return. In verse 27 he says, 'As lightning cometh out of the east, and shineth even unto the west; so shall the coming of the Son of man be. For wheresoever the carcase is, there the eagles be gathered together.'"

Ruthie knew that verse very well. She looked at Trump Tower and noticed something odd. Two birds were circling round and round in front of the building. They were swift and graceful as they flew, almost as if they were partners.

"You're looking at two eagles," the man said.

"Are they eagles? I can't tell. They're too far away to see."

"Look closely. You will see."

She opened her eyes wide and focused in on the birds. She still couldn't tell. "Help me see Lord," she said to herself. Suddenly she had an idea. She grabbed her phone and pointed it in the direction of the birds. She took a picture. Next, she enlarged the picture. By enlarging it, she could clearly see it was two eagles.

"If I didn't know better I'd say those birds were mates. The way they circle each other tells me they must belong to one another."

The man watched the birds silently, but under his breath he was saying something. Ruthie listened carefully, wondering what he was muttering. As she listened she was sure she heard numbers. He muttered, "Five, six, seven".

"Are you counting?"

"Yes", the man said. In a flash the birds flew over the building and out of view. "Seven times."

"What do you mean?"

"The birds flew in a circle seven times," the man stated. "It's just like the Bride and Groom at a Jewish wedding. The Bride circles the groom seven times, and this symbolizes the beginning of a new family. It also **symbolizes _a wall_ of protection for the Bride and Groom**."

"Did you say wall?" Ruthie asked.

"Yes, a wall."

"But, that sounds like…"

"Jericho?" the man asked.

"Yes, like Jericho! The Israelites circled Jericho 7 times on the 7th day and then the wall fell down. Only Rahab was spared when the city was destroyed."

"Did you mean to say _the Bride_ was spared?"

Ruthie got quiet. At this point she was sure the story of Jericho foreshadowed the rapture. Did this man know too?

"There's another Jewish wedding tradition you should know about," the man explained.

"What is it?"

"The stomping of the glass."

Ruthie looked at Trump Tower, covered in beautiful glass.

"What is the stomping of the glass?" she asked, still looking at the tower.

"At the end of the wedding ceremony a Jewish couple will stomp on a glass and break it with their feet. This symbolizes the destruction of the Temple in Jerusalem. Some couples will say, 'If I forget thee O Jerusalem, may my right hand forget its skill', or 'Set Jerusalem above my highest joy.' Once the glass is broken, the wedding ceremony is complete, and it's time for the celebration."

Ruthie couldn't stop staring at the glass on the building. She couldn't help but wonder what was in store for America and the rest of the world. God must have big plans for Israel, Jerusalem and the Temple. Was Jesus going to return soon? If so, how soon?

"Ruthie, I know you have many questions, and you've seen many signs. There is only so much God will tell us. We don't know exactly how he will use our nation, or our President. I know most people think everything has to result in peace in order to be effective. But God can use division, insurrection and war to bring about change, and lead to a greater plan. We know in the last days there will be strife, confusion and suffering. But, God holds the key to all things. The *full purpose* for the rulers he chooses is not always completely clear. He makes the rules and knows the how the game will end. And only he knows the timing. But I do know one thing."

"What's that?" asked Ruthie, finally looking away from the building.

"We've got to prepare people. Most people are asleep. They can't see the signs, even though they are right in front of them. Likely, they won't see the signs until…."

"Until what?"

"Until lightning strikes."

"Do you mean the rapture?"

"Exactly. Even though there will be time to turn back to God after the rapture, it will be the scariest time on earth. Jesus wants to *hide his Bride* from all the torment and chaos."

"I know. He's shown me over and over that he wants to spare his Bride, just like he did for Rahab. Just like Rahab's house. **It was hidden in the wall**. But her house was spared, and she and her family were the only ones saved. It was the only part of the wall left standing."

"You will figure out what to do Ruthie. Just keep looking up and you'll know. Remember this about the eagles' wings. Unlike some birds, the eagle flies with its wings held straight out. Many other birds fly with their wings in a V shape. Not the eagle. He only uses the V shape to power his flight. **But, once he's flying his wings stay straight**."

She looked up, and to her surprise, the two eagles she saw circling earlier were now high above her head, circling again. Their wings were straight.

"Trust in the Lord with all thine heart; and lean not unto thine own understanding," the man quoted from Proverbs.

"The voice of him that crieth in the wilderness, Prepare ye the way of the Lord, make straight in the desert a highway for our God," Ruthie quoted from Isaiah 40. She looked at the eagles in awe.

"Whatcha looking at?" asked Thomas, as he set down a box of donuts and two cups of coffee.

"What? Where did you come from?"

"Uh, what do you mean? I went to get some food. Remember?"

Ruthie looked all around. Where was the man she was speaking with earlier? No sign of him. He was gone. Why was she surprised?

"Eat up quick. We gotta be at Grand Central Station by 10:30."

Ruthie grabbed a donut and looked back at the sky. She could still see the eagles. Could they see her? Probably not. But knowing they were there was comforting. Knowing God had a plan was comforting too. He would make the path straight, even if she didn't know all the details.

CHAPTER 22
Grand Central Station

When Ruthie and her family reached Grand Central Station, they were not surprised to find it was buzzing with people. Everyone looked like busy bees traveling from one terminal to another. It was kind of overwhelming.

"What are we going to do here?" Ruthie asked.

"I just thought you guys might want to take in the architecture, and the sights and sounds of this place. It's a piece of New York's transportation history. Over 750,000 people come through Grand Central Station a day," Thomas answered.

"Look at the clock!" Jonah exclaimed, running over to it.

"That's the famous *Grand Central clock*. It's the one everyone meets at in the movies," Thomas laughed. I think there's even a saying that goes, '*Meet me at the clock.*'"

The clock was quite beautiful. Adorned with a gold color and *four opal faces*, it had the look of wealth and prestige. It bore some resemblance to the clock near Trump Tower, but this one had some differences. It sat atop an information booth, monitored by busy workers, all helping passengers who had questions about train stops and schedules.

"You know, that clock holds a secret," a man passing by said to Jonah.

"What do you mean?"

"See the top of the clock and how it's slightly pointy? Well, that's actually a compass. The clock is always lined up with true north. The faces of the clock are lined up with the four compass points of this building."

"Awesome! Did you hear that Mom and Dad?"

"We heard."

"That's not all either. Did you know there's a spiral staircase *hidden* inside the information booth the clock rests on top of? The workers in the information booth can *escape*.... Oops, I mean go down the stairway to get to the next level."

Ruthie wondered why the man said "escape" by accident. The staircase was **hidden** from everyone else's view, but he said it was *an escap*e. She thought about God's "hiding place" in heaven. It would be an escape from Earth. Not only that, as she looked at the four clock faces, she realized it would all be timed precisely by God. Even the compass on top of the clock made her think of heaven. It pointed North. Heaven was as far north as you could come.

"Hey Mom! Remember the movie, ***Back to the Future***?"

"Yes, you mentioned it at Trump Tower. What about it?"

"Remember in the movie when the clock tower was struck by lightning, and then the clock stopped running?"

"Yes, I remember that part. You told me earlier."

"Remember when Doc Brown used the lightning storm to power the *DeLorean* so Marty could go back to the future? The **lightning** hit the clock tower at exactly **10:04 p.m**. But, Doc had already connected some wires from the tower to the car so the lightning would zap the wire, and then give the car electrical energy. Next thing you know- BAM- **the car was gone**! Then, in Part 2, the DeLorean is struck by **lightning** while Doc Brown is hovering in the air. In a flash, in the twinkling of an eye, **it's gone again**!"

Ruthie nodded her head in agreement. Jonah used the words, "**in a flash, in the twinkling of an eye**". She couldn't help but see the similarities between what happened to the car, and the biblical event known as the Rapture. The lightning....the swiftness....even the clock itself. Wasn't the rapture timed by God, who uses lightning to manifest his power? Yet, the Lord warns the Rapture will be quick, and catch many off guard.

"Who can forget the *DeLorean*? It was such a distinctive car. All stainless steel, with falcon wing doors," the man said.

"Falcon wing doors? What do you mean?" Thomas asked the man.

"Well, most car doors open horizontally, or outward. But falcon doors open upward, like when a falcon moves its wings up and down."

"Oh yeah," said Jonah. I remember that from the movie. The doors moved up instead of out! I wish we had a car like that!"

"I believe *Tesla* cars have falcon wing doors," Thomas added.

"You are correct. And don't forget *Tesla* cars *are electric*," the man said, looking right at Ruthie.

Ruthie knew it was a clue. The cars are **electric**. And what about the doors? **Falcon wings**? She already knew raptors, or birds of prey, were a reminder of the rapture. Raptors, such as the falcon, were birds that seized their prey quickly and forcefully from the sky. One day Jesus would snatch his Bride in the blink of an eye. **It would be swift, like electricity moving through a wire, or lightning zipping from the cloud to the ground.**

Thomas turned to Jonah. "*Back to the Future* is a great movie Jonah, but what does that have to do with **this clock** here at Grand Central Station?"

"I don't know. I just thought of the *Hill Valley Clock Tower* when I looked at it."

Ruthie thought it was strange for Jonah to mention *Back to the Future* two times. Also, here was this man *who just happened* to connect the movie to things she already knew about the rapture. It seemed like a *hidden message* of some sort. She knew lightning was God's power and glory, and when Jesus returned there could be lightning, and perhaps thunder. His return for the Bride would be quick, and the timing would likely line up with his holy feasts. The Bride wouldn't go back to the future though. Instead, they'd be going **to their future** in heaven. Time for the Bride would change. In heaven, time wouldn't be linear. It wouldn't exist the same way it did on Earth.

"By the way, this is one of America's busiest train stations. More than 750,000 people come through here a day. And it's not called *Grand Central Station*. It's actually called **Grand Central <u>Terminal</u>**," the man said with a wink.

Thomas shrugged his shoulders and said, "Why don't we walk around for a bit to get a good look at everything, and then we'll be off to tour Wall Street, and the Museum of Natural History."

"I don't know why we're going to see *a wall*, but I love the museum," Jonah said.

"It's not an actual wall Jonah. It's called Wall Street. Though truthfully, the history of Wall Street started with a wall."

"Huh?" Jonah said, looking perplexed.

"Just wait till we get there and I'll explain," noted Thomas.

Ruthie looked up the word **terminal** on her phone. It said, "final, last, concluding, closing, end." At some point, **the world as everyone knew it would be terminal. The old would pass away. Then, the new would come.** But before this, there was a journey the Bride would take. It would be faster than a speeding bullet, or a train. Like the clock in Grand Central, where people from all walks of life met, there would be **a meeting in the sky- a Grand Central of sorts**. The destination? Heaven. Would everyone be going? No. Only those who were **ready** for the trip would be going.

She started following Thomas when the man walked up to her and whispered something.

"Did you know falcons have been clocked at speeds of over 240 miles per hour as they dive downward to grab their prey? In comparison, lightning travels **<u>upward</u>** at a speed of 220,000,000 miles per hour. That's called the **<u>return</u> stroke**." *The man emphasized the word return.* "Don't forget it," he urged.

Ruthie could picture Christ in the sky, coming for his Bride, then **returning** with them to heaven in a bright streak of light. The whole sequence too swift for the human eye to behold. One blink and it would be done.

"I won't forget," she answered.

She looked up at the listing of train stops and times on the screens of the information booth. Next, she looked at the clock. *Yes, it would all be on God's clock, but he was giving clues along the way.*

"You ready Ruthie?" Thomas asked, wondering why she was standing in place.

"Of course I am," she responded, but she wasn't really responding to Thomas. She was responding to God.

Author's Notes about Lightning:

Most people don't realize lightning has a return stroke. The strike comes down, and then goes up. The speed of the return stroke is so quick it occurs in the blink of an eye.

In the Bible, lightning is a manifestation of God's power, and it denotes his presence among the people. God actually followed the Israelites in the wilderness as A CLOUD. Exodus 13:22 says "Neither the pillar of cloud by day nor the pillar of fire by night left its place in front of the people." We also know that Jesus will return riding on the clouds at the Second Coming. Revelation 1:7 says, "Look, he is coming with the clouds, and every eye will see him, even those who pierced him." The Day of the Lord is described as being a day of dark clouds. Zephaniah 1:15 says, "That day is a day of wrath, a day of trouble and distress, a day of wasteness and desolation, a day of darkness and gloominess, a day of clouds and thick darkness."

Keep in mind that clouds and lightning go hand in hand. The electricity is within the clouds, and manifests itself as lightning. The strike is a powerful force- beautiful, yet also destructive. The Rapture, and the Second Coming, will be events that showcase God's power, light and judgment. The removal of the Bride will be a move of force and power. Raptors (birds of prey) remove their prey with great force and power. It is swift and rarely does the prey escape. Luckily for the Bride, she is taken by force, but for the purposes of *escaping the judgement* falling upon the Earth.

Psalm 97:2 says, "Clouds and thick darkness surround Him."

Job 22:14 says, "Clouds are a **HIDING PLACE** for him."

Job 37:15-16 says, "Do you know how God controls the clouds and makes his lightning flash? Do you know how the clouds hang poised, those wonders of him who has perfect knowledge?"

Job 26:9 says, "He covers the face of the full moon (*his throne*), spreading his clouds over it."

Nahum 1:3 says, "The clouds are the dust beneath His feet."

Revelation 14:14 says, "And I looked, and behold a white cloud, and upon the cloud one sat like unto the Son of man, having on his head a golden crown, and in his hand a sharp sickle."

October 21, 2015 was marked as **BACK TO THE FUTURE DAY**. In the movie (*Back to the Future Part 2*), on this date, Marty Mc Fly and Doc Brown travel to the future in the time machine (the DeLorean). In the movie (Part 2), Marty travels to the future- **October 21, 2015,** to save his children. These children hadn't been born yet, as Marty is living in the year 1985, but Doc told him his "future children" were in trouble. Keep in mind, this movie was released in 1989, so the October 21, 2015 date was still 26 years away at the time. When the day finally came in 2015, people celebrated with parties and get-togethers.

2015 was also the year there were two blood moons- one on April 4, 2015 (on Passover), and one on September 28, 2015 (Feast of Tabernacles). The *Back to the Future* celebrations happened a month after the last blood moon. One day Jesus will come back to save his "children". Luckily, we don't have to ride in a time machine to see the future. It's already in the Bible. God already knows the end. It won't be a DeLorean riding on the clouds- it will be Jesus!!!

CHAPTER 23
Water Landing

After a long day in New York City, everyone felt tired, especially Thomas.

"Ugh, I feel like a train ran over me," he said, plopping down on the bed.

"Did a train run over you at Grand Central?" Ruthie joked.

"I'm serious babe. My head is killing me and my body is aching."

"Oh no! I hope you don't have the flu."

"I don't know what I have, but I gotta get to bed."

Thomas went to bed within a few minutes. She figured they should all do the same. They had a long day tomorrow. Ruthie tucked Jonah in, and then she went to bed. She was out like a light.

Halfway through the night she felt Thomas moving around. He turned to one side, then the other. He repeated this over and over again. Ruthie felt his head, but he didn't have a fever. No sooner had she done this, when he woke up, looking overwhelmed and upset.

"What's wrong Thomas?"

He shook his head. "I don't know."

"What do you mean? You look disturbed."

"I guess that's what you'd call it."

"Come on. Just tell me."

"It was just a dream."

"Well, for it just being a dream, you look mighty upset. What was the dream about?"

"It involved a plane."

"A plane?"

"Yes, a plane going down."

"Going down where?"

"In the water."

"Were you on the plane?"

"Yes."

"Who else was on the plane?"

"The President."

"Ok, instead of playing 20 questions, just tell me the whole dream Thomas."

"The flight began smoothly. No turbulence. No problems. But then things changed."

"How?"

"The plane started moving side to side. Turbulence began. The whole plane was shaking."

"Go on."

"The pilot did his best to alleviate the shaking and erratic movement. But, to no avail. The more buttons he pushed, the worse the turbulence became. He started sweating profusely, and he even took off his hat. He pulled out the flight manual and frantically looked through it. The turbulence increased and then the plane began to dive slightly. The pilot called air traffic control, but they were no help. They were all arguing in the background about what to do. So, the pilot hung up."

"What did the pilot do?"

"He kept trying to stabilize the plane. In the dream it seemed like he was working for hours and hours on keeping the plane in the air. But, in reality, it was just a few minutes. Finally, he said, 'I have to ditch the plane.'"

"Ditch the plane? What do you mean?"

"He meant he had to land the plane in water."

"In water?"

"That kind of sounds like the movie *Sully*."

"Yes, it does. Anyway, the pilot had no choice. He landed the plane in the water. But the plane was destroyed. The pilot turned to me in the dream and said, 'It's gone.' He looked numb and exhausted."

"Wait a minute. Earlier you told me the President was on the plane. Where was the President?"

"The pilot was the President."

Ruthie felt a knot forming in her stomach. Even though it was a dream, she knew it meant something. Perhaps the President needed lots of prayer. After all, he was the leader of a country that was in great political turmoil. He had the hardest job on the planet. He was piloting an entire country through what some called "The Great American Divide." Navigating through the terrain must be difficult, and at times impossible.

"Thomas, I know the dream was disturbing. Maybe we just need to pray for the President, and for our country."

"You're right Ruthie. Honestly, it seemed like the dream had a symbolic meaning. I feel like the plane represented the United States. It all felt so real. I could feel the President's stress. But, no matter how hard he tried, the plane kept descending at a rapid rate. I could feel the hopelessness of it all. "

"What do you mean?"

"I mean, **it felt like the plane was our country,** and it was going to crash. The President tried but he couldn't keep the plane in the air."

"Thomas, nothing is hopeless. We have the one true hope. He's our real pilot."

"I wish I had faith like you Ruthie."

"Having faith means believing something you can't see in front of you. It's the hope you have for what you want to come to pass. I just believe there's something bigger and better on the way for those who believe in Jesus. The world may fail, but he will not. In the meantime, we need to pray for the President, our leaders and the country. We need to pray for God's will to be done."

"What if God's will is for our country to crash?"

"Thomas, only God knows what is best. His plan doesn't always fit **our ideas** for what's best. That's why I pray for his will to be done in this situation."

"I suppose you are right."

"I've never been more right in my life," Ruthie said. "Let's get back to sleep. Hopefully you'll feel well enough to *sight see* one more day."

Author's Note:

In the chapter above Ruthie mentions that Thomas' dream reminds her of the movie SULLY. The principal photography for the movie SULLY began on **September 28, 2015**. Principal photography **involves shooting all the scenes of a movie script**. The actors are on location, and scenes are shot using video cameras, lighting and sound. These are the scenes that will end up in the movie. Without principal photography, you have no movie.

On **September 28, 2015** the last blood moon of the 2014/2015 tetrad occurred. All four blood moons occurred on Jewish/Feasts of the Lord. The blood moon on **September 28, 2015** occurred on the Feast of Tabernacles. Keep this fact in mind as you read the coming chapters, especially chapter 28.

CHAPTER 24
Wall Street

§

THE NEXT DAY THOMAS WOKE up feeling better. He was feeling so well he immediately began rushing everyone to get up.

"Come on you guys! The day is new. Let's get out there," he said exuberantly.

"Really?" Ruthie asked. "Just last night you thought you had the flu!"

"That was then. This is now. I feel great. Let's get going!"

Ruthie was glad Thomas felt better, but she felt a bit worn down herself. She didn't get much sleep last night with Thomas tossing and turning. Nonetheless, she got up and dragged her clothes on. She needed coffee. Strong coffee.

"Here's a cup of coffee," Thomas said, handing her a piping hot travel cup.

"When did you have time to get this?" she asked.

"I woke up early with a surge of energy. I feel like electricity is running through my body."

She raised an eyebrow. Electricity again?

"Why do we have to visit that place called Wall Street?" Jonah asked. "Why can't we go straight to the museum?"

"Wall Street is America's financial center. It's the home of the New York Stock Exchange. Our economy rises and falls based on the stock market. Wall Street is the epitome of American Capitalism. And Federal Hall is nearby. That's where George Washington took his very first Presidential Oath," Thomas declared.

"So, are you saying Wall Street has something to do with money?" Jonah asked.

"Yes, it has everything to do with money!" Thomas answered.

"Then I'll go because I love money."

"I know. You love to spend it too," Ruthie added.

"It's settled then. Let's get out there and see how money's made," Thomas said, with a little too much enthusiasm.

They all made it out the door quickly, at Thomas' urging. Before they knew it they were standing in front of the New York Stock Exchange.

"Well, here we are at 11 Wall Street," Thomas said, looking at the New York Stock Exchange.

Ruthie stared at the building. The architecture resembled buildings she'd seen from Ancient Rome. It was similar to the Roman Pantheon, with its massive columns. Above the columns was a large triangle, called a pediment. Inside were carved figures of people. A figure in the middle resembled an ancient God of some sort, similar to a Greek or Roman God she had seen in world history books.

"The building is very impressive. Imagine- inside that building stocks are being traded every second. All the buyers and sellers of the world converge here to make deals, and basically determine the prices of everything we buy. It all starts and ends at the New York Stock Exchange," Thomas said.

"How long has this building been here?" Jonah asked. "It looks old."

"The New York Stock Exchange was founded on March 8, 1817, but not at this location. Well actually, the New York Stock Exchange goes back *even before that* to March 1792. Twenty four prominent merchants had a secret meeting at a place called Corre's Hotel here in New York City. They met again on May 17, 1792 and signed an important document called the Buttonwood Agreement."

"That's a weird name," Jonah said.

"They called it that because their usual meeting place was under a buttonwood tree somewhere near 68 Wall Street. A buttonwood tree is a type of sycamore tree. Anyway, this agreement stated these merchants would only trade amongst themselves, and they would set trading prices. I guess you could say it was a mini Wall Street Stock Exchange. They even called themselves the New York Stock and Exchange Board. In 1817, the New York Stock Exchange began meeting in a room located at 40 Wall Street. That's where the Trump Building is located now."

"Did you say Trump Tower?" Ruthie asked.

"No, I said the Trump Building. Trump Tower is located on 5th Avenue. The Trump Building is located at 40 Wall Street. It's just a three minute walk from the Stock Exchange. They are two different buildings, but both are owned by Trump. Anyway, when the NYSE started meeting at 40 Wall Street, it was before the Trump Building was constructed. Before Trump owned the building at 40 Wall Street, it was known as the Bank of Manhattan Trust Building, and also the Manhattan Company Building. Trump didn't buy the building until 1995."

Ruthie thought it was interesting that the current President owned a building on the same site (land) where the members of the first stock exchange met.

"What happened to the **_original building_** the Stock Exchange met in on 40 Wall Street?"

"The Great Fire of New York happened in 1835 and it spread over 17 city blocks. About 600 buildings were destroyed, including the building the NYSE (New York Stock Exchange) was meeting in. The fire wreaked havoc. I read one account that said they could hear _walls tumbling down like avalanches._ And the water in the bay nearby was described like a sea of blood. There were a lot of new businesses with copper roofs destroyed, and witnesses say they saw the metal melting and dripping."

Ruthie pictured the walls tumbling down like avalanches. "More Jericho symbolism," she thought.

"The Stock Exchange had to move locations a few more times until it finally ended up here at 11 Wall Street," Thomas said.

"Dad, all I asked was how long THIS building has been here. Why do you have to give all that history? My head hurts," Jonah complained.

"Thomas, how do you even know all that stuff?" Ruthie asked.

"I told you I was up early and full of energy. I did some research."

Ruthie shook her head. Thomas had gone from deathly sick to a factual genius.

"Well, can we just go inside Dad?" Jonah asked impatiently.

"Sorry buddy. We can't go in. After the September 11 attacks, no one can go in unless they are on a special tour that has security clearance."

"That stinks. We only get to look at the outside."

"Turn around and look behind you. That's Federal Hall. See the statue of George Washington?" Thomas said.

"Yes, I see it. Why is it there?"

"That spot is where our first President, George Washington, took his first oath of office on April 30, 1789. It was also where our first Congress met, and it housed the Supreme Court. It even held the Executive Branch offices. At one time it was also part of the U.S. Treasury."

"Was George Washington a Christian?" asked Jonah.

"As far as I know, he was. I've read lots of historical documents which show he had great faith. He placed his hand on the Bible when he took the oath of office. That's why most Presidents place their hand on the Bible when they take the oath. Washington's inaugural address mentions God, and after he took the oath, he went to St. Paul's Chapel to pray for our nation."

"What's an oath?" asked Jonah.

"It's a sworn promise," said Thomas.

"That means you're not supposed to break it right?"

"You're not supposed to break oaths Jonah, but unfortunately people sometimes do."

"But God never breaks oaths does he?" asked Jonah.

Thomas looked at Ruthie as he answered. **"God never breaks an oath Jonah."**

Ruthie couldn't help but think of Rahab. An oath was sworn to protect her, even though she was a foreigner, a sinner and an outsider. But, she had the scarlet cord hanging from her window. The walls fell down, but she escaped. Those who knew Christ as their Savior had that same scarlet cord. It was an oath that would not be broken. It was their ticket to safety in the shelter (the hidden place) of the Most High.

Author's Notes:

Wall Street gets its name from the fact that there used to be a wooden wall (palisade) in the area, built by the Dutch to form a boundary of protection against Native Americans, pirates and the British. In 1685, Wall Street was laid out *based on where the original palisade (wall) was located*.

On **April 30, 1789**, George Washington took his oath of office on Wall Street at Federal Hall.

One World Trade Center, the new tower that replaced the old Twin Towers, became the tallest building in New York City on **April 30, 2012**. Regarding "tower"- there was one page of the Bible found at the Ground Zero wreckage of the original Twin Towers- it was a page showing Genesis 11- the Tower of Babel

The Louisiana Purchase, which doubled the size of the United States land, was made on **April 30, 1803**. (LAND DEAL)

April 30, 2003- Release of roadmap for a permanent two state solution for Israel and Palestine (LAND DEAL). This has not happened yet, *but these are the blueprints for it*. Hopefully, this does not come to pass at the hands of the United States.

It's ALWAYS bad to mess with God's land- a permanent two state solution "messes" with God's land! If the U.S. messes with God's land by trying to broker a land "deal" in Israel, it is likely he will mess with ours and I can assure you it WILL BE A BIG, HORRIBLE MESS when he's done!!!! Oh, I forgot to mention, on **April 30, 1907**, the idea to build *Titanic* was conceived over dinner. As you know, *Titanic* sank! The roadmap for a two state solution, an idea put forth publically on **April 30, 2003,** is no different than *Titanic's* plans. It will bring destruction to all those who try to accomplish it. "Many are the plans in a person's heart, but it is the Lord's purpose that prevails."

CHAPTER 25
Golden Eagle

Ruthie and her family toured a few more places on Wall Street, and then moved on to the Museum. Jonah enjoyed this part the most. The amount of displays to explore seemed to go on forever. After a few hours of exploring, they moved on to Central Park for a quick tour. Exhausted and tired they made their way to a cozy dinner spot, and then headed back to the hotel.

"We'll be heading back tomorrow morning," Thomas reminded everyone.

"So soon? We just got here," whined Jonah.

"It was just a short trip this time. We'll be back again," he promised.

Ruthie wanted to see more sights, but she knew Thomas had to be back at work.

"Why don't we watch a quick movie before we go to bed," suggested Jonah.

"I suppose we could," answered Thomas, picking up the remote. He began flipping through channels.

"Wait! Stop on that station," Jonah begged.

"Which one?"

"Go back, go back. Stop right there! You got it! It's *Back to the Future*!"

Ruthie watched as Michael J. Fox emerged from the *DeLorean* time machine.

"It's the falcon wing doors," Jonah yelled.

"That's pretty cool Jonah, especially since we were just talking about that movie at Grand Central Station."

Ruthie found it odd that *Back to the Future* just happened to be on. "Coincidence or divine timing?" she wondered.

By the time the movie was over, it was midnight. "Ugh, we're going to be tired in the morning," Thomas stated. With that, everyone rushed to bed, with lights out in record time.

Morning came quickly and just as Thomas predicted, everyone was tired.

"Why do you always book early flights," Ruthie complained.

"Hey, you guys were the ones who wanted to watch the movie."

"You had the remote!"

"Let's quit arguing and get moving. We have to be at *La Guardia* by 8:00 a.m."

Ruthie switched into high gear and gathered the rest of her things. A quick shower, a little make-up and she was out the door.

"Are you going to wait for us?" Thomas asked, still trying to gather his things.

"You said to get moving so I did," she laughed.

They were out the door and in *La Guardia* Airport ahead of schedule.

"We didn't even have to rush. We have 45 minutes to spare," said Ruthie to Thomas.

"Yes, it's nice to have some time to relax for once. I can actually check my email and look at the news….. Oh no!"

"What is it?"

"My phone only has 2% charge left."

"I thought you charged it at the hotel."

"I must have forgotten. I'm gonna see if I can find an outlet to charge it."

"Do what you have to do," Ruthie said, as Thomas walked away.

She glanced at Thomas' open seat and noticed something gold and shiny. It looked like a coin. Thomas must have been sitting on it the whole time. She picked it up and investigated it carefully. It definitely was a coin of some kind, though she'd never seen one like this before. The front of the coin showed the image of a woman carrying a torch in one hand, and an olive branch in the other. The word LIBERTY was written along the top of the coin. The other side had two eagles. One eagle carried an olive branch, and was flying above a nest with a female eagle and her babies. UNITED STATES OF AMERICA was written along the top of the coin.

She knew it had to be an American coin, but she still didn't know which one. It wasn't a quarter or half dollar. She decided to search on her phone. She typed in the description, and the words AMERICAN GOLD EAGLE COIN popped up on the screen. She looked at the link and sure enough, she did have an American Gold Eagle coin. She read through the information to fully understand the coin's value and history.

She found out she had a valuable coin. The American Gold Eagle is the official gold bullion coin of the United States, and is made from gold mined in the U.S. The value of the Gold Eagle coin was based on how many ounces of gold it was made with, as well as the year it was minted.

She looked back at the coin in her hand. This coin was made in 2016. She wondered how many ounces it was. The value of the coins varied, but a one ounce gold coin could go for as much as $1000.00. Suddenly, she wondered if someone lost it. This wasn't the type of coin you would just let fall out of your pocket.

As she looked at the coin, she saw an older woman hurrying toward her, her eyes wide.

"Excuse me, but you didn't happen to see a beautiful gold coin with eagles on it did you?"

"Why yes. In fact, I have it right here. It was lying in this seat," Ruthie said, holding the coin in her hand.

"Oh thank goodness! I was sick to my stomach when I realized the coin was gone. I only took it out for a moment, but I thought I….."

"Here's your coin back," Ruthie said, a little sad to give it up.

"Thank you so much. You know, this coin cost me $1,300.00. I just bought it last week."

"That's a lot of money for a coin. I guess it's because it's pure gold."

"It's one ounce of pure gold. I decided I'm going to buy as many as I can because you never know when American paper currency will lose its value."

"Yes, I worry about paper currency too. Every time I go on the national debt clock I get worried. The last time I checked we were almost at 20 trillion! Ugh."

"Well dear, it's only a matter of time. China and Russia are already trading without U.S. dollars. And they aren't the only country doing this. The plan is to do away with the dollar. In a few years America may no longer be the reserve currency. That's why I'm buying gold. It doesn't lose its value."

Ruthie put her head down. She felt a sudden tinge of worry in her spirit. What would she do if American money lost all its value?

"Oh, I shouldn't have worried you dear. I'm so sorry. You know, money isn't the most important thing in this world."

"I know that," she said. "It just makes me sad when I think about what can happen to our economy, and our people."

"I want you to do something dear," the woman said. She handed Ruthie the coin. "Take a look at the two eagles on the coin."

Ruthie looked at the eagles.

"I want to share some things about eagles with you."

"Sure, go ahead."

"First of all, an eagle can fly at very high altitudes. In fact, there are few birds that can fly to the height of an eagle. Secondly, eagles have magnificent vision. They can spot prey up to five kilometers away. An eagle's eyes are packed with millions of special light sensitive cells, which help them see with great detail. When an eagle finds a fish he wants, he will keep his eyes glued on it until he gets it. This is a difficult task because fish are hard to detect in the water. They blend in with their surroundings."

Much of the information the woman shared sounded very familiar. She felt like she'd heard it before.

"That's just the tip of the iceberg. Did you know eagles can fly through thunderstorms? When the winds of a storm rage, an eagle can actually use the wind to help lift him above the clouds. **The eagle can soar above the storm.**"

"Wait! I *have* heard these things before."

"I hoped so. But, you've forgotten them. You have to remember Ruthie."

"I know. It's just there are so many things to remember lately. Tell me more to remind me. And by the way, how do you know all these facts about eagles?"

"I used to do some volunteer work at the Audubon Rehabilitation Center. We had a few eagles there. We've had a few eagle babies to take care of as well. What's interesting about eagle babies, or eaglets, is that ***they live in a nest full of thorns***."

"I have heard that, but I don't know all the details. How can they live in a nest full of thorns?"

"The mother eagle builds a big nest high on the edge of a cliff. She makes the nest from large branches and thorns. She covers the branches and thorns with fluffy, soft feathers. She keeps it this way for a while. But, eventually the time comes for the babies to leave the nest. The mother will slowly remove feathers day by day. The babies will become uncomfortable as the soft feathers are removed. Soon, they will want to leave the nest. The feeling of the thorns will become unbearable. The mother eagle knows if she doesn't make the eagles leave their cozy nest, they will never try to fly. They'll never take the leap of faith needed to soar. When the baby can no longer stand the uncomfortable nest, he/she will jump out of the nest. With no prior flying experience, most baby eagles would plunge to their death. But, never fear! The momma eagle will swoop down and rescue the baby. She will do this over and over again until finally, the baby can fly on its own."

"I remember now. **God's people are like the eagles**. God puts us high upon a cliff to keep us safe. But at some point we have to venture out. We get pricked and torn up by life's circumstances, but God never lets go of us. If we stick with God we will soar high like eagles."

"**Those who wait upon the Lord shall renew their strength; they shall mount up with wings as eagles; they shall run, and not be weary; and they shall walk, and not faint,**" the woman said, quoting Isaiah 40.

"Now I see. No matter what we face in this world, God will help us keep going. He'll carry us on his wings like the mama eagle."

"**As an eagle stirreth up her nest, fluttereth over her young, spreadeth abroad her wings, taketh them, beareth them on her wings,**" the woman said, quoting a verse from Deuteronomy. "God will make sure we are prepared for the battle ahead."

"I believe you are right," Ruthie said.

"The Bride will know what to do when the time comes. Then, one day she will be **stolen**."

"**Like the eagle steals fish, the Bride will be stolen by Christ, who is the fisher of men**," Ruthie added.

"I knew you would remember. Don't lose heart. Jesus has overcome the world. And remember, other birds look over their shoulder, but **an eagle never looks back**. Stay the course. Follow the straight path," the woman exclaimed. She began walking away.

"Wait! Your golden eagle coin. It's worth a lot of money."

"I want you to keep it as a reminder. The people of God are the eagles, and gold is the prize- the gold streets of heaven!" the woman said. "Oh, but I almost forgot to tell you something else."

"What is it?"

"Have you seen the movie *Sully*? Here we are in *La Guardia* airport and I got to thinking about that incident back in 2009. It was a **bird strike** that took down the plane right?"

Ruthie gave the lady a quizzical look. She thought of Thomas' dream. The pilot had to land in the water. Sully had to land in the water.

"All pilots need prayer. All leaders need prayer," she said, walking away.

"My phone's all charged. Who was that lady?" Thomas asked, sitting in his seat.

"She lost her coin, but then found it."

"What?"

"She lost a golden eagle coin."

"Really? Those coins are worth a lot of money."

"I found it in your seat. When she asked about it, I gave it to her. But then she gave it back to me."

"What? Are you kidding me?"

Ruthie handed Thomas the coin. "There's an ounce of gold in the coin."

"Wow! This is your lucky day Ruthie. I must say, weird stuff is always happening to you."

"Yeah, I know. I didn't think you noticed."

"Looks like it's going to be another stormy flight. The weather is reporting thunderstorms in the area."

"That's ok," she said, looking at the gold eagle coin. "If eagles can handle it, then so can I. After all, eagles can soar above the storm."

CHAPTER 26
Raptors

The flight to Orlando from New York was turbulent. As Thomas predicted, the weather was stormy. But, Ruthie handled it well. She kept thinking about what the woman at the airport said about "flying above the storm". As she sat on the plane, she wished she had something to read. That would get her mind off the turbulence.

"You got anything to read?" she asked Thomas.

"Sorry babe," he said, half asleep. I don't. Why don't you check the compartment in the back of the seat?"

"Ok, but I don't see how you can sleep during a thunderstorm," she said, sifting through the compartment. Bingo! She found a magazine in the bottom. It was pretty wrinkled, but it would do.

"*Travel Treasures*," she said, reading the front cover. "I like to travel. Maybe it will give me some ideas," she thought. She flipped through the pages, trying to decide what to read. As she flipped through she noticed some pictures of birds. "Oh boy! Birds, of all things. Do I really want to know more about birds? I think I'm birded out! Eagles… hawks….birds all the time," she argued in her mind. She decided to turn to something else. "Ahh, Paris, France. That's more like it. I've never been to Europe. Why not read about where I dream to go?" she thought.

She started to read the article. Unfortunately, a nagging thought interrupted her reading. "Oh, just ignore it. Think Paris, France." She continued to read. But again, the nagging thought surfaced. "Ahh, you might as well give in. Just turn to the page about birds," she mumbled to herself.

"Are you talking to me," Thomas asked, looking confused.

"Sorry babe. No, I was just…. Never mind."

Thomas shrugged his shoulders and went back to sleep.

She turned to the page about birds. The first thing she noticed was a picture of what looked like a horde of birds flying through the sky. There were so many, the sky looked black in the picture. She read the title of the story. *Israel: A Bird Watcher's Paradise*. "This could be interesting," she thought.

She read the entire article thoroughly. The first paragraph stated, "Each year, more than one billion birds will fly over the ancient land of Israel. **It is home to one of the largest bird migration paths in the world.** In one morning, more than 10,000 eagles can be seen flying across the land."

"What? Did it say 10,000 eagles?" she said loudly.

"Are you talking to me?" Thomas asked. He looked annoyed.

"No. Sorry. Go back to sleep."

She kept reading. "Bird enthusiasts from around the world come in droves to see the birds. Some of the best sites to see the spectacular migration are the Jerusalem Mountains, the Carmel coast, the Gaza coast and even the *ancient city of Jericho*."

"Jericho! Are you kidding me? Jericho!" she said out loud. A few passengers looked in her direction.

"Sorry," she mouthed. She couldn't help herself. She couldn't believe the connection. The world's largest bird migration flies over Jericho? She suddenly thought about raptors. Raptors were birds of course. Eagles were raptors and they were part of the migration. She scanned the rest of the article, looking for anything *specifically* about raptors. Sure enough, she found something. "Israel acts as a **<u>raptor rapture</u>** for the world's raptors. **Above Israel you can see more than 30 species of raptors, which include many varieties of eagles, buzzards, and sparrow hawks.**"

She couldn't believe the article used the word rapture. She knew the Lord was showing her how raptors were a reminder of the rapture. Here she was reading about Israel having one of the largest raptor migrations in the world! Not only that, Jericho was one of the hotspots! Raptors and other birds flew over Jericho during their migration. Jericho was an allegory about the rapture. What were the chances?

She read more. "The number of raptors flying over Israel is difficult to see anywhere else in the world," one expert said. "There are raptor watch points where the birds are counted as they fly through. It is estimated that approximately **90% of the world's population of raptors travels through Israel in the Fall."**

Ruthie covered her mouth. If she didn't she knew she would scream. How could this be? Why didn't she know this before? 90% of the world's raptors migrate through Israel in Autumn? In the Bible, the season known as Autumn (Fall), represented the **harvest** of God's people. **The rapture would be a harvest of God's people.** The Bride would be snatched quickly and forcefully. Usually, raptors grabbed their prey with their powerful talons. The Bible constantly references Jesus having the enemy under his feet. In Ephesians 1:22 it says **God has placed all things under Jesus' feet**. Not only that, when Jesus returned to Earth for the Second Coming, he would set his feet on the Mount of Olives. One day Jesus would snatch away his Bride. Later, he would return to Earth and set everything straight at the Second Coming.

Ruthie read the rest of the article. "Israel channels all the birds and raptors that come from three different continents. Birds fly from Asia and Europe, and then move southward toward Africa. Israel is in the perfect spot for these birds. It's the safest, easiest route to take on their migration path. The path hasn't changed for thousands of years and has been heavily documented."

She was astounded. **She knew Israel was the timeclock for the end times**. The rapture was certainly part of end times. She had a thought. Revelation was the last book of the Bible, and it described the end times in detail. Wasn't there something in Revelation about birds of prey? (*raptors*) Yes, she was sure of it. She pulled out her phone to look it up. She realized she had no signal. She wished she had her Bible.

"Excuse me, but would you like to borrow my Bible?" a passenger seated across from her said.

"Huh? Why do you ask?" *Could this passenger read her mind?*

"I heard you say Jericho earlier. Did you want to read about Jericho?" She passed the Bible to Ruthie.

"Thanks," Ruthie said, feeling awkward, yet grateful. But, she didn't need to read about Jericho. Instead she quickly flipped to Revelation. She knew she should look at the chapters near the end. She scanned Revelation 17, then 18 and finally 19. As she read 19, she saw it. It mentioned birds of prey.

"And I saw heaven opened, and behold a white horse; and he that sat upon him was called Faithful and True, and in righteousness he doth judge and make war. His eyes were as a flame of fire, and on his head were many crowns; and he had a name written, that no man knew, but he himself. And he was clothed with a vesture dipped in blood; and his name is called The Word of God. And the armies which were in heaven followed him upon white horses, clothed in fine linen, white and clean. And out of his mouth goeth a sharp sword, that with it he should smite the nations: and he shall rule them with a rod of iron: and he treadeth the winepress of fierceness and wrath of Almighty God. And he hath on his vesture and on his thigh a name written, KING OF KINGS, AND LORD OF LORDS. And I saw an angel standing in the sun; and he cried with a loud voice, **saying to all the fowls that fly in the midst of heaven, Come and gather yourselves together unto the supper of the great God: That ye may eat the flesh of kings, and the flesh of captains, and the flesh of mighty men, and the flesh of horses, and of them that sit on them, and the flesh of all men, both free and bond, both small and great…….. and all the fowls were filled with their flesh.**"

"Did you find what you were looking for?" the passenger asked.

"Yes… yes I did," Ruthie answered, handing the woman her Bible.

Ruthie couldn't get over it. One of the largest raptor migrations in the world happened over Israel. Not only that, someday in the future,

there would be a huge feast for all the raptors of the land. When the Lord wiped out the enemies of Israel, the scene wouldn't be pretty. Dead bodies would lie everywhere. Eagles, owls, kestrels, vultures and other birds of prey would have their fill. Where would this final battle take place? Wasn't it called Megiddo, or the Valley of Jehoshaphat? Where exactly was this located? Right now she didn't have Wi-Fi so she couldn't look it up. She'd make a mental note of it. Unfortunately, the image was a grim reminder of the judgement that would take place on all those who rejected God. At least the Bride would not succumb to this fate. The Bride would be hidden in the time of trouble, and protected.

CHAPTER 27
The Final Battle

THE REST OF THE PLANE ride was fairly smooth, though Ruthie felt shaken inside. Revelation 19 was somewhat disturbing in its details. She tried to put thoughts of it aside as she exited the plane with her family. She had to switch gears quickly.

"Home sweet home," Thomas said.

"Yeah, but I still wish we could've stayed longer in New York," Jonah answered.

"Like I said, we'll go back again."

They made their way out of the airport and drove home. As Ruthie looked out the window, she noticed a large group of Ibises flying across the sky. She wondered where they were flying, and where they'd been. Immediately she thought of the bird migrations she'd read about on the plane. She read Revelation 19 and that chapter highlighted the day of God's judgement against the nations that plundered Israel. **All those nations who stand in direct defiance of God would become food for the birds of prey**.

She thought, "Where would this great feast occur?" She quickly searched for the answer to the question on her phone. She typed in-*where will the final battle for Earth take place?* Megiddo, also known as the Jezreel Valley, was the answer that popped up in several detailed articles. As she read, she found out many things.

Megiddo is located in Northern Israel, and is often known by the name **Armageddon.** Revelation 16, verse 16 says, "And he gathered them together into a placed called in the Hebrew tongue Armageddon. In Greek, the word means "the hill of Megiddo." Even though Armageddon is only mentioned once in the Bible, Megiddo is mentioned 12 times in the Old Testament.

Megiddo is made up of a 15 acre summit and currently contains the ruins of different kingdoms. Megiddo was once an important Canaanite city, but was also an important city in the Kingdom of Israel. Its location was prized by many rulers because it sits on a pass which leads to Mount Carmel and the Mediterranean. It was an invaluable trade route as well. Megiddo lies within the Jezreel Valley, which is the site of Gideon's miraculous victory against the Midianites and Amalekites. It is also the location where King Saul and his sons died, and the Israelites were defeated by the Philistines.

Several historical battles took place at the site. Thutmose III, who was one of Egypt's greatest military leaders, fought the Syrians here and was victorious, thus earning himself a very fertile and prosperous area. This is also the site where King Josiah, a great ruler of Judah, battled the Egyptians and subsequently lost his life. More recently, in September of 1918 (during World War I), a battle was fought between the British Empire and the Ottoman Empire. The British won, causing history to change in moments. This victory put the British in control of the area. That would eventually allow for the creation of a Jewish homeland, which would be *fully realized* in the years to come. In fact, one of the first Jewish settlements was in the Jezreel Valley on **September 11, 1921.**

Ruthie realized there were a lot of important battles and events that took place in Megiddo and the Jezreel Valley, but by far the most significant would be the Battle of Armageddon. It is here where Jesus Christ would wipe out the enemies of God and Israel. Ruthie looked up a few verses that correlated with the final battle of the Lord.

"Come near, ye nations, to hear; and harken, ye people, let the earth hear, and all that is therein; the world, and all things that come forth of it. **For the indignation of the Lord is upon all nations**, and his fury upon all their armies: he hath utterly destroyed them, he hath delivered them to the slaughter. Their slain also shall be cast out, and their stink shall come up out of their carcases, and the mountains shall be melted with their blood. And all the host of heaven shall be dissolved, and the heavens shall be rolled together as a scroll: and all their hosts shall fall down, as the leaf falleth off from the vine, and as a falling fig from the fig tree…. And their land shall be soaked with blood, and their dust made fat with fatness. For it is the day of the Lord's vengeance, **and the year of recompences for the controversy of Zion** (Israel)….. The wild beasts of the desert shall also meet with the wild beasts of the island, and the satyr shall cry to his fellow; the screech owl also shall rest there, and find for herself a place of rest. There shall the great owl make her nest, and lay, and hatch, and gather under her shadow: there shall the vultures also be gathered, every one with her mate." **Isaiah 34 (verses 1-4, 7-8, 14-15)**

"Who is this coming from Edom, from Bozrah, with his garments stained in crimson? Who is this, robed in splendor, striding forward in the greatest of his strength? It is I, proclaiming victory, mighty to save. Why are your garments red, like those of the one treading the winepress? I have trodden the winepress alone; from the nations no one was with me. I trampled them down in my anger and trod them down in my wrath; their blood spattered on my garments, and stained all my clothing. It was for me the day of vengeance, the year for me to redeem had come…..I trampled the nations in my anger; in my wrath I made them drunk and poured their blood on the ground." **Isaiah 63, 1-6**

The more she read, the more she realized just how bloody the final battle would be. The winepress would be full at harvest time. There would certainly be plenty for the raptors to feast upon. According to the information she read on the bird migration, northern Israel is where the majority of these birds would be. She quickly looked up "bird migration sites in Northern Israel," and found an area called the Hula Valley. This area is a region with large amounts of fresh water, and more than 500 million birds and 500 species stop here during the migration.

In this perfect spot they can rest and recuperate before moving on to their final destination. North America, which is more than 1000 times the size of Israel, doesn't see migrations even close to this amount. By contrast, it wouldn't be unusual to see over 100,000 birds *at one time i*n the Hula Valley.

Within the Hula Valley there is a lake called Lake Merom, which was where Joshua had a decisive victory over the Canaanites. It is at the waters of Merom where the Lord said to Joshua, "'Do not be afraid because of them, for tomorrow at this time I will deliver all of them slain before Israel: you shall hamstring their horses and burn their chariots with fire'. … the Lord delivered them into the hand of Israel………they struck them until no survivor was left." **Joshua 11:5-8.**

The book of Joshua told the stories of how God delivered Israel from her enemies, and how Israel inherited her land from these enemies. Ruthie couldn't help but see a connection to End Times. Right now the enemies of Israel were lining up to destroy her. Currently, it was behind the scenes, though some countries made no qualms about their hatred for Israel. Iran literally wrote it on their missiles! Many others such as Lebanon, Syria, Turkey and Yemen had publically voiced their desires to wipe Israel off the map. The battles of the Old Testament were rearing their head again. But, the Bible stated clearly these enemies would be wiped out. God would have his day of vengeance, and the birds of prey would be part of that plan. Armageddon took place in the northern part of Israel, and so did this bird migration. God had it set up well ahead of time. His word always confirmed his plan. It didn't matter what the world leaders wanted. The land belonged to Israel and God would redeem it all. In Isaiah 41:15, the Lord says, **he will make Israel into a "threshing sledge, new and sharp with many teeth. They will thresh the mountains and crush them and reduce the hills to chaff"** Who were the mountains and hills? The enemies of God and Israel. **"Therefore wait ye upon me, saith the Lord, until the day that I rise up to the prey: for my determination is to gather the nations, that I may assemble the kingdoms, to pour upon them**

mine indignation, even all my fierce anger: for all the earth shall be devoured with the fire of my jealousy." (Zephaniah 3:8)

The rapture. Raptors. It was all so symbolic. Christ would snatch his Bride at just the right moment, just like a raptor grabs its prey. His people, also known as eagles, would be gathered to him. Christ's followers (the eagles) would know it was **his body (carcass)** that laid in the tomb and rose again, only to return for his Bride on a day of redemption. The Bride would be hidden away during a time of great turmoil. The Earth would be trampled and judged, but not the Bride. The raptors (birds of prey) would be part of God's plan to rid the Earth of the carcasses of Israel's enemies. It would come full circle.

Suddenly, Ruthie pictured Lot and his wife, leaving the evil city of Sodom and Gomorrah. Lot moved straight ahead, knowing the city would be destroyed by God's wrath. But, his wife looked back at the city. She should have kept going, looking straight ahead like Lot. But, she turned around. One more glance. She turned to a pillar of salt.

Then Ruthie remembered. Eagles always fly straight ahead. They don't look back. God's people needed to stay on the straight path and follow God. Looking back would do no good. Following the world would do no good. God's plan for the Bride and Israel was imminent and eternal. **Even the raptors knew that.**

CHAPTER 28
Flight 1549

§

Even though Ruthie missed New York, she was glad to be home. "There's no place like home," she thought. The first thing she wanted was a big cup of coffee.

"I'll take a big cup of coffee," said Thomas, reading her mind.

"Great minds think alike," she nodded.

With coffee in hand they went to the living room to relax. Thomas turned on the T.V., per his usual routine. He flipped through the stations over and over.

"Just pick one," complained Ruthie.

Thomas stopped on what she liked to call "the documentary channel." It was Thomas' favorite station. Being a history major, he reveled in events of the past, present and future. Sure, he was a fireman, but he had a historian's heart.

"This looks interesting. I can't believe it's already been eight years since this happened," Thomas said.

Ruthie listened to the narrator introducing the program.

"Flight 1549, piloted by Captain Chesley B. "Sully" Sullenberger, went down in the Hudson River on January 15, 2009. There were 150 passengers and three flight attendants aboard the aircraft that day. With pilot and co-pilot included, there were **155** total."

Immediately Ruthie felt a small burst of static electricity run up her arm. The lady at *La Guardia* airport had mentioned the movie *Sully*. Now, as soon as she gets home from her return flight out of *La Guardia*, Thomas *just happens* to turn on a documentary about Sully.

"Just three minutes into its flight, the plane struck a flock of Canadian geese, resulting in a complete loss of engine power. Both engines shut down, and engine thrust ceased. Interestingly enough, the birds had not been on the departure controller's radar screen."

The first thing Ruthie took note of was how quickly it happened. One minute the plane was ascending normally, and the next it hit a flock of geese. All this within a few minutes. *There was no warning before the birds hit. They weren't even on the radar before it happened.*

"The pilots reported their view was obscured with large birds, and the passengers stated they heard 'very loud bangs'. Many reported seeing flames spewing from the engines. The strong smell of burning fuel trickled through the plane. Captain Sullenberger contacted the New York Terminal Radar Control and let them know he lost thrust in both engines. Air traffic control advised Sullenberger to turn around and land at *La Guardia's* **Runway 13**. But, he knew *there was no time*. He simply responded, 'Unable.'"

Ruthie couldn't imagine the stress the passengers must have felt-just the sheer fear would have killed her! And what about the pilots?

"Knowing he didn't have time to turn back, Sullenberger looked for other options, such as landing in New Jersey's *Teterboro Airport*. Unfortunately, he realized this option wouldn't work either. There just wasn't time, and there were too many buildings in the way. The plane was already flying too low and there wouldn't be any way to maneuver safely. The only viable option was a **water landing** in the Hudson. At this point, the plane had been in the air for barely five minutes, and now it was on its way over the George Washington Bridge, and into the Hudson River."

Ruthie looked at Thomas, who was staring intently at the TV screen. She wondered if he was thinking about his dream? After all, in his dream the pilot landed in the water. The pilot had done everything he could to keep the plane airborne, but it wasn't good enough. The plane went down.

"Before the plane hit the water, the Captain advised everyone, '**Brace for impact**.' At 3:31 p.m. the plane descended into the Hudson and landed while at a speed of approximately 140 miles per hour. The landing was described as a 'hard landing with one impact and no bounce'. Immediately the Captain and crew evacuated the passengers. The plane was taking on water quickly so it was important to get everyone out of the plane. The Captain checked the plane several times to ensure all passengers were out. Passengers piled onto the plane's wings, as well as inflated slides. The air and water temperatures were a frigid 20 degrees."

Ruthie wondered what was worse- the shock of the landing, or evacuating the plane to find oneself in freezing temperatures?

"Captain Sullenberger ditched the plane in a strategic spot. The area he landed in was frequented by boats. Sullenberger knew this would give the passengers the best chance for survival, as there would be boats nearby to help facilitate rescue efforts. The first boat on the scene was the *Thomas Jefferson*, NY Waterway's ferry, captained by Vince Lombardi, which arrived within minutes of the crash. The passengers on the wings were rescued first, followed by those on the life rafts. By **3:55** p.m., ***all passengers had been rescued.***"

As Ruthie listened to the story, she realized just how miraculous the incident had been. An unpowered ditching of a full plane into the Hudson River, and not a single death. In her spirit she knew this story held a rich meaning. The hand of God must have been on that plane, as well as on the pilots. Miracles like this don't just happen.

"Though the Captain had little time, he planned the landing well, and made the best possible choice. Because of this, not a single passenger or crewmember perished. In addition, the ferry boat crews who arrived to help knew exactly what to do. They had been trained for emergencies and they jumped into action. The first rescue boat was alongside the plane within four minutes. Things happened at lightning speed, but the actions of the captain and rescue crews were timed perfectly," the narrator stated.

It happened at lightning speed, but the rescue came quickly. The passengers were on the wings. Once the birds struck the engines, the plane went down. No turning back. As Ruthie reviewed these things in her mind, she couldn't help but think of the rapture. After all, when the rapture happened it would be quick- *no turning back*. God's people would be whisked away in the blink of an eye. After the rapture, the world below would be in turmoil. Planes would literally be crashing as Christian pilots suddenly disappeared, along with Christian passengers. The rescue would come quickly for those who belonged to Jesus. They would soar high on the wings of eagles. Just like the passengers who were rescued from the wings of the plane, the people of God would be covered under the wings of God. Ruthie could hear Psalm 91, verse 4 in her head, *"He will cover you with his feathers, and under his wings you will find refuge."*

"Captain Sullenberger was trained in flying gliders while he was a student at the United States Air Force Academy. He became an instructor for the glider SOARING program while he was there. He also had done some glider training after the Academy. This must have helped him glide Flight 1549 into the Hudson River. After all, gliders are aircraft designed to fly without using an engine. Sully lost power in both engines, forcing him to 'glide' into the Hudson. Birds such as eagles fly in a similar manner. In fact, eagles can fly for extended periods of time without flapping their wings. Some eagles have been observed flapping their wings no more than three minutes per hour while in flight. They choose to spend their time gliding rather than flapping. The eagle soars on thermals as they climb to a high altitude. Then they will glide across the sky, wings straight and outstretched, flying effortlessly ahead."

"I guess you could say Sully was like an eagle that day," Thomas said, his eyes glued on the T.V.

As soon as Thomas said that a picture formed in Ruthie's mind. She saw the beautiful eagle on the electrical pole. The eagle sat perched up high, its wings spread. The electrical pole was across from the neighborhood entrance marker that read *Lake Lagrange Heights*. She had the urge to go outside and see the electrical pole and the neighborhood entrance marker. She got up from her spot on the couch and ran outside.

"Hey, where are you going?" Thomas asked.

"Be back in a second. I've gotta see something," she said.

She ran quickly to the spot, hoping she would see the eagle. She had only seen it on Facebook, but she longed to see it for herself, *in person*. She looked up at the electrical pole. She couldn't believe it. There, perched atop the pole, was an eagle. It was beautiful. Large and bold, the eagle sat silently, looking to the sky with a sheer calmness. She glanced at the neighborhood entrance marker, and then at the street sign. It said ***Dawley Avenue***. She never thought about the name of the sign before. She found herself wondering what Dawley meant. She pulled out her phone and looked up the meaning of the word **dawley**. The definition said, "**a group of people gathered together for a common purpose. A gathering.**" Ruthie almost dropped her phone. A gathering of people? A common purpose? Wasn't the rapture a gathering of God's people? The purpose of the gathering was to literally fly to heaven. She already knew eagles were used in the Bible (symbolically) to represent God's people. There was also the verse, "As lightning cometh out of the east and shineth even unto the west; so shall also the coming of the Son of man be. For wheresoever the carcase is, there the **eagles be gathered together.**" She couldn't believe it. The eagle, the electrical pole, the name of the street sign. It all fit together like the pieces of a puzzle. It was a giant parable staring her in the face. Her phone began ringing. It was Michael.

"Hi Michael. How are you?" She was always glad to hear from her son. He was currently going to school at the U.S. Air Force Academy in Colorado Springs, Colorado. Oddly enough, it was Michael who was with her when the lightning strike happened while he was visiting on leave. It was also Michael who pulled up the picture of the eagle on Facebook that day.

"I'm great Mom. You'll never believe what happened."

"What happened? Tell me."

"I got the job!"

"The job? What job?" Ruthie asked.

"I'm going to be a **glider pilot**! I got a position as a SOARING instructor at the Academy. I'm going to be teaching students how to fly gliders!"

Ruthie felt a lump form in her throat. Did he just say GLIDER pilot? An image of flight 1549 entered her mind. She could see Sully. He too was a glider SOARING instructor at the United States Air Force Academy. What were the chances?

"Did you hear me Mom? I'm going to be teaching students how to fly gliders!"

Ruthie looked up at the eagle on the electrical pole. She noticed a number on the pole, just below where the eagle was perched. **The number was 13**. There was something familiar about the number. What was it?

"Mom! Are you still there?" Michael asked.

"Yes, Michael, I'm here. I'm staring at this beautiful eagle right now. What are the chances you call me at this perfect moment. After all, eagles are the masters of gliding. You are going to be teaching students to glide like an eagle."

"Wow! That's great timing. I wonder if it's the same eagle I saw on Facebook."

Just then the eagle flew off the electrical pole. Ruthie watched it as it soared high, riding the thermals of the Florida air. As it flew higher, it started circling.

"I'm so proud of you Michael. I know you're going to do great things," Ruthie said.

Michael would do great things. She was sure of that. So would God's people, known in the Bible as eagles.

"Well, I gotta go Mom. I have to be at the airfield in **13 minutes**."

Thirteen. There it was again. What did it mean? Another puzzle. Another parable. She looked in the sky. The eagle was still circling. Why did eagles circle so much? Did it help them fly better? Every answer seemed to lead to another question. "This is like a wild goose chase," she said to herself. A wild goose chase? Did she really say that? She thought of the Canadian geese that struck the engines on Sully's plane.

Ruthie hung up the phone, astonished with the timing of everything. She looked at the number 13 on the electrical pole. She typed *the biblical significance of 13* on her phone's search engine. What she saw made her heart jump out of her chest. **"The city of Jericho is associated with the number 13. The Israelites marched around the city for <u>six</u> days, circling the city <u>one time each day</u>. On the seventh day, they marched around it <u>seven</u> times. The grand total of all the marching (in circles) was 13 times."**

"Jericho! Thirteen is tied to Jericho! And the rapture is foreshadowed in the story of Jericho! Rahab represents the Bride of Christ, who is spared from the destruction of the city. The walls of the city fell, but she and her family were spared. Here I am standing at a neighborhood entrance marker that looks like a wall, near a sign that says *Dawley*, <u>which means gathering</u>. Not to mention, I just saw the eagle on the electrical pole across from the marker. Eagles represent the people of God! And to top it off, I can see the eagle still circling in the air," she said aloud.

"Who are you talking to Ruthie?" Thomas asked.

"Where did you come from?" she asked, startled.

"You just ran out of the house. I wanted to make sure you were ok. Are you watching that eagle?" he said, looking upward.

"Yes, I was watching the eagle," she said, not really wanting to explain.

"You'd think the eagle would fly straight ahead all the time, ***but circling actually helps the eagles fly through the thermals, or rising air.*** If the eagle turns when he finds a thermal, he can stay inside it. The thermals help his body move and he can eventually fly forward to where he wants to go," Thomas explained.

"Circling is a good thing then," she said. "I guess I should go back inside. I lost track of the time out here."

As they walked back, something caught Ruthie's attention. An American flag waved in the wind, not too far from where the eagle was circling.

"I've got a trivia question for you," Thomas said.

"Shoot," she answered.

"How many stripes are on the American flag?"

"I forget. How many?"

"Thirteen."

Ruthie turned to Thomas. "Thirteen?"

"Yes, there are seven red stripes, and six white." *Ruthie recognized the six and seven from Jericho, as well as the thirteen.*

"I just thought of something else," Thomas said. "Our <u>original national flag</u> was adopted by the Congress on **June 14, 1777**. That one had <u>thirteen stripes on it, but it also had thirteen stars, standing for thirteen colonies</u>. Anyway, isn't Donald Trump's birthday on **June 14?** That's kind of interesting when you think about it. It's like he's tied to our nation in some sort of numerical way."

Ruthie looked at Thomas. She was stunned. How in the world did he know when the flag was adopted, and why did he know the President's birthday? Those weren't things most people knew off the top of their head. What was even stranger is that the President's name was the actual word **trump, which meant shofar,** or **alarm**. The trumpet was associated with Rosh Hashanah, and the rapture. Jesus would return with the sound of the last trump. She just realized the number **13 was tied to Jericho and the rapture**. Not only that, the national symbol for America is the eagle! How could all these things be tied together?

"How do you even know all those facts Thomas?"

"I don't know. I do a lot of reading I guess, and I watch a lot of *Jeopardy*. Anyway, this year, on **June 14, 2017** our flag will be **240 years old**. Wait, I think I read somewhere it took *Titanic* **2 hours and 40** minutes to sink. Uh oh, all this numbers talk is making me connect unrelated things now."

Only Ruthie wasn't sure if it was unrelated. She knew an awful lot about *Titanic*. She knew the passengers of *Titanic* had no clue the ship would hit an iceberg. They had no clue the ship would sink. In the case of US Airways flight 1549, the passengers aboard had no clue either. The bird strike happened and before they knew it, they were going down. Luckily, a skillful, calm pilot knew what to do, and they were spared.

"Oh wait! I've got another number connection for you!" Thomas remarked.

"Really?"

"Since we were talking about the number 13 earlier, this came to mind. After the bird strike, Air Traffic Control asked Sully if he could turn around and land at **Runway 13** at *La Guardia Airport*."

"Oh yeah. I forgot about that."

"*Guess once you go forward, you can't go back,*" Thomas said.

Just then, out of nowhere, a big duck flew toward them both. It flew low to the ground, gaining speed, and heading right for them.

"Get down," Thomas shouted. Ruthie ducked. The duck just missed them by inches. Ironic- *ducking for a duck.*

"What in the world? I've never seen a duck flying straight toward people before! Good thing we ducked!" Thomas said.

"Are you sure it wasn't a goose?" she added, thinking about the Canadian geese that struck Flight 1549.

As Ruthie walked to the house, she couldn't help but marvel in the signs she'd seen. Even street signs were SIGNS! It was unbelievable how each piece of the puzzle fit with the next one- in sequence, and timed oddly well.

Upon approaching the door, she noticed something on the ground. It was a five dollar bill.

"Looks like you dropped some money Thomas."

"You mean YOU dropped some money. I'm not usually careless when it comes to money."

"And I am?" she asked, feeling insulted.

"No, you're not careless. You're just…."

"What?"

"Well, sometimes your head is in the clouds."

"Really? Thanks a lot!"

"No, it's just you seem to get distracted a lot. It's like you're day-dreaming or something."

Ruthie let out a loud sigh to let Thomas know she wasn't pleased. How dare he! She wasn't day dreaming. If he knew half the things she'd seen and connected lately he wouldn't say those things. As she grumbled to herself and walked into the house she noticed two more five dollar bills on the floor by the threshold of the door.

"More money on the ground? Seriously? Do you think money grows on trees Ruthie?"

"What? I'm telling you, I didn't drop that money. I haven't even opened my purse since we came home from our trip."

"Well, I know I didn't drop it."

"Maybe Jonah did!"

"Jonah, did you drop any money on the floor?"

"Money? What money? I want some."

"You mean this isn't yours?" Thomas asked.

"No, but I'll be glad to take it off your hands," Jonah said, with a big grin.

"I know I didn't lose it. It wasn't here when I left to find you," Thomas stated emphatically.

"If it wasn't there when you left to find me, then how could I have lost it?"

Thomas realized she had a point.

"Well, I don't know how money just appears out of nowhere. Three five dollar bills. That's 15 bucks."

Suddenly Ruthie had a thought. Maybe there was some meaning behind the five dollar bills. All three of them were fives. Where had she heard about the number five recently? "Five," she said to herself. "Come on, where did I see fives?"

Thomas overheard her and said, "Weren't **155** passengers saved on Flight **1549**?"

Ruthie ran over to Thomas and kissed him. "You're a genius Thomas!"

"If you say so. While we are on the subject of five, I also heard the documentary say the last passenger on Flight 1549 was taken from the plane at **3:55**. Do I get another kiss?"

"Yes, of course!" she said, grabbing Thomas and kissing him again.

"How about five kisses?"

"Don't push your luck. You accused me of daydreaming and losing money."

"Yeah, I was just kidding. Anyway, have fun with all this stuff about fives. I have to run down to Station 5 to drop off my gear. Ha! Look what I said- **Station 5**! I am really on a roll today," Thomas said.

Ruthie wondered about the fives. There were **155** passengers saved from Flight **1549**. That's two fives in 155, and three fives in the Flight number- 1549- *the 15 equaled 5 times 3*. The last passenger was picked up at **3:55**. Two fives again. The burning question was, what did it mean?

She knew God assigned special meanings to numbers in the Bible. God was the inventor of all math, and he always used numbers to convey his perfect order to the world, and the timing of all events. What did five show in the word of God? Only one way to find out. Search!

She searched on the computer, sifting through Bible websites and study articles. Certain things came up over and over again. **The number five pointed to God's grace, or favor.**

In the book of Exodus, God used **five in the design of the tabernacle**, which represented his holy dwelling among the people. He commanded there be *ten* curtains, with **five** of them joined together at a time. There had to be **50 loops on the curtains**, along with **50 gold clasps** to fasten the curtains together. **Fifty** equaled *ten sets of five*. In addition, the crossbars of wood for the frame of the tabernacle had to be made in **sets of five**. An altar of wood was built that was **five cubits long** and **five cubits wide**. The west end of the courtyard had to be **50**

cubits wide, as well as the east end. There had to be curtains that were **fifteen cubits long** on both sides of the entrance of the courtyard. Even the height of the court inside the tabernacle was **five cubits**. The tabernacle represented God's grace toward the people, as he would forgive their sins through the sacrifices made at the Tabernacle. In addition, his presence would reside there.

The Ten Commandments, made up of ten specific laws of God, were written in a unique and symbolic way, pointing to favor and grace. The **first five commandments** highlight our relationship with God, and how we should treat him as a Holy God. The **next five commandments** highlight our relationship to others. These five describe how we should deal with our "neighbors". Following these commandments is an act of obedience that keeps us within God's grace, or favor. They also allow us to grant grace and favor to others. Turning from them leads us into trouble, much like a sheep wandering away from the Shepherd. *Though we can't earn grace, the commandments keep us in the safe borders of God's grace and favor. God's only son Jesus would come to Earth and fulfill the commandments, offering grace to all who accepted and followed him.*

There were **five offerings Israel could give to God as a sacrifice**. There were burnt offerings, meal offerings, peace offerings, sin offerings and trespass offerings. These offerings would gain favor from God during Old Testament Times (before Jesus died on the cross).

The Holy anointing oil used in the Tabernacle was composed of five parts, and each part was measured in **increments of five**. The components were **500 shekels** of liquid myrrh, **250 shekels** of cinnamon, **250 shekels** of calamus, **500 shekels** of cassia and a hin of olive oil. This sacred oil would be used to anoint all the things inside the tabernacle. Instructions for making the components in the anointing oil are given by God himself in Exodus.

The Jubilee year marked every **50th year (5 times 10),** and was tied to the land. Every 50th year, any land that was lost had to be returned to its original owner. Even if the owner had lost the land due to poverty or debt, the land would be returned. In addition, prisoners and slaves would be freed in this year. Thus, God granted grace by commanding the land be returned, and by allowing those in captivity to be released. ((Leviticus 25 is where we find the rules for Jubilee in the Bible- note the 25, which is five fives- the number of grace)

There are **five books containing God's Laws**, also known as the Torah. These books are Genesis, Exodus, Leviticus, Numbers and Deuteronomy. When Jesus came to Earth, he came to fulfill the Law, and to extend grace to those who accept him as Lord and Savior.

Perhaps the most famous miracle in the Bible is when Jesus feeds the **5,000** with just **five loaves** of bread and two fish. By providing food, he was showing his grace and favor to the people. He is actually referred to as the bread of life and was born in Bethlehem, which means "house of bread".

Jesus became the ultimate sacrifice on the cross, allowing us to receive grace and favor, while he paid the entire cost. *While hanging on the cross*, **he received five wounds**. Both of his hands were pierced separately, accounting for two wounds. Two wounds occurred on his feet when nails passed through both on the wooden beam. The fifth wound occurred on his side. A soldier's spear pierced his side to ensure he was dead. **These five wounds represent the final expression of God's grace.** He sent his only son to die on the cross for the sins of the world. This one act of grace would save all those who accepted him as the Savior of the world, and grant eternal life to all who believed.

It was obvious to Ruthie that **five represented grace and favor**. She realized the passengers on Flight 1549 were granted an amazing gift of grace. They had a skilled, competent pilot, who knew what to do in an emergency. 155 souls were saved that day- *that equaled 31 groups of 5!* Grace abounded on that icy winter day. Even the date of the accident screamed grace. It happened on **January 15**. (Three fives) And what about the **3:55**? All the passengers and crew exited by 3:55, and all of them were alive! Talk about grace!

The rapture itself would be the ultimate act of God's grace and favor. He would literally remove the Bride from a chaotic, sinful world and take her to a paradise in heaven. She would be spared from the judgment coming upon the world. Like Christ, who was resurrected on the third day, the people of God, like eagles, would be swept away in the biggest thermal in history! The altitude would extend beyond Earth, and into the hidden place. Jesus would be our wings, allowing us to soar with him to heaven. There would be no need to turn back. There was only forward.

Suddenly, Ruthie thought of something. She knew raptors were a symbol of the rapture. She wondered what day God created birds. Could it be the fifth day? Quickly she grabbed her Bible and looked it up. Sure enough, <u>birds were created on the **5th day**</u>. *These beautiful winged creatures that soared in the sky were a foreshadowing of God's gift of grace to his followers- flying away at the rapture.*

Rosh Hashanah was a biblical feast that foreshadowed the rapture. It occurred in the Fall, at harvest season. 100 trumps were sounded as a reminder of God's mercy. The 100th trump was called the Last Trump. Jesus would return at the sound of the last trump! What feast number was Rosh Hashanah? Ruthie looked it up on the computer. Sure enough, **it was the 5th biblical feast**. How amazing was that? Even the 100 trumps pointed to five and grace because 20 times 5 equaled 100.

She knew more than ever God never missed a beat. He had everything in the universe lined up according to his will and grace. One day, that grace would hit planet earth head on. Some people would be ready, while others would not. Just like the days of Noah, many would be blinded to the signs. But others would have their eyes wide open, just like a raptor searching for its prey. After all, contrary to popular belief, most raptors were **diurnal.** That meant they hunted **during the day.** They were not all hunters of the night. Ruthie thought of 1 Thessalonians 5.

"But of the times and seasons brethren, ye have not need that I write unto you. For you yourselves know perfectly that the day of the Lord so cometh as a thief of the night. For when they shall say, Peace and safety; then sudden destruction cometh upon them, as travail upon a woman with child; and they shall not escape. But ye brethren, are **NOT IN DARKNESS**, that this day should overtake you as a thief. Ye are all children of the LIGHT, and **CHILDREN OF THE DAY: WE ARE NOT OF THE NIGHT, NOR OF DARKNESS."**

As Ruthie looked at the scripture again, she realized it was from the **5th chapter of Thessalonians,** and it was describing the rapture. The true Bride of Christ would not be asleep. They would be awake and ready. They would know the times and seasons, which meant they would know *the Lord's times and seasons. The Lord's times and seasons were his holy feasts.* Christ had fulfilled four of the feasts, but there were three left. The next one to be fulfilled would be the rapture. Our high Priest, Jesus, would only come like a thief to those who were asleep. Like the high priest of ancient times, Jesus would know who was falling asleep on the job. Those who were awake, and in the light, would receive a great reward. Those who were asleep would face "the fire," just like those who fell asleep on the job in ancient times. Just like Jericho, which was burned to the ground, those left behind would endure a terrible time on Earth. But, not the Bride. The Bride of Christ would see grace before their very eyes.

Like a plane falling from the sky, the world would go down. But, not the people of God. They would go on to be with the Living Water- Jesus. Like Sully's plane, as it went down in the water, they would be spared. The whole thing would be quick, just like Flight 1549. The plane was only in the air about five minutes. There was no way to turn back and go to Runway 13.

"Wait, I think I see the 13 again," Ruthie realized. She counted the number of letters in the word **Thessalonians.** There were 13 letters! Just when she thought she could be shocked no further, yet another connection. God never stopped surprising her.

Author's Notes: The first boat to come to the rescue of Flight 1549 was called the *Thomas Jefferson.* Tying in the theme of five and grace, think about this....Thomas Jefferson is on the nickel, or five cent coin.

The plane missed the George Washington Bridge by a mere 900 feet. *Can you imagine if it hit the bridge?* It's the nation's busiest motor vehicle bridge, carrying over 100 million vehicles per year. Yikes, can you say catastrophic! (900 feet- that's 180 sets of five)

The temperatures on the Hudson that day were freezing. If passengers stayed in the water more than a few minutes, they could surely die. *Titanic* passengers suffered this fate. There weren't enough lifeboats to carry everyone and many succumbed to the frigid water. But, most of the passengers on flight 1549 *climbed on the <u>wings</u> of the plane*, and luckily the rescue boats came in less than **five minutes. No one froze.**

Captain Sullenberger's full name is **Chesley Burnett Sullenberger**. The name **Chesley means meadow, or field.** In the Bible, meadows and fields represent the world, and are tied to the harvest of God's people. Think of the verse that mentions, **"Two are in the field, one is taken and the other is left"-** this refers to the rapture. And think about all the instances in the Bible where Jesus refers to landowners of fields. There is always a lesson about taking care of the field, or about being workers in God's fields. The kingdom of heaven is even referred to as a treasure hidden in a field in **Matthew <u>13</u>:44.** The Bible tells us to sow good seed in our field. **In Matthew <u>13</u>:38, Jesus actually states the world is a field. He says, "The field is the world; the good seed are the children of the kingdom; but the tares are the children of the wicked one."** (Did you catch the 13 above?)

Even though the story of Flight 1549 is essentially about the rescue of what some would call a "doomed flight", I see so much more within it. I see a parable of the world. As the world (plane) goes down into icy waters, we have a pilot who guides us to safety and helps us take refuge in his wings (**Psalm 91**). Jesus, essentially, is our pilot. He leads us by the still waters (Psalm23), and he rescues us from calamity. The world still turns and keeps moving forward, but at some point Jesus will return for his Bride. At that time, many may have "fallen asleep". But, the true Bride will be awake in the field, ready to be harvested. And speaking of Psalm 91…..**13 times 7 equals**……wait for it…………**91.**

There's the 13 again, tied in with Psalm 91 (wings). 13 is also tied to Jericho because the Israelites marched around the city a total of 13 times! The Israelites were victorious, the city was taken and *only Rahab and her family were spared.*

The principal photography for the movie *Sully* began on **September 28, 2015, the same date as a blood moon, and during the Feast of Tabernacles.** This feast symbolizes dwelling with God forever, and foreshadows the Millennial Reign of Jesus Christ.

Oh, and I forgot to mention: Flight 1549 landed between Manhattan and **Weehawken,** New Jersey. Do you see the word **HAWK.** A hawk is a **raptor.** A coincidence I'm sure, but who knows????

On the subject of the **symbolic meaning of five:** Most people are familiar with the characteristic look of an eagle: the stunning white feathers on their head, in contrast to the dark feathers on the rest of their body. But, did you know it takes **FIVE YEARS** for an eagle to get their beautiful white feathers? Up to that point, the head area is a dingy brownish black color. Think about God's people- the eagles. Just the fact that we are forgiven and saved by Jesus allows us to have "white feathers", or to be cleansed and redeemed. The number five points to grace, and the eagles of God received grace through Jesus. Even nature shows us numerical secrets..................

True story: On **January 15, 2016**, I went outside and found my neighbor's flagpole on the ground. During a storm, the pole had snapped, and the American flag was on the ground, being drenched by the rain. Seeing the flag on the ground gave me an eerie feeling. About six months prior, I had written about a similar event in my book *What are the Chances?* I had described a situation where an American flag is struck by lightning. When I wrote this in my book I was picturing my neighbor's flagpole, which is located on Kingfisher Drive. This part of the story was fictional. But then, something similar happened. Some of the details were different, but the flagpole did come down in a storm, and the flag fell on the ground. I didn't notice the date until I started writing about flight 1549, about two years later. The date of the incident was **JANUARY 15, 2016.** The *Miracle on the Hudson* (Sully), takes place on **JANUARY 15, 2009.** So, I witnessed this flag incident **SEVEN years** after Flight 1549 went down into the Hudson.

The name of the airport Flight 1549 took off from was **La Guardia.** The words *La Guardia* mean **The Guard.** In the Bible, a recurring theme is "being on guard." We are told to be on guard for the coming of Jesus. He will come like a thief and if we are not on guard we will not be ready. We are also told to be on guard for the schemes of the enemy. **Think about this:** In Arlington National Cemetery there are guards posted 24 hours a day at the Tomb of the Unknown Soldier. Rain or shine, sleet or snow, even during hurricanes- there is always a Sentinel marching around and guarding the tomb. There are no days off- not even holidays. The Tomb of the Unknowns is guarded by volunteer Sentinels, but they must be the best of the best! Their uniforms must be impeccable and without blemish. Every move must be precise. They are trained to ignore any and all distractions when they are on guard.

As followers of Christ we are to stay on guard no matter what "weather" comes our way. The storms of life will come, but we must stay on guard. The world will distract us and try to take our attention away from Jesus, but we must stand firm and **STAY ON GUARD**. We are covered by the blood of Jesus, which makes us impeccable and perfect in the eyes of God. But, we can't just take a day off because it's a holiday. We have to keep marching until our day of redemption. The Tomb of the Unknown Soldier is designated to remind us **to remember** our fallen soldiers FOREVER. They will never be forgotten. When you are covered by the blood of Jesus, you are never forgotten. **He will remember you at the sound of the last trump!**

CHAPTER 29
The Diary

§

Ruthie felt a sense of happiness and awe as she got ready for bed that night. The word grace flowed through her mind like a gentle breeze. The feeling of peace was unlike anything she'd experienced before. Usually, she went to bed with worries or questions lingering in her mind. But not tonight. She laid her head on the pillow and within five seconds she fell asleep.

An unusual dream of vivid detail began. A quiet street near a canal. A beautiful chestnut tree in full bloom. And a tall tower atop a church. Next, a tall building with multiple rectangular windows. A door opens and she steps inside.

Immediately she is drawn to the stairs. She climbs two flights, arriving at a hallway. At the end of the hallway is a bookcase. Reaching out to grab a book, she senses movement. She steps backward, only to notice the bookcase has shifted. The entire bookcase swings open like a door. Intrigued and a little frightened, she walks through the doorway, only to see another staircase, as well as rooms to the left and right. Unsure of where to go first, she decides to head to the room on the left.

Entering inside, she immediately notices the pictures in the room. Slightly tattered and scattered along the wall, it is evident they were important to someone. She sees two simple beds, one with a bear neatly placed on the pillow, the other with a newspaper lying across it. Her gaze is fixed on the bed with the bear. As she moves past the beds she notices a small desk with a lamp. A book covered with a bright red checkered pattern lay on top of the desk. The book's metal clasp is undone. Instinctively, she opens it. Each page is hand written and labeled with dates. She turns to the first page dated **JUNE 14, 1942**. She runs her fingers over the date several times, pausing to study it. She flips though the book, stopping on the last page, dated *August 1, 1944.* After staring for several seconds, she takes the book and places it close to her heart, folding her arms and hands in such a way as to embrace it. It was as if the very book were alive- part of her very soul. She didn't want to let it go.

Ruthie woke up with her arms wrapped around her body, immediately aware she was no longer holding the book. She was in her room. No bookcase. No desk. "No diary," she said out loud.

It was a diary she held in the dream. But whose diary? **JUNE 14, 1942.** She remembered the date from the first page of the diary. Quickly she jumped out of bed, dashing to grab her phone. The search topic: *famous diaries*. The first listing: **The Diary of Anne Frank**. "Anne Frank?" she thought to herself. "She's the girl who went into hiding with her family, but was later found by the Nazis and placed in a concentration camp and…….." Her train of thought switched. The date. The date! **June 14, 1942 was the first entry in Anne Frank's diary**. Where did she know the date from?

"What are you doing Ruthie? Why are you on the phone in the middle of the night?" Thomas mumbled, half asleep.

It was Thomas! Now she remembered. Earlier that day Thomas said **June 14 was the President's birthday, and it was also the date our <u>first flag</u> was adopted by Congress in 1777**. The dates were the same. Different years, but the same dates. What did it mean?

"Ruthie, you gotta get some sleep. Put your phone away and come to bed."

Only she didn't see how she could sleep. Something needed figuring out. She knew coincidences often meant God-incidences. Still, she knew Thomas was right. Perhaps with a full night's sleep, her brain would have what it needed to figure this out.

Author's Notes: Here's something else about the **JUNE 14** date

Everyone is familiar with the PLEDGE OF ALLEGIANCE. This was originally written by Rear Admiral George Balch in 1887, and then revised by Francis Bellamy in 1892. It was later adopted by Congress in 1942. *But, the words* **UNDER GOD** *were not added until JUNE 14, 1954.* Interesting coincidence- (See more about this in the back of the book under THE PLEDGE OF ALLEGIANCE.) The other June 14 dates in this book were**: June 14, 1777**- the adoption of our nation's original flag- 13 stars and stripes signifying 13 original colonies. **June 14, 1946**- Donald Trump's birthday (our 45th President). **June 14, 1942**- Anne Frank's first official diary entry. Every year on June 14 the United States celebrates Flag Day.

CHAPTER 30
Grace

After tossing and turning most of the night, Ruthie felt groggy in the morning. She tried to sleep, but her mind kept moving in circles, and back to the same questions. How were the June 14 dates related?

"Coffee?" asked Thomas, poking his head in the room.

"Of course," she said. She figured she needed at least five cups.

"Well, get up so we can share a cup together before I leave for work."

She dragged herself out of bed, got dressed and headed to the kitchen. As she sat at the table, she noticed her Bible sitting on the placemat. She picked it up and opened it to a random spot. She scanned the page, her eyes falling on **Romans 6:14. "For sin shall not have dominion over you: for ye are not under the law, but under grace**." She nodded to herself as she read it. "That's so true, and I surely need it this…." She stopped mid-thought. She looked back at the scripture number- Romans 6:14. Wait a second! There was something familiar. "Ah ha! I've got it! 6:14 as a date is 6-14, which is June 14." She clapped her hands in delight.

"Well thank you. This isn't the world's best cup of coffee, but it certainly comes close," Thomas said, handing her the coffee.

"Thank you my love," she answered, thoroughly pleased with herself. Something stood out from the scripture. What was it? What was it? "Ah ha! Grace! Grace is it!" she exclaimed boldly.

"I'm not sure what that has to do with coffee," Thomas answered.

She gave him a kiss and said, "Thanks for the coffee babe. But, I have to do something. Have a great day at work." She dashed off into the den and plopped down in front of the computer. Thomas shrugged his shoulders and didn't argue.

She wasn't exactly sure what she was looking for. She just knew she needed to understand more about Anne Frank, and her life. She began by gathering the facts.

Anne Frank lived in Germany, but had to move to the Netherlands because of Anti-Semitism and severe persecution in Germany by the Nazis. She and her family lived there several years. Eventually, the Nazis occupied the Netherlands as well, and persecutions increased in number and severity. Shortly after her **13**th birthday, Anne and her family went into hiding. They called their hiding place the Secret Annex, since it was cleverly concealed. The building itself was nestled between several houses, forming a quadrangle. It was actually an extension of the main building, which was used for Anne's father's business. Mr. Frank sold his business to his non-Jewish business associates Jo Kleiman and Victor Kugler, since Jews were not allowed to own businesses. When the time came to hide, his associates agreed to help. By July 6, the Franks had gone into hiding. **The first thing Anne packed was her precious diary.**

The Franks weren't the only family to go into hiding. They were joined by the Van Pels family, as well as Fritz Pfeffer. In all there were **eight people** who hid in the Secret Annex. For two years, the family hid there. Anne used the diary she received for her **13**th **birthday** as a way to express her feelings about the war, and to describe her everyday experiences from being in hiding. At some point during her stay, she heard a radio broadcast that encouraged people to keep diaries, letters and journals so the war could be documented. Anne decided she would write as much as possible about her experiences, hoping perhaps her diary would be published as a historical document. **Little did she know her diary would become famous throughout the world**. Over 30 million copies of the diary have been sold, and it has been translated into at least **67 languages**. **The diary became a symbol for**

the war and Anne became the most familiar face associated with the Holocaust. Unfortunately, Anne would not live to see her dreams become a reality. She and her family were arrested on August 4, 1944 and taken to concentration camps. The only family member to survive would be Anne's father, Otto Frank. He would be the one to retrieve Anne's diary and have it published.

Ruthie loved the story of Anne Frank. It inspired her on so many levels. Anne was a symbol for the war, and the Holocaust. She began writing in her diary on the same date (*June 14*) as our new President's birthday, and technically the birth of our flag as a new nation. What did it mean?

She closed her eyes so she could think. Within moments a vision filled her mind. She saw Anne Frank holding her diary close to her heart. Next she saw what looked like stars and stripes, circling all around her. Strangely enough, it was as if the American flag were encircling Anne Frank. Round and round it went. In the vision Anne was smiling. She seemed comforted. Then she spoke. She said, "Romans 11:15". Then, the vision was gone.

Ruthie opened her eyes. What a strange, yet powerful vision. She knew she had to look up the verse she heard Anne describe in the vision- Romans 11:15. The King James version said, **"For if the casting away of them be the reconciling of the world, what shall the receiving of them be, but life from the dead."** The New International version said, **"For if their rejection brought reconciliation to the world, what will their acceptance be but life from the dead."**

She put her Bible down for a moment. "Who is 'them' referring to in the verses?" she wondered. She went back and read all of Romans 11. She read verse one and two aloud. "I say then, Hath God cast away his people? God forbid......God hath not cast away his people, whom he foreknew."

"It's the Jewish people. This verse is referring to God's people, the Jews." She read aloud verses five and six. "Even so than at this present time also there is a remnant according to the **election of grace.** And if by grace, then is it no more of works: otherwise grace is not grace. But if it be of works, then it is no longer grace; otherwise grace would no longer be grace."

There was the word grace. She remembered Romans 6:14, which said we are no longer under the law, but **under grace.** She read on.

"What then? Israel hath not obtained that which he seeketh for; but the election hath obtained it, and the rest were blinded. According as it is written, God hath given them the spirit of slumber, <u>eyes that they should not see,</u> and ears that they should not hear; unto this day."

Ruthie realized these scriptures were saying that many of the Jews do not see the truth of who Jesus is because of a spirit of blindness. The spirit of blindness came upon them after Jesus, their Messiah, was rejected.

She read verse 10. "Let their eyes be darkened, that they may not see, and bow down their back away. I say then, Have they stumbled that they should fall? God forbid: but rather through their fall, salvation is come unto the Gentiles, for to provoke them to jealousy."

"So the Jewish people who rejected Christ have a spirit of blindness. But, this does not mean they are lost forever, and it certainly doesn't mean they've been rejected by God. Through the grace of God, salvation has come to the Gentiles (non-Jews/foreigners), even though we were once lost to God. But it came to us through God's chosen people- the Jews. And as they see our faith in Messiah, and as they watch us in action, this is supposed to cause a stirring within them- a stirring in their heart for the Messiah," Ruthie said to herself. She knew she had to keep reading all the way to verse 15.

"Now if the fall of them (the Jews) be the riches of the world, and the diminishing of them the riches of the Gentiles; how much more their fullness? For I speak to you Gentiles, inasmuch as I am the apostle of the Gentiles, I magnify mine office; If by any means I may provoke to emulation them which are in my flesh, and might save some of them. For if the casting away of them be the reconciling of the world, ***what shall their fullness be, but life from the dead***?"

Ruthie thought about these last verses. The rejection of Jesus by the Jewish people was a crushing blow to God. His only son, sent to save the world, was rejected by the very people he came to save. Jesus was Jewish after all. Yet, through that rejection, the Gentiles were saved. The Gentiles, like Rahab of Jericho, were foreigners, and a sinful people. They were people who did not follow God and didn't deserve his grace. But Christ dying on the cross changed all that. Grace came through Christ's death and resurrection.

"Resurrection!" Ruthie practically yelled. "That's it! When Christ rose from the grave, or resurrected, he saved the world. One day, Christ is going to return for the Bride. **The Bride includes all those who love and know Jesus as Savior (both Gentile and Jew).** At the rapture, Christ would snatch his Bride like a thief in the night. When this occurred in the blink of an eye, the world would know something astonishing had happened. Many would be deceived about the event, yet many would know. Their eyes would be opened. **This one monumental event would open the eyes of millions of people in the world, particularly the Jews! It would literally be 'life from the dead' as the Bride is taken from the Earth- a form of resurrection,"** she said.

The number 144,000 popped into Ruthie's mind. "The 144,000 Jewish witnesses," she thought. Quickly she turned to Revelation 7 in the Bible.

"And after these things I saw four angels standing on the four corners of the Earth, holding the four winds of the earth, that the wind should not blow on the earth, nor on the sea, nor on any tree. And I saw another angel ascending from the east, having the seal of the living God: and he cried with a loud voice to the four angels, to whom it was given to hurt the earth and the sea, Saying Hurt not the earth, neither the sea, nor the trees till we have sealed the servants of our God on their foreheads. And I heard the number of them which were sealed: and they were sealed **a hundred and forty- four thousand, of all the tribes of the children of Israel."**

Ruthie was very familiar with this chapter. 12,000 from each of the 12 tribes of Israel would be sealed. It would be these Jewish servants **who would preach the truth of Jesus Christ to all those who were left on Earth during the Tribulation.** Would this happen right after the rapture? Could it be that the part of the verse in Romans 11:15 which said "life from the dead" meant the rapture would bring about this event? During the rapture there would be **"life from the dead" because the bodies of believers would be resurrected.** This would usher in the Tribulation on Earth. Those who were left behind would need guidance about what happened. They would need to hear the truth! These 144,000 Jewish witnesses would have their eyes fully opened. There would be no blindness in them. They would be used by God to tell the world about his son, and give the world a second chance to be redeemed. Who better to preach this gospel than God's ancient people, the Jews? They were God's first chosen people after all. As a nation they did not accept Jesus as Messiah when he died on the cross. But, how amazing that they would be used in the end times to convince a lost world that Jesus was the only way- he was the only King, and the only one who would save mankind. God's plan would come **full circle**. The 144,000 Jewish witnesses would be a testament to the redemptive nature of God.

Ruthie's mind went back to Anne Frank. She, of course, was Jewish. In World War 2, America played an important part in defeating Hitler. America helped create a home for the Jews as well, by recognizing Israel when it became a new nation on May 14, 1948. Since then, America had stood by Israel and the Jews by defending them politically or physically. But, in recent years, America was slowly turning from Israel- from asking her to give away land in 2005, to stabbing her in the back on recent United Nations Resolutions. But, since the election of the new President, things seemed to be looking up. The President vocally supported Israel, and even mentioned he would like to move the U.S. Embassy to Jerusalem, Israel's capital. But, the world wasn't making it easy on the President. The countries surrounding Israel were Hell-bent on destroying her, and the Jews.

In the vision Anne Frank was being circled by the stars of the American flag. Ruthie thought about Jericho. The Israelites circled Jericho **13 times**. Interestingly enough, Anne Frank received her diary on her **13th birthday**. And weren't there **13 original colonies**? America began as 13 colonies! And what about the eagle she saw on the electrical pole? It was on pole 13.

In the vision, Anne Frank pressed her diary close to her heart. She was embracing it. Ruthie looked up the word embrace in the dictionary. It said, "to take or clasp in the arms; press to the bosom; hug." It also said, "to encircle, surround or enclose." Anne was holding her diary close to her bosom, or chest.

Ruthie wondered how often the word embrace was used in the Bible. She looked up the word embrace in Strong's Concordance. The entry number assigned to embrace was **2263**. The Hebrew word for **embrace** was chabaq. She looked through the concordance for instances where the word embrace was used in the Bible. The first example she read about was the meeting of Jacob and Esau, which occurs in Genesis 32 and 33.

Many years had passed since Jacob had seen Esau. Their last interaction had been bitter and hateful. Jacob, after all, had stolen Esau's birthright. He had also stolen his brother's blessing, given by his father Isaac. Esau had every reason to hate his brother Jacob. The time came when they would meet again. Jacob expected Esau to want vengeance, and to treat him with great contempt. But, the opposite happened. In Genesis 33, verse 4, it says, "And Esau ran to meet him, and **embraced** him, and fell on his neck, and kissed him; and they wept." Instead of contempt and hate, Jacob received grace and love.

Ruthie knew Jacob represented Israel in the Bible. After all, God changed Jacob's name to Israel, and he became the father of all the tribes of Israel. But, what about Esau? Could he represent the Church, made up of Jews and Gentiles who had accepted Christ? Since the crucifixion and resurrection of Jesus, the Christian church had grown by leaps and bounds, yet the majority of the Jewish community did not accept Christ. It was considered "un-Jewish" to believe in Jesus. This had caused great animosity between the two groups. History proved deadly for the Jewish people through events such as the *Inquisition*, and the *Holocaust*. Persecution of the Jews continued throughout history, and often at the hands of the Church. Yet, the Church and the Jewish people were not meant to be enemies. **They were meant to be brothers, or family. They are both part of the Branch, which is Jesus. They are both part of the olive tree, which is vividly described in all of Romans 11.** Yet, in the story of Jacob and Esau, even after years of treachery and animosity, the brothers embrace. They hold each other close together, their hearts pulled tight, and their bond restored. The symbolism was uncanny.

Another example where **embrace** is used in the Bible is in the story of Joseph, when Israel (the father of Joseph), blesses Joseph's two sons, Ephraim and Manasseh. Starting in Genesis 48, verse 10 and on through verse 20 it says,

"Now the eyes of Israel were dim for age, so that he could not see. And he brought them near to him; and he kissed them, and **EMBRACED** them. And Israel said unto Joseph, I had not thought to see thy face; and, lo, God hath shewed me also thy seed. And Joseph brought them out from between his knee, and he bowed himself with his face to the earth. And Joseph took them both, Ephraim in his right hand toward Israel's left hand, and Manasseh in his left hand toward Israel's right hand, and brought them near unto him. And Israel stretched out his right hand, and laid it upon Ephraim's head, who was younger, and his left hand upon Manasseh's head, guiding his hands wittingly; for Manasseh was the firstborn. And he blessed Joseph, and said, God, before whom my fathers Abraham and Isaac did walk, the God which fed me all my life long unto this day. The Angel which redeemed me from all evil, bless the lads, and **let my name be named on them, and the name of my fathers Abraham and Isaac**; and let them grow into a multitude in the midst of the earth. **And when Joseph saw that his father laid his right hand upon the head of Ephraim, it displeased** him: and he held up his father's hand, to remove it from Ephraim's head unto Manasseh's head. And Joseph said to his father, Not so, my father: for this is the firstborn; put thy right hand upon his head. And his father refused, and said, I know it, my son. I know it; he also shall become a people, and he also shall be great: but truly <u>his younger brother shall be greater than he, and his seed shall become a multitude of nations.</u> And he blessed them that day, saying, In thee shall Israel bless, saying, God make thee as Ephraim and as Manasseh: and he set Ephraim before Manasseh."

Ruthie saw something amazing in this story. She noted how Israel (Joseph's father) b*lessed the youngest son before the older one.* He blessed Ephraim, who was younger, before Manasseh. In biblical times, it was customary to bless the firstborn first, then each child on down by age (oldest to youngest). Why would Israel do this? She searched her mind for any verses she'd read that might explain this. In her spirit she felt like Colossians 1:18 was significant. She quickly looked it up. It said,

"And he is the *head of the body, the church*: who is the beginning, the *firstborn from the dead*; that in all things he might have the preeminence."

From that verse Ruthie was reminded that the Church (made up of Gentiles and Jews who knew Christ as Savior) *was considered the firstborn.* When Jesus rose from the dead, the Church accepted him as Savior. Much of the Jewish people at that time did not accept this fact. **But, the Church EMBRACED it.** He became their Savior and Lord. <u>Once they embraced him, they were resurrected to a new life. Just like when Jesus rose on the Feast of First Fruits (Easter as we know it), the Church too became the first fruit, or the firstborn from the dead. They had new life.</u>

In Hebrews 12, verses 22-23 it says, "But ye are come unto Mount Zion, and unto the city of the living God, the heavenly Jerusalem, and to an innumerable company of angels, To the general assembly and **church of the firstborn**, which are written in heaven, and to God the Judge of all, and to the spirits of just men made perfect."

Ephraim represented the firstborn, thus spiritually representing the Church, made up of both Jewish and Gentile believers in Messiah. The firstborn would be "harvested" first. Like Christ was the firstborn, the Bride (the true Church) is also the firstborn- united with Christ. Jesus himself says in John, "I say unto thee, **except a man be born again**, he cannot see the kingdom of God."

Ruthie had a thought. Was the tribe of Ephraim mentioned as one of the 144,000 in Revelation? After all, 12,000 from each tribe would be sealed, and the 144,000 would be on Earth during the Tribulation, to preach the gospel to the unbelieving world. If Ephraim was the Bride (both Jew and Gentile believers in Christ), why would this tribe be mentioned as being one of the 144,000? If the rapture had already taken place *before the Jews were sealed*, how could Ephraim still be on Earth?

She turned to Revelation 7, to see what tribes were listed. "Of the tribe of **Judah** were sealed twelve thousand. Of the tribe of **Reuben** were sealed twelve thousand. Of the tribe of **Gad** were sealed twelve thousand. Of the tribe of **Asher** were sealed twelve thousand. Of the tribe of **Nephthalim** were sealed twelve thousand. Of the tribe of **Manassaes** were sealed twelve thousand. Of the tribe of **Simeon** were sealed twelve thousand. Of the tribe of **Levi** were sealed twelve thousand. Of the tribe of **Issachar** were sealed twelve thousand. Of the tribe of **Zabulon** were sealed twelve thousand. Of the tribe of **Joseph** were sealed twelve thousand. Of the tribe of **Benjamin** were sealed twelve thousand."

As she searched the list, she did not see Ephraim. Manasseh was mentioned, and even the tribe of Joseph, but not Ephraim. Perhaps Ephraim *symbolically* represented the Bride (the Church) in the story of Israel blessing Joseph's sons. Interestingly enough, even Joseph tried to correct the mistake by telling Israel to bless the oldest son first. But, Israel refused and blessed the younger son first. Israel went on to say that the older son Manasseh would be great, but the younger son Ephraim shall be greater and his seed would become a *multitude of nations*. This "greater" meant Ephraim would be made up of <u>many kinds of nations from all over the world- a great variety of Gentiles and Jews</u> *would be within* this symbolic tribe. The truth in all this was clear in Ephesians 1, verses 4-6 which says, "According to faith he hath chosen us in him before the foundation of the world, that we should be holy and without blame before him in love: Having predestined us unto the **ADOPTION of children by Jesus Christ to himself**, according to the good pleasure of his will."

Ruthie realized that when Israel embraced Manasseh and Ephraim, he was actually **foreshadowing** the future of the Jews and Gentiles. He was essentially, wrapping his arms around them, pulling them close to his heart. **His love encircled BOTH the Jew and the Gentile**. Israel represented God, and his love for the world. "For God so loved the world that he gave his only son, that whosoever believeth in him shall not perish, but have eternal life."

The harvest of the Church (Jewish and Gentile believers in Messiah), and the nation of Israel (the Jews who do not believe Jesus is Messiah), <u>would come at different times</u>. The rapture would be the harvest of the Church, and this would happen first. The tribulation would come afterward and bring about the salvation of the majority of the Jewish people, as well as those Gentiles who were not believers before the rapture.

Anne Frank was Jewish and she suffered during one of the worst times in history for Jewish people. Some Christians helped, while others looked the other way. Some even tried to justify the killing, saying it was biblical. But Ruthie knew the truth. **GOD WANTED THE CHURCH TO EMBRACE THE JEWISH PEOPLE. GOD WOULD NEVER FORGET HIS COVENANT PEOPLE, THE NATION OF ISRAEL**. One day, the world would come against the Jewish people again and who would stand in for them? Who would circle them with love and hold them close, protecting them from harm? Ephraim, the youngest brother, MUST do this. The true Church would remember their spiritual brother.

And what about the United States, whose flag was adopted on the same date as Anne Frank's first diary entry? Just like during World War 2, **the United States must stand by the Jews.** The United States is seen as a light to the nations, full of immigrants from all nations around the world. Surely, this light to the nations would embrace Israel (the Jews) tight, and never let it go. **The United States must be the "secret annex" the Jews needed when the world became dark again.**

Ruthie heard a word in her mind. It was the word **BRACE**. The word **embrace had the word brace in it.** Was this why the word came to mind? She closed her eyes. She saw a plane. It was going down into the water.

"Sully! Flight 1549!" she practically screamed. Before the plane went down Sully said, **"Brace for impact."** The flight attendants also told the passengers to "**BRACE**," as well. This meant people needed to prepare themselves, and to lock their bodies in the right position for a crash landing.

Ruthie knew the Bride would be taken from the Earth like a flash of lightning, as the world headed for collapse and tribulation. The rapture would happen quickly and the world would be unprepared. They wouldn't have time to brace themselves. The unbelieving world, who didn't embrace Jesus, would be left behind.

Ruthie looked back at Strong's Concordance and scanned the page giving information about the word embrace. She saw the entry number once more. "**2263**," she said to herself. "Something is familiar about that. Did it have something to do with Anne Frank?" she thought.

She quickly pulled up a webpage on Anne Frank. As her eyes searched the page, she read, "Anne Frank's hiding place in the Secret Annex was located at **263** Prinsengracht, in the Netherlands. The number 263 was at the end of the concordance number. A coincidence, or a God-incidence? Whatever the case may be, the message was clear. The Bride had to brace for what was coming. The Bride had to speak the truth to everyone about Jesus, especially to the Jewish people.

Author's Notes:

Each year the Jewish holiday, **Tisha B Av** is observed. This is a time to commemorate the destruction of the first and second Jewish Temples, which occurred on the 9th of AV (Hebrew calendar). It is also on this date (9th of AV) that the Jews were expelled from Spain in 1492 (the same year Columbus came to America). On this date the Jewish people will fast and mourn, and remember the hardships of their ancestors. THIS YEAR (2017) THE LAST DAY OF TISHA B AV FALLS ON **AUGUST 1. The last entry in Anne Frank's diary is August 1, 1944.** Perhaps we should be taking notice of the Jewish people **right now,** and praying for the peace of Jerusalem. The story of Anne Frank is well known here in the United States. We should be ready to stand with the Jewish people of our nation, and Israel. *2017 marks 50 years since Jerusalem was unified during the Six Day War in 1967.*

A solar eclipse occurs just 20 days after Tisha B Av this year on August 21, 2017.

Incidences of fives (**the number of grace**) in the story of Anne Frank:

The square footage of the Secret Annex was **500** square feet

The family was in hiding for a total of **25** months (2 years 1 month)

Anne was **15 years old** when she passed away (may not seem like grace, but her death and diary became a symbol for the Holocaust and allowed people to sympathize with the Jewish people, and learn about the Holocaust for generations)

Anne Frank's diary was published on June **25**, 1947- See the 25? Five fives

This year, on June 14, 2017, it will be **75 y**ears since Anne first wrote in her diary

Though Anne Frank was in hiding for 25 months, she was able to see small bits of the outside world from the Annex's attic window. It was here she often passed time by looking at a chestnut tree. She also could see the clock from the Westerkerk Protestant Church. In her diary she often wrote how the chiming of its bells brought her comfort.

As we remember the 75th anniversary of Anne Frank's first diary entry, I can't help but think of that clock, and how the time of redemption must be near. Though Anne did not survive, **little did she know how her diary would change lives around the world.** The clock is ticking for God's ancient people, and it's up to us to fight for them when their voices can't be heard. Just like Anne's voice, that was heard from her diary, **we are the voices for the Jewish people. We received grace, and they too need to be shown grace.**

There were eight people who hid in the Anne Frank House. Eight in the Bible points to a new beginning. There were eight people spared on Noah's Ark. When God remakes the Earth, it will be known as the 8th great day.

CHAPTER 31
PI

JUST WHEN RUTHIE'S MIND COULD take no more, the doorbell rang. She wasn't expecting anyone. Who could it be?

She opened the door and to her surprise it was her neighbor, Mrs. Goldman. "I made a pie for you Ruthie," she said, handing it to her.

"For me? What's the occasion?"

"Give your neighbor a pie day!" she laughed. "No occasion really."

The pie looked scrumptious. Layered with almonds and whipped cream, it looked irresistible.

"It's a pineapple key lime pie."

"Yum! I've never had that combination before."

"There's always a first time," Mrs. Goldman laughed.

"Thank you so much," Ruthie said, giving her a big hug.

"Let me know if you like it."

"I'm sure it's going to be fantastic."

Ruthie took the pie inside. It looked amazing. Should she eat a slice now, or wait till after dinner? It only took her two seconds to decide. She began to cut a slice. As she did this, she heard the word, "Pie" in her mind over and over. "Duh, this is a piece of pie," she laughed to herself. Still, she kept sensing the word, only she wasn't sure it was the same word. "What other word for pie is there?" she thought. She stared at the pie, hoping for a light bulb to turn on in her mind. Minutes passed.

"I've got it. The word isn't pie, as in a dessert. It's **PI**, *as in the mathematical term*," she said to herself. She knew the word from studying geometry. But, she'd forgotten what **PI** represented. She grabbed her phone and looked it up. *"PI is the ratio of a circle's circumference to its diameter,"* the definition stated.

"Oh yeah. I remember now. In geometry, we learned about circles. We would find the radius and diameter by measuring across the circle, but to get the *circumference* we used the **formula for PI**," she thought. She continued reading the information.

"The number representing PI is usually expressed as 3.14, but this is the number rounded. **The number for PI goes on <u>forever.</u>** Computers have calculated the number PI to trillions of digits, but <u>**the number is infinite**</u>," the text read.

Ruthie thought about this for a few seconds. It made sense that PI went on forever because circles went on forever too. The ring forming a circle continued in its curvy path without stopping. It just went around and around, around and around.

In that moment she realized something amazing. **Circles and PI were infinite**! Where had she read about circles before? **JERICHO!** When the Israelites crossed the Jordan into Jericho they were on the threshold of their land inheritance. Before they could claim it they had to follow God's instructions perfectly. What did God say? He said to march around Jericho **IN A CIRCLE** for seven days. The first six days they would CIRCLE once. The seventh day they would **CIRCLE** seven times, for a total of 13 CIRCLES.

She always wondered why God asked the Israelites to CIRCLE Jericho. She wondered about the spiritual significance. God is symbolic in his ways, and in his word. Now she realized why he commanded CIRCLES. First of all, a circle represents infinity. When the Israelites circled Jericho he was telling them the inheritance they would receive is **INFINITE**- it was an **everlasting, forever covenant**. Even the number 13 was significant. The first six times of marching around represented man, since six is man's number. On the last day they marched around the city seven times. This represented God's perfect order. When man followed God's perfect instructions, victory followed!

After the seventh day of marching, the walls fell down and the Israelites entered into their promise land.

Ruthie knew **Jericho represented Israel's inheritance, but it also symbolized the rapture**! When the walls fell down, the city was destroyed, but Rahab and her family were spared. At the rapture, the world would be thrown into chaos, but the Bride would be spared. The **circling** done by the Israelites represented the idea that the Bride would be **FOREVER** in heaven. Heaven itself would come to Earth during the Millennial reign of Jesus Christ for 1000 years. After the 1000 years the New Jerusalem would arrive and the world would be **forever** reconciled. But, before the Earth could be reconciled, the Bride would be snatched away, and taken to the "Secret Annex", or "the hiding place" in heaven. This one event would set God's plan for redemption in motion. The end goal would be to bring God's perfect kingdom to Earth. **Like a circle, it would not end.** Jesus would **reign forever** with his people- his Bride. The scarlet cord Rahab hung from the window of her house in the wall was a reminder of the covenant the Bride has with Jesus- **it doesn't end.**

But, there was more. The word **embrace**. It meant to fold your arms **around** and hold tightly to your chest. Like a shepherd, who holds a sheep close to his body, Jesus would embrace his Bride at the rapture. Ruthie could picture an eagle, circling in the sky, looking for his prey. As soon as he spotted the fish in the water, he would swoop down and snatch it. His eagle eyes wouldn't miss it. He'd been watching for a long time. He wouldn't miss when the time came. Jesus wouldn't miss when he came either. While the world **BRACED** for disaster, Jesus would **EMBRACE** his followers. The **grace** of God was infinite. The wedding ring would be on the Bride's finger, symbolizing eternity in heaven. But, God's grace would not end with the Bride. His ultimate goal would be redemption for the world, but *especially his chosen people, the Jews.* **The Tribulation would bring about this final harvest, where all of Israel would embrace (circle around and hold close to their hearts) his son, Jesus, the Messiah.**

"All this from a pie," she laughed, eating the first bite. "And it tastes just like a piece of heaven."

Author's Notes:

If you read the story of Jericho in the book of Joshua, you'll see that the land of Jericho was the **first piece of land** the Israelites conquered. This was the first piece of land included in their inheritance. It was only AFTER THEY FOLLOWED GOD'S SPECIFIC INSTRUCTIONS, that they were able to go into the Promised Land and claim their inheritance. The instructions God gave the Israelites sound unusual- circling round and round, day after day. For six days they circle around once, then on the 7th day, circle seven times. Six, then seven.

At the rapture the Bride of Christ will be taken quickly- whisked away to be with Jesus FOREVER- like a never ending circle. After this happens it will open the door for something else- Israel. Once the Bride is taken, the land of Israel will need to be **fully redeemed**. The inheritance of Israel will need to be claimed by Jesus, the Messiah. Like God's instructions for defeating Jericho, there is a perfect order to all this. **The Bride leaves (circling around- walls fall down). Then, the Tribulation begins (fire and destruction to all of Jericho- except Rahab who is spared-The Bride). Finally, the land will be claimed and redeemed just like the Israelites did in Jericho-(but in the end times it will be Jesus himself who redeems it. The Promised Land will be claimed by Jesus for his people when he returns to Earth at the Second Coming.)**

Remember the 6 and 7 (six days of circling, then seven)- Well, in 1967 (June 7, 1967, or 6-7-67) Israel claimed a key part of her inheritance (land). Israel claimed East Jerusalem during the Six Days War. See the 67 in 1967? Jerusalem is prime real estate for God's Kingdom, and holds the key to the return of Christ. On **JUNE 7, 2017, IT WAS THE 50 YEAR ANNIVERSARY OF ISRAEL CLAIMING THIS KEY PIECE OF REAL ESTATE! IT IS THE MOST IMPORTANT PIECE OF THE PIE. The 6 and 7 of Jericho is coming full circle to planet Earth! Keep your eyes open watchmen!!!**

CHAPTER 32
Eclipse

THE NEXT DAY RUTHIE WOKE up refreshed. The light of a new day had come. The sun was up, and not a cloud in the sky. It was certainly a day to seize. What should she do?

A beeping sound came from her phone. A text message from her friend Barb came through, as if on cue.

"Want to go to lunch? I'm in town for the day."

"Definitely!" she texted back. "Where and what time?"

"How about noon at *Seasons 52*?"

"Love that place. See you at noon."

Ruthie figured she'd do a few chores before she met Barb for lunch. A quick load of laundry, unloading the dishwasher, and the usual clutter clean up were on the list. She worked quickly and in no time it was already 11:30. Time to leave. She grabbed her keys and headed for the door. As she passed the by her front door, she noticed a small book. It was called, **In God We Still Trust**. Where did it come from? It wasn't a library book. It had no bar code. She picked it up. She didn't have time to look through the book because she needed to meet Barb. She stuck the book in her purse, figuring she'd look at it some other time.

She arrived at *Seasons 52* right at noon. "Hey Barb, it's great to see you! I feel like it's been forever!"

"It has been forever! I've been so busy with work, not to mention my kids. Things are never ending!"

Blink

"Like a circle," Ruthie said.

"Yeah, like a circle. They just go round and round and I'm dizzy from it all," she laughed. "So, what's new with you?"

"Just trying to keep up with everything too. Husband, kids, God… you know."

"God? You're trying to keep up with him? Good luck with that one. Keeping up with God is like racing with a cheetah. He's always a million steps ahead."

"True. I guess I'm just trying to keep up with his word, and understand it."

"I know what you mean. I'm in several Bible studies and it seems no matter how much I read and study there's always more God wants to show me. He's like…."

"A circle?"

"Yes, a circle!" she agreed. "Speaking of circles, there's something I wanted to ask you about."

"What is it?"

"Well, as you know, the *big circle in the sky* is going to be blocked out on **August 21**."

"Huh? What are you talking about? *Big circle in the sky*?"

"Come on Ruthie! Big circle in the sky….the light of the SUN is being blocked out….everything goes dark….?"

"Oh yeah, the solar eclipse! How did I forget?"

"We should go see it together!"

"Great idea! It's going to be an extraordinary event! It's being called **THE GREAT AMERICAN ECLIPSE."**

"That's because it is traveling all the way through the United States. If you look at the map of where the eclipse is going, it literally cuts the United States in half. The path of totality starts in Oregon, between Lincoln County and Newport. From there it travels through the middle of the United States, and then it exits out of Charleston, South Carolina," Barb explained.

"What does the path of totality mean again?"

"The path of totality includes **all the areas the eclipse hits directly with its shadow**. In these areas the sun will be completely blocked out, *causing complete darkness to fall upon the land.*"

"That actually sounds kind of spooky. Darkness falling upon the land."

"Well, it is a **shadow** on the land."

They were both silent for a moment. Though they didn't say it, they were both wondering if a solar eclipse hitting U.S. land was a good thing.

"Anyway, we need to get to one of the cities in the path of totality. The states the path of totality is passing through are Oregon, Idaho, Montana, Wyoming, Nebraska, Kansas, Missouri, Iowa, Illinois, Kentucky, Tennessee, Georgia, North Carolina and South Carolina."

"That's a lot of states!"

"It's fourteen states actually."

Again they were silent, realizing the depth and breadth of the eclipse. It was passing through the heartland of America, traveling west to east.

"I think we should watch it from Charleston or Columbia South Carolina," Barb suggested. "My mother in law lives in Charleston, so we could just stay with her."

"What are the chances? The last city the solar eclipse hits just happens to be where your mother in law lives. Come to think of it, **isn't Charleston where Ft. Sumter is? That's where the first battle of the Civil War took place. In fact, I believe it was South Carolina that was the first state to secede from the Union during the war.**"

"You're right. We could see the eclipse from Ft. Sumter if you wanted."

They both got quiet again. Ft. Sumter. The first battle site of the Civil War. What did that mean? Right now the country was divided in so many ways. The Presidential election had been vicious and unprecedented. For the first time in American history a President was elected who had no prior political experience. He won against all odds. A divided nation received a very different kind of leader. Would he be able to unite the country again? Would political, religious and spiritual division tear the country apart? The solar eclipse map **showed a shadow that was bisecting the country**. It looked like a dividing line. Perhaps God was saying, "Wake up! Civil War is upon you." Even the first county the eclipse touched echoed Civil War. The eclipse passed through **Lincoln County** as it first entered U.S. land.

"You know, even though this eclipse seems a bit spooky, I think we should see it. God controls the sun, moon, earth and stars. And this will be the first total solar eclipse to come through **ONLY THE UNITED STATES**, since our founding in the year 1776. At least that's what I read on a website called **The Great American Eclipse**," Barb added.

"Earlier we were talking about circles," Ruthie said. "I've read that the sun's corona is only visible during a solar eclipse."

"What's the corona?"

"I'm going to read something from this space website I found. It says, "the corona is a circle of gases around the Sun. The corona **encircles** the Sun, but most times it is **hidden** by the bright light of the Sun's surface. But, during a solar eclipse **the corona is *suddenly visible and no longer hidden***. It is seen as a bright white glowing light around the Sun. The Sun is now hidden behind the moon, with this crown of light circling it."

"A crown of light circling the Sun? Wow! That description makes me think of Jesus. He's the King and he's the light," Barb stated. "In fact, I believe the word **coronation, which means to crown a king**, comes from the Latin word corona, which means wreath or crown."

As Barb spoke Ruthie was thinking about something else. The information said **the corona is usually hidden**. It is only visible during a solar eclipse. **The "crown" shape of the corona could only be seen during a solar eclipse.** She couldn't help but visualize the rapture. At Jericho the Israelites circled the city and the walls fell down. Then, they were able to claim their Promised Land. Someday, Jesus would fetch his

Bride and take them to a **hidden** place. Then, the crowned King would return to claim the land of Israel once and for all. The land would be reinstated to the Jewish people, and the heirs of Christ would share in this blessing. The land would be freed. No more sin- **no more shadow**. It would finally be finished. What if the solar eclipse was a reminder that our crowned King is coming soon? After all, Rosh Hashanah is called the Hidden Day, and it fore**shadows** the rapture. The Sun's light is **hidden** during a solar eclipse, **but the crown/corona is visible**.

"Oh my goodness! There's more I need to tell you. I almost forgot," Barb insisted.

"What else could there be? A solar eclipse is fascinating enough."

"How about **two** solar eclipses?"

"What? Two? What do you mean?"

"You already know about the total solar eclipse on **August 21, 2017**, but can you believe there's another one coming **seven years after that one**!"

"Really? You mean another solar eclipse is touching U.S. soil?"

"Yes! Seven years later, on **April 8, 2024, <u>ANOTHER</u> TOTAL SOLAR ECLIPSE HITS AMERICA**!"

"Give me the details!"

"Well, this second one coming on April 8, 2024 will take a different path than the one in 2017. Instead of only hitting the United States, it will pass through Mexico first, then through the U.S. and exit through Canada. Basically, the eclipse is passing through NORTH AMERICA."

"That's interesting because it's hitting one specific continent. Also, America, Canada and Mexico form what's theoretically called the *North American Union*. Though there's no *official* union of the three, people have been saying for decades that America, Mexico and Canada should have open borders, and share the same currency."

"I've heard about that. But right now our country is adamant about closing our borders because of terrorism and illegal immigration. It's all about America first."

"Yeah I know. Our country is talking about building a wall and we are trying to get Mexico to pay for it…" Ruthie stopped herself. She thought about the wall of Jericho and how the wall fell down.

"I wonder if the solar eclipse means we will have open borders one day?" Barb asked.

"Maybe it means we are in for **big changes** here in America, and in North America as a whole. What U.S. states is it passing through?"

"Let me pull up the website with the map," Barb said, checking her phone. "Ok, I've got it. Let's see….it goes through Texas, Arkansas, Missouri, Illinois, Kentucky, Indiana, Michigan, Ohio, Pennsylvania, New York state, Vermont and New Hampshire."

"So, the path is going from south to north this time."

"Yes, the August 21, 2017 eclipse runs west to east, but this one on April 8 goes south to north."

"If I'm picturing this in my head correctly, it seems like if you put the two eclipse paths on a map together they would form a big X."

"A big X? What do you mean?"

"I mean the paths would intersect each other on the map like a big X. I guess it would kind of look like the United States is being **crossed out**."

"Crossed out? What do you mean? Are you saying the U.S. might not exist in the future?"

"I'm not saying anything other than the fact that the two paths of the eclipses form a large X that goes across the United States. I don't know what it means. A big X can mean other things too. For instance, in Greek, the letter X means Christ. Also, in ancient Semitic languages X stood for the cross. An X can also mean intersect, which is when two roads cross each other. But, intersect also means *to divide by passing through*."

Looking worried, Barb studied the eclipse map on her phone. It showed both paths of the eclipses.

"There is one particular place where the paths of **both eclipses** intersect."

"Where do the paths intersect?"

"Makanda, Illinois."

"I've never heard of Makanda, but I know a lot about Illinois," Ruthie said.

"Isn't Illinois where Lewis and Clark began their journey to explore the land we acquired during the Louisiana Purchase?" Barb asked.

"You know your history Barb. Yes, they started out from Camp Dubois, which is in Wood River, Illinois. Most people don't realize how important their expedition was. They mapped and documented the land we bought from France. **We doubled the size of our land as a nation when the Louisiana Purchase was signed**. *This one transaction literally put America on the map*- it made America a superpower."

Both Ruthie and Barb were silent. They were thinking about America's land. Two solar eclipses were hitting the land within seven years of each other. The eclipses were hitting Civil War battle sites, and historical landmarks that were tied to the acquisition of the land. Suddenly Ruthie thought of something.

"I just thought of something else about Illinois. Isn't its nickname **LAND OF LINCOLN**?"

"I didn't know that. Why? Was he born there?"

"No, but he moved to Illinois in 1830 and lived there until he became President in 1861. He also represented Illinois in the House of Representatives and was a member of their Legislature for four terms. His home in Springfield, Illinois is registered as a National Historic Site. His tomb is in Oak Ridge Cemetery, which is also in Springfield."

"Did you say his tomb is in Illinois?"

Ruthie was quiet for a few moments. *Lincoln's tomb was in Illinois.* The eclipse paths intersected in the state of Illinois. She thought about the United States today. It was so divided right now. The government and the people were at odds. One only needed to turn on the news or look at Facebook to figure this out. The nation was like a ship splitting in two- like the ***Titanic***. Were the paths of the eclipses signaling a warning to a country about to split apart?

"Where did Lincoln give that famous speech? Oh, what was it called? It was something about being divided," Barb said.

"It's called **A House Divided**. Oh yes, other than the Gettysburg Address, that's Lincoln's most famous speech. In the speech he says the United States cannot remain a country if it divides itself. He said a house divided against itself cannot stand. At the time when he gave the speech our country was divided over slavery. The divide between the states and politicians had become as deep as the Grand Canyon. Lincoln took his inspiration for the speech from the Bible. In Matthew 12:22 Jesus says, **"Every kingdom divided against itself is brought to desolation, and every city or house divided against itself will not stand."**

"I just looked up the speech on my phone. Lincoln gave it in **Springfield, Illinois**," Barb stated.

They were both silent again.

"Barb, I think these eclipses mean something. In a total solar eclipse the sun is blocked, covered and darkened. It's hidden."

"Yes, and?"

"Well, when we watch an eclipse at first we have to cover our eyes with those special solar eclipse glasses. That's because if we look at the sun before it is completely covered we could damage our eyes. But, once the sun is completely covered we can take the glasses off- sort of like taking off a blindfold. Then we can look at the sun directly. We even see the corona, which is usually hidden. At no other time can we look at the sun directly without risking damage to our eyes."

"What are you getting at with this?"

"I'm saying that maybe these eclipses are what God is using to open our eyes- to open America's eyes. Our nation seems to be blinded by their own sins and idols. We are so steeped in sin and idolatry we can't even see God anymore. God is light. He is our Sun! But, our nation doesn't look to him anymore. It's like he's hidden. But, these solar eclipses will be seen by everyone. The first one is being called *The Great American Solar Eclipse. The second one is the Great North American Eclipse.*"

"You know what I just thought of?"

"I'm afraid to ask."

"I just saw a news show the other day and it said Illinois is going bankrupt. Right now Illinois has the lowest investment grade rating and the lowest credit rating of any state. The eclipse center line is going through Illinois in 2017, and the intersection of both eclipses (2017 and 2024) is located there also. And I forgot to mention that **the 2017 eclipse lasts the longest in Illinois**. There's a spot in the Shawnee National Forest, near Carbondale, Illinois, where the eclipse's duration is the greatest. It's going to last for 2 minutes 42 seconds. I'm starting to realize this eclipse is more than just an eclipse. The media is saying the eclipse in 2017 will be the most watched eclipse in our nation's history," Barb said.

"It's time for America to take off their glasses. These eclipses are meant to reveal the things that were once concealed."

They were both quiet for a few moments.

"Well, do you want to go see the eclipse together on August 21, 2017?" Barb asked.

"Of course! I can't miss a divine appointment."

"We might as well be part of history," Barb said.

Just then the waitress brought the bill for Ruthie and Barb. There was an X at the bottom of the bill where Barb had to sign her name.

"Hey look Ruthie. It's an X," she laughed.

Ruthie smiled, but inside she was kind of worried. She wanted America to turn back to God and to be ready for what God had planned. The big question was, *what* is he planning?

Author's Notes: THESE ARE IMPORTANT TO READ!!!!!!!!!!

THINK ABOUT THIS! The solar eclipse coming ONLY to American soil on August 21, 2017, will touch our land at 10:15 a.m. ABRAHAM LINCOLN was shot at 10:15 p.m. on April 14, dying on April 15. That's a 12 hour difference between the solar eclipse touching land 10:15 a.m., and the time Lincoln was shot at

10:15 p.m.- 12 in the Bible points to divine order and government. Keep in mind, on April 15, 2014 a total LUNAR eclipse already happened on Passover (Lincoln's death date anniversary)- and it's also the anniversary of Titanic's sinking! DID YOU KNOW IN 2017 ABRAHAM LINCOLN WAS RANKED AS #1 from among all the U.S. Presidents, according to a C-SPAN SURVEY which polled 91 historians? The qualities considered in the rankings were presidential leadership, international relations, crisis leadership, economic management, public persuasion skills and whether they pursued equal justice for all. (source- *CBS news article*). Regardless of this survey, Lincoln is always listed in the top five in most surveys of the American Public, or among scholars.

October 15, 1924 – 10-15- Presidential Proclamation declares the Statue of Liberty a national monument -(shadow touching land at 10:15.)

The speed of eclipse's shadow will be moving faster than a jet plane- (Remember Sully....)

The first state the eclipse touches on August 21, 2017 is Oregon. Oregon is the last state Lewis and Clark passed through before they reached the Pacific Ocean. They were responsible for mapping and documenting the new land the U.S. acquired in the Louisiana Purchase. This was the first land we purchased/acquired as a new nation.

I repeat, ***The eclipse touches down in Oregon first****.* The Oregon state quarter was released on June 6, 2005. In 2005 the United States helped Israel broker a land deal with the Palestinians in which Israel gave away land- the Gaza Strip, and portions of the West Bank. Not long afterward, our land was struck by Hurricane Katrina, which up to this date, is the **COSTLIEST NATURAL DISASTER IN OUR HISTORY.** I find it interesting that the **Oregon** quarter (MONEY) was released in this same year. Why? Because God has repeatedly said DO NOT TOUCH MY LAND. Now, the world is asking Israel to give Jerusalem back- to give its most precious piece of land back to terrorists! The shadow of the eclipse is touching our land and I believe the

Lord is saying HANDS OFF MY LAND. The quarter was released **June 6,** 2005 and Israel claimed East Jerusalem on **June 7**, 1967. 6 and 7

Notes about the paths of both eclipses:

The two solar eclipse paths, when placed on the map, form an X. Interestingly enough, X is used to represent **transformations** in mathematics. It is often represented as f(x) in the equation. In addition, when referring to electricity, an X is often used to abbreviate the word **transformer**- written as **Xformer.** With respect to electricity, transformers change or convert electricity by increasing or decreasing the amount of voltage. Transformers "change" the voltage, so electricity can safely enter power lines that will be running through your home.

The word transform itself means to go through a dramatic change in appearance and/or form. Synonyms include transfigure, metamorphose, remake, renew and revolutionize. Perhaps the X being formed by the two total solar eclipses is a reminder of something we need to do as a nation. **We need to be transformed to the image of Christ. Also, when Jesus returns at the last trump it says we will all be CHANGED. In fact, our bodies will be resurrected! Talk about a transformation. At the rapture we will all be changed/transformed in the blink of an eye.** Not long before I wrote this chapter a transformer blew outside my window. I heard loud zapping and sizzling sounds. I could see green lights flashing outside. Later, I looked up the word transformer and that's when I noticed the connection to the X.

Other meanings for X: *keep in mind that an X is formed over U.S. land by the two solar eclipses*

XX means to double-cross or betray someone.

X marks the spot on a treasure map

An X is on railroad crossing signs. *This sign indicates a train crosses over the road. The motorist must stop when the train is crossing.* Ignoring the railroad crossing could mean death for a motorist.

X in Roman numerals means 10- There are 10 commandments in the Bible. Also- the story of the 10 Virgins at Midnight- the five that were ready went with Jesus. The five who were not were left behind.

What does INTERSECTION mean? (an X)- It means a crossroads or a point at which a life altering decision must be made that will have *far-reaching, long standing, possibly irreversible consequences.*

Here's another meaning for X- a very IMPORTANT and SYMBOLIC meaning! In the Bible the word **threshold** is used often. It refers to the wood beam under a door's entrance. When a person comes into their home, or in some cases their barn, they CROSS OVER the threshold. Their body literally CROSSES OVER the threshold of the door as they walk in. In essence, they are intersecting the threshold. Many Jewish people will place a Mezuzah on the doorpost of their homes. This tradition goes back to Deuteronomy 6:9, and 11:20, which says to "write the commandments of God on the doorframes of your houses, and on your gates." This reminds them that the Lord is King over their homes. As they cross the threshold of their door, they walk in remembrance of this and apply this in the teaching of their children, and how they run their household.

To get even more specific, the threshold goes all the way back to King David, who purchased a threshing floor for the Temple of the Lord.

The threshing floor is a place where grain would be threshed and winnowed. This is where the grain would be harvested. The grain would be separated from the chaff. The grain was good for eating, but the chaff was burned up. This is symbolic of what happens when people are harvested by God. The grain (seed) is harvested and this represents the people of God, but the chaff (inedible part of the grain) is thrown away and burnt up. Often, when threshing was done in a barn, a large piece of wood was placed at the door. This piece of wood was called a threshold. This wood kept the grain from falling out of the barn.

So, crossing the threshold is in essence, crossing into God's plan. Either you are with him, or you are against him. You are either the good grain, or the chaff. If you are the chaff, you are "burnt up".

Did you know the Temple Mount in Jerusalem is the threshing floor King David bought? David's son, Solomon would later build the first Jewish Temple to worship God at this very site. Today, it is the

MOST CONTESTED place in the entire world. Jews, Christians and Muslims all lay claim to this sacred place- the threshing floor of Jerusalem. We know the truth. One day Jesus is going to step foot on this threshing floor and set it all straight. It is his land. Interesting, because threshing was often done using feet.

Perhaps the X formed by the two solar eclipse paths are a reminder that we have two choices. We can cross over with him, or without him. But, without him we are doomed. The Israelites had to cross the threshold of the Jordan before they could inherit the Promise Land. **But, they couldn't cross without God. The Ark/Lord went before them. Also, the eclipses could be a reminder that we are reaching the threshold when it comes to Jerusalem. The enemies of Israel want to take the land. We are at a crossroads. Some people will be sheep and stand with God, and some will be goats and go against him. But, those who cross without God will be doomed. Jerusalem belongs to JESUS, whose name Christ is signified with an X (in Greek). X marks the spot for Jesus' land.**

Also, according to tradition, a **BRIDE** should be carried by the **GROOM** over the **THRESHOLD** of the front door of their new home. They are CROSSING over into their new lives together!!!

When I think of a shadow crossing our land, forming an X, I also think of SHADE. The word shadow is synonymous with the word shade. The shade can be a covering, or protection from the sun. An umbrella is something we use to cover or protect us from the sun and rain. An umbrella is actually made using EIGHT SPOKES that converge at a common point on the top of the umbrella. If not for the point bringing them all together, they would all *intersect* and form lots of X shapes. But did you know that God is our shade- our covering? He's the only one who can protect us in all circumstances.

Facts about Illinois: (the state in the CROSSROADS-intersection- of the two eclipses)

As far as the August 21, 2017 solar eclipse is concerned, Illinois is the state that will be able to view the eclipse for the **longest amount**

of time. The point of greatest duration is in the **Shawnee National Forest** (just south of Carbondale, Illinois- Makanda -*mentioned in the chapter*- is part of the Carbondale area). This area will have **2 minutes and 42 seconds** of full totality- full eclipse of the sun!

Louis Albert Bowman was an attorney/chaplain from **ILLINOIS**. He was the first person to initiate adding UNDER GOD to the Pledge of Allegiance. He first recited the pledge with **UNDER GOD** added to it while at a meeting in Illinois. He said he was inspired by Abraham Lincoln's Gettysburg Address.

Illinois is considered the **most nuclear state in America**. They have six nuclear power plants and 48% of their electricity is generated with nuclear energy. **It's the largest producer of nuclear power in the country.**

Illinois is part of the **New Madrid Seismic Zone**. This zone is credited with producing four of the largest earthquakes in North America. The New Madrid fault caused a devastating series of earthquakes in 1811-1812. More than 1000 earthquakes occurred during this time. The earthquakes were so strong the Mississippi River was diverted. The ground undulated and sand liquefaction occurred (the sand/soil loses stiffness and "structure", causing it to behave like a liquid, rather than a solid.) The aftershocks of the quakes were felt over 1000 miles away. Missouri is also in this zone. The path of the solar eclipses of 2017 and 2024 both travel through Illinois and Missouri. This land is historic as well since it goes back to our beginnings as a newly formed nation- The Louisiana Purchase and Northwest Territory were both tied to land we received once we broke free from England as a new nation. If an earthquake(s) were to occur in the New Madrid Seismic Zone at this point it would be ABSOLUTELY CATASTROPHIC. Back in 1811-1812 there were no nuclear sites or oil pipelines. In addition, the population was nothing like it is today. The amount of homes, businesses, bridges, buildings, etc that would be destroyed is unfathomable. The Mississippi River would be greatly affected by seismic activity. Keep in mind the Mississippi passes through, or borders the states of Tennessee, Arkansas, Mississippi, Louisiana, Minnesota, Wisconsin, Missouri, Illinois and Iowa. The watershed of the Mississippi River includes all or part of 31 states.

Illinois was once part of the Northwest Territory (though it wasn't called Illinois back then). The Northwest Ordinance of 1787 created the Northwest Territory. This was **THE FIRST ORGANIZED TERRITORY of the United States.** Previously this land had been in the hands of the French. But, when England won the French and Indian war, this territory became their possession. Later, when the colonies won the war (during the American Revolution) and the Treaty of Paris was signed, the newly formed "America" now gained ownership of this large territory. So, in addition to the thirteen colonies, now there was also the Northwest Territory, which included what we now know as ILLINOIS, OHIO, INDIANA, and WISCONSIN. According to the book, *How the States Got Their Shapes*, by Mark Stein, the land gained during the French and Indian War (the Northwest Territory- what we now know as Illinois, Ohio, Indiana and Wisconsin) became a big influence on how America's future land (states) would be divided. Of course, in the years that followed America's development, the Louisiana Purchase would lead to an astonishing amount of land being "placed" into American hands. Napoleon would sell America 828,000 square miles of land on April 30, 1803. The land of the Northwest Ordinance, as well as the Louisiana Purchase, would put America on the map as a superpower- **a nation with a lot of land! So, Illinois was quite important in the beginnings of our nation because it influenced the borders of our future land.**

The first total solar eclipse comes to America on **August 21, 2017**. On **August 21, 1959,** Hawaii became our LAST state! **Hawaii is the last piece of land we have acquired as a nation**!!! The 50th state……………..50 in the Bible is tied to the land because it represents JUBILEE. In the Jubilee year all land was returned to the rightful owner. Well, if you ask me GOD is the rightful owner of America's land. But, he can take it away at any time. He has sovereignty, and he is the real estate agent forever! Our land will be blessed if we follow God, and if we bless the nation of Israel.

Texas is the first state the eclipse touches on the **April 8, 2024** eclipse (*7 years after the August 21, 2017 eclipse)*. The LAST BATTLE OF THE CIVIL WAR was fought in TEXAS in 1865. Robert E. Lee had already surrendered at Appomattox Court House in Virginia a month before and that was considered the last *MAJOR* battle. But, the Battle of Palmito Ranch in Texas *was the last engagement*. So, think about this: The last state the first eclipse (August 21, 2017) touches is South Carolina, which is where the **first shot** of the Civil War was fired. The first state the second eclipse touches (Texas) is where the **last shot** was fired in the last engagement. Coincidence?

See the back of this book for more details about the intersection of the two eclipses

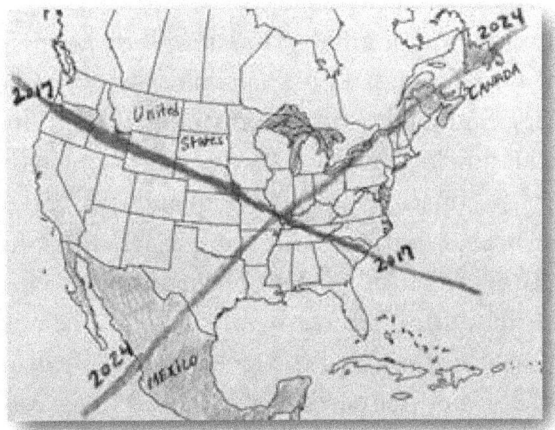

My son Jonah created a map above showing the two eclipse paths. It's not perfectly to scale, but you can see the general direction of the paths. For detailed maps check out greatamericaneclipse.com

CHAPTER 33
Civil War

§

When Ruthie got home she felt both exhilarated and worried about the eclipses. On the one hand, it would be an exciting celestial event. On the other, it could be foreshadowing trouble and division in the land. It may just be a warning, but Ruthie didn't feel good about it. Even though the United States had a new leader, the spiritual condition of the country was at an all-time low. The laws of the nation did not reflect the laws of God. The America of today was not the America of our founders. Suddenly Ruthie remembered the book in her purse. She pulled it out quickly. In one fell swoop the book fell to the ground, landing with pages open. She picked it up and read the title of the page the book landed on. "**National Blessing**," she read. She saw a picture of **Abraham Lincoln** at the bottom of the page as well.

She found the timing interesting, being that she and Barb had just discussed the solar eclipse, and the fact that it was exiting not far from Ft. Sumter, where the first battle of the Civil War was fought.

As she read the page over, she learned that **Abraham Lincoln declared a National Fast Day on March 30, 1863**. The country was in the throes of a civil war, and Lincoln knew it needed the power of God to stay afloat. The war ravaged the nation. Brother fought brother. Blood spilled in every field. Lincoln realized it was time to call out to God. The nation needed healing. Some have called this Fast Day a "Yom Kippur" to the Lord. For thousands of years the Jewish people had observed the Day of Atonement, or Yom Kippur, every year after

Rosh Hashanah. Yom Kippur would occur 10 days after the start of Rosh Hashanah. **In Israel, this is the day the High Priest would make atonement for the sins of the nation (in biblical days).** The priest would appeal to God through sacrifice and prayer. On this day God would sit on the mercy seat of the ark and pronounce Israel's fate. If atonement was made, God showed mercy and forgave the nation for that year. Once Jesus came, *he became the High Priest* and the *rituals* of the old covenant were not necessary. All believers could ask Jesus for forgiveness *directly* and receive mercy. But, Abraham Lincoln had great respect for the ancient laws and feasts of the Bible. In his own way, he was calling out to God through his ancient feasts, still celebrated by the Jewish people today.

Lincoln began by saying, "Whereas, the Senate of the United States, devoutly recognizing the Supreme Authority and just Government of Almighty God, in all the affairs of men and of nations, has, by a resolution, requested the President to designate and set apart a day for National prayer and humiliation. And whereas it is the duty of nations as well as of men, to own their dependence upon the overruling power of God, to confess their sins and transgressions, in humble sorrow, yet with assured hope that **genuine repentance will lead to mercy and pardon**; and to recognize the sublime truth, announced in the Holy Scriptures and proven by all history, <u>**that those nations only are blessed whose God is the Lord.**</u>"

"And, insomuch as we know that, by His divine law, **nations like individuals are subjected to punishments and chastisements in this world**, may we not justly fear that the awful calamity of civil war, which now desolates the land, **may be but a punishment**, inflicted upon us, for our presumptuous sins, to the needful end of our national reformation as a whole People? We have been recipients of the choicest bounties in Heaven. We have been preserved, thee many years in peace and prosperity. **We have grown in numbers, wealth and power, as no other nation has ever grown. But we have forgotten God. We have forgotten the gracious hand, which preserved us in peace,**

and multiplied and enriched and strengthened us; and we have vainly imagined, in the deceitfulness of our hearts, that all these blessings were produced by some superior wisdom and virtue of our own. Intoxicated with unbroken success, we have become too self-sufficient to feel the necessity of redeeming and preserving grace, **too proud to pray to the God that made us.**"

Ruthie stopped reading. Even though Lincoln wrote this over 153 years ago, the words were so applicable to America right now! In the proclamation Lincoln mentioned how the United States was richly blessed by God. Its very existence owed to God. Yet, as a nation, we have forgotten God. **Lincoln mentions how the Civil War in the land was surely brought on by our own sins as a nation.**

The solar eclipse hitting our land. The shadow dividing our land. Ruthie couldn't help but wonder what this meant for America. Yes, there were many Christians in America, but how many truly EMBRACED Jesus? Many can say they've accepted him, but how many truly believe his message, and are truly folded into his arms? How many churches were actually ready for the rapture? In the book of Revelation, seven churches are mentioned, but only two are ready for the return of the Groom. The timing of finding this information about Lincoln was right on target.

Back in 2014, 2015 there were four blood moons (total lunar eclipses) that occurred and were visible from the United States. Interestingly enough, the first blood moon, which occurred on **April 15, 2014, was the same date Lincoln died.** He was shot on April 14, 1865 and died on April 15, 1865. This was also the date *Titanic* sank in the North Atlantic in 1912. Since the blood moons, there had been unprecedented unrest in the United States and the world. From terrorist attacks, to civil disobedience- things were getting darker here in America, and it looked like America could be the *Titanic*.

While things looked dreary, there was one good thing about all of this. The shakings of this day and age were all precursors to the return of Christ. He would be the only one to set things straight. No

President or world leader would be able to do this. God could certainly use world leaders to bring about his plan, but God would be in charge of it all.

Ruthie grabbed the book *In God We Trust* and turned the page. There she saw a familiar song, but one she hadn't thought about in quite a while. It was called *Battle Hymn of the Republic*. It was written in 1861 by Julia Ward Howe, during the Civil War. The song was originally called John Brown's body, and paid homage to famous abolitionist John Brown. Brown had been hung for his role in the Harper's Ferry slave uprising. When Julia Howe heard the song it was suggested to her that she should write the song with new words. That night Howe went to bed, but awoke at early dawn, or twilight. Her mind was bombarded with the new words for the song. Even though it was still dark and she could not see, she wrote the words down. Her version of the song became the most popular song of the Civil War, and to this day remains an American favorite.

Ruthie read the words to the song aloud:

Mine eyes have seen the glory of the coming of the Lord;
He is trampling out the vintage where the grapes of wrath are stored;
He hath loosed the fateful **lightning** of His terrible swift sword;
His truth is marching on.
Glory, glory hallelujah,
Glory, glory hallelujah,
Glory, glory hallelujah
His truth is marching on.
He has sounded forth the **trumpet** that shall never call retreat;
He is sifting out the hearts of men before his judgment seat;
Oh, be swift, my soul, to answer Him; be jubilant, my feet!
Our God is marching on. (*Repeat chorus above*)
In the beauty of the lilies Christ was born across the sea,
With a glory in his bosom that **transfigures** you and me;

As He died to make men holy, let us live to make men free;
While God is marching on, *(Repeat Chorus)*
He is coming like the glory of the morning on the wave,
His wisdom to the mighty, He is honor to the brave;
So the world shall be his footstool, **and His faithful He shall save**;
Our God is marching on.

After she finished reading she was stunned. This song was perhaps the most famous anthem of the Civil War. Was it about men fighting? No, it wasn't. Was it about world leaders saving the nation? No! Was it about the political issues of the states during the Civil War? NO. **It was about JESUS. It was about the RETURN OF JESUS, and the judgment that would be inflicted upon an unbelieving, sinful world**. In the song Christ was trampling the grapes and sounding the shofar. He was coming to save the faithful.

Was America headed for Civil War? Was it a physical war, or just a spiritual one? What would the final consequences of this war be? Would a war happen before the rapture, or after? Were we already in the beginning stages of this war? Ruthie didn't know, but there was one thing that stood out to her like a blaring siren. Whatever happened, Jesus would rescue the faithful ones who embraced him as savior.

Julia Ward Howe wrote this song in the dark, but through it she was bringing light to the world. Jesus was the light in the darkness. The Civil War would claim more than 600,000 lives. There were few people in the country at that time who did not know someone who perished in the war. The President called on the nation to repent, and rightly so. **Without repentance, the country would divide and dissolve.** The ancient Israelites knew this type of fate. Their kingdom was split in two, and then eventually destroyed. But, God brought them back to their Promised Land after long years of suffering and division. After World War II the nation of Israel became a country once more. In 1948, they became a nation again.

It was obvious God had blessed the United States and Israel as well. But, God expected obedience. His ultimate goal was redemption. Even if things had gone awry, it was never too late to turn back to God. Ruthie just hoped her country would fully embrace God's son, Jesus, before it was too late.

AUTHOR'S NOTE:

The Civil War is known as America's bloodiest war. The loss of life is estimated at around 620,000. It also took a heavy economic toll. The cost of four years of war is estimated at over eight billion dollars in today's money. On <u>April 15, 1861</u>, President Lincoln tried to end the rebellion before it turned into all- out war. He sent 75,000 soldiers to put down the rebellion of the Southern states. It didn't work. Things escalated and the country headed into the bloodiest conflict in their history. Flash forward, 51 years later, to <u>April 15, 1912</u>. *Titanic* **sailed into icy waters, not aware of the doom and death awaiting her. If only there had been enough lifeboats……**

Think about the design of the Confederate flag. **<u>It has a large X on it</u>**! This was the flag of the South- the Confederate states. This flag is a reminder of the South's decision to secede, or leave the Union. It is a reminder of a war that almost tore our nation apart. (*<u>The solar eclipse paths form an X</u>*)

The solar eclipse occurring in the United States will happen on the first day of the month of Elul. (August 21, 2017). On the Hebrew calendar the month of Elul precedes the Jewish Feast known as Rosh Hashanah, or Feast of Trumpets. During the month of Elul the shofar (trumpet) is played once each day for all 29 days of the month (though some synagogues will skip the 29th day). This trumpet blast is meant to be an AWAKENING BLAST. It is meant to wake up the heart of every believer to repent and turn back to God. When Rosh Hashanah arrives, believers should be ready to usher in the New Year, and in Jewish tradition, believers names are written in the Book of Life. As Christians, our names are written into the Book of Life when we receive Christ. However, the Feast of Rosh Hashanah foreshadows the return of Christ for his Bride. The Bride will have repented (and been forgiven by Jesus), and be ready for the Groom (Jesus) when he returns at the Rapture. In fact, we are to search our hearts every day as believers in Christ so **we are always ready** for our Groom.

The fact that this eclipse is occurring on the first day of Elul may very well be an awakening blast for all of America. God could be calling out to our nation to repent and turn back to him. Between the first day of Elul and Yom Kippur (Day of Atonement) is 40 days. This is because Yom Kippur occurs 10 days after Rosh Hashanah. **It is said that on Rosh Hashanah it is written, but on Yom Kippur it is sealed.** National atonement for sins was made by the High Priest on the Day of Atonement/Yom Kippur in ancient Israel. It was this day when the High Priest went into the Holy of Holies to meet with God and atone for the sins of the nation. If all went well, the sins were forgiven and God granted mercy. As a nation, America will see this eclipse- **this shadow-** going across our land from west to east. It will happen during Elul. Seven years later we will witness another one! Our national sins are great. But God is a fair and just God. He will give us the opportunity to repent and turn back. His son Jesus, **who is our High Priest and atonement**, is ready and willing to forgive our sins as individuals, and as a nation.

The prophet Jonah went to the ancient city of Nineveh and prophesied to the people they needed to repent. He did this for 40 days. Some scholars say he began prophesying to the people on the first day of Elul. The people had 40 days to repent and get themselves right with God- this would put the timing at Yom Kippur. **At that point their fate would be sealed.** In the case of Nineveh, they did repent. They were spared, **at least this time around**. But later they forgot God again and were destroyed. What will the United States do?????????

Jonah, Chapter 3

And the word of the Lord came unto Jonah the second time, saying, Arise, go unto Nineveh, that great city, and preach unto it the preaching that I bid thee. So, *Jonah arose, and went unto Nineveh, according to the word of the Lord. Now Nineveh was an exceeding great city of three days' journey. And Jonah began to enter the city a day's journey, and he cried, and said,* **YET FORTY DAYS AND NINEVEH SHALL BE OVERTHROWN.** *So the people of Nineveh believed God, and* **proclaimed a fast**, *and put on sackcloth, from the greatest of them, even to the least of them. For the word came unto the King of Nineveh, and he arose from his throne, and he laid his robe from him, and covered him with sackcloth, and sat in ashes. And he caused it to be proclaimed and published through Nineveh by the decree of the king and his nobles, saying, Let neither man nor beast, herd nor flock, taste any thing: let them not feed, nor drink water: But let man and beast be covered with sackcloth, and cry mightily unto god: yea, let them turn every one from his evil way, and from the violence that is in their hands…. And God saw their works, that they turned from their evil way; and God repented of the evil, that he had said he would do unto them; and he did it not.*

It is possible there was a solar eclipse during the time of Jonah's preaching. This may have urged the King to heed Jonah's warnings to repent.

On Yom Kippur it is customary for the Jewish people to fast for the entire day- the city of Nineveh fasted as a form of repentance as well

The second solar eclipse on **April 8, 2024**, first passes through Mexico, then America and finally Canada. **The last place it touches is the Newfoundland coast. Newfoundland is considered Britain's oldest colony. The eclipse will exit from the eastern coast of Newfoundland**. Of course, keep in mind that Britain (England) is our mother country. Through the English our nation was founded. If our nation does not repent and follow God's plan, we are going to be like the ***Titanic.*** The *Titanic*, by the way, was found approximately 400 miles east of Newfoundland, lying 12,000 feet below, on the depths of the cold ocean floor!

Break down Newfoundland and you get NEW FOUND LAND.

HISTORICAL MESSAGES: Paul Revere is famous for **warning** the colonists the British were coming. He rode on his horse to ALARM the countryside, and deliver an important message. Because of this, the colonists were ready for the war (Revolutionary War). This famous ride took place at midnight on April 18, 1775. Soon after, the famous SHOT HEARD ROUND THE WORLD occurred at Lexington and Concord. The first shots of the war were fired and the road to revolution began. Freedom would be the final result. One day, when Jesus returns, we will witness **THE SHOFAR HEARD ROUND THE WORLD**. That's when true freedom will arrive!!! Oh, and by the way, Jesus will be on a horse too- a pure white one!

CHAPTER 34

Connections

RUTHIE'S MEETING WITH BARB HAD been a real eye-opener. She realized the solar eclipse coming on August 21, 2017, and the one on April 8, 2024, was something important to note. The fact that four total lunar eclipses had occurred just a few years ago, in 2014 and 2015, was important as well. These lunar eclipses had occurred on the Jewish holidays of Passover, and the Feast of Tabernacles. The first total lunar eclipse happened on **April 15, 2014**, and lined up with the sinking of *Titanic*, which occurred **April 15, 1912**. In addition, Abraham Lincoln died on **April 15, 1865**, after being assassinated. Not only that, the concentration camp which held Anne Frank was liberated on **April 15, 1945**. Unfortunately she died just before it was liberated, but her diary lived on as a legacy.

The second total lunar eclipse occurred on **October 8, 2014** on the Feast of Tabernacles. John Hancock, best known for being the first delegate to sign the Declaration of Independence (and the biggest signature as well), died on this date in 1793. The new design for the 100 dollar bill went public on **October 8, 2013**. The bill features Benjamin Franklin, as well as liberty bells. The hundred dollar bill is the largest bill in circulation (as far as denomination). Benjamin Franklin is the only politician to have signed all four documents that essentially created our nation - The Declaration of Independence (1776), the Treaty of Alliance with France (1778), the Treaty of Paris (1783), and the U.S. Constitution (1787). He is also credited with showing that lightning is a form of electricity. (*Think of the lightning verse*)

The third total lunar eclipse also occurred on Passover again, but on **April 4, 2015**. This eclipse lined up with several historical events. On **April 4, 1945** the United States liberated its **first** concentration camp near the end of World War II. All of Hungary was liberated on **April 4, 1945** as well. NATO was formed on **April 4, 1949**. Martin Luther King Jr. was assassinated on **April 4, 1968**. The original World Trade Center Towers were dedicated to the public on **April 4, 1973**.

The last total lunar eclipse of the tetrad occurred on **September 28, 2015**, on the Feast of Tabernacles. This date lined up with the Battle of Yorktown on **September 28, 1781**. This was the most important battle of the Revolutionary War because it was a decisive victory for the Americans. It led to the signing of the Treaty of Paris, thus ending the war. This one victory led to the forming of the United States of America, free of British rule. Interestingly enough, the battle was financed by a Jewish broker by the name of Haym Soloman. He single handedly financed the battle. Without funds to fight, the Americans would not have won.

On **September 28, 1870**, famous **Civil War** general Robert E. Lee suffered a stroke, which led to his death on October 12. Though the South lost the war, Robert E. Lee has been noted as one of the best generals in American History. Also, the land Arlington National Cemetery sits upon used to belong to Lee and his wife. It was seized during the Civil War and eventually used as a place to bury the dead. The war had claimed so many lives there wasn't enough space to bury them. Lee's property was used for this reason.

The timing of the four total lunar eclipses (blood moons), and the upcoming solar eclipses were no coincidence. Two solar eclipses on American soil within seven years of each other wasn't coincidence! **It seemed more like God was putting his handwriting on the sky. He was signing his name across the <u>American sky</u> in particular. A warning perhaps.**

The year 2017 was already a significant year in God's eyes for Israel. After all, on November 2, 2017, it would be **100 years since the**

Balfour Declaration was signed. This document set aside land for a national homeland for the Jewish people. It wouldn't be fully realized until midnight on May 14, 1948, when Israel officially became a nation.

Ruthie thought the 100 revealed something interesting. In the Bible, 100 pointed to a significant event. Abraham was 100 years old his promised son Isaac was born. Later Abraham would go to Mount Moriah to sacrifice Isaac. He was fully prepared to do this when God provided a ram instead. This foreshadowed that God would send his only son Jesus, to die on the cross for our sins. The ram pointed to the shofar, or trumpet, because a ram's horn is what is used to make the shofar. The feast of Rosh Hashanah foreshadowed the rapture because the trumpet was blown 100 times and the last time was called the Last Trump. One day Jesus would return at the Last Trump.

It also pointed to the story of the lost sheep. The story says that if there are 100 sheep in the pasture and one gets lost, the shepherd will go after that one sheep. Still, there was something else about the 100. She tried to think of what else reminded her of 100. As she thought, she looked down. There, on the floor, with a shiny glint, was a penny. "Ah ha! A penny!" she said. "Now, what does it mean?" She knew it took 100 hundred pennies to make a dollar. A strange thought popped into her head. "Vice President Pence," she thought. She suddenly realized the Vice President had a last name that sounded very much like "penny". She looked up the word pence and found out it meant the plural form of penny.

She couldn't help but wonder. It was interesting how President Trump's name meant "shofar" and on Rosh Hashanah, the **100th Trump** was called The Last Trump. Here was Trump's Vice President with a name that means **"100"**, or penny.

Something told her to look up Mike Pence's birthday. His birthday was **June 7, 1959**. The date June 7 was very familiar to her. On **June 7, 1967**, Israel claimed East Jerusalem in the Six Days War. Thus, the capital was unified. The Israeli Defense Forces came through the Lion's Gate on that day, and even hung the Israeli flag near the Temple

Mount. This fulfilled Biblical prophecy since the Lord's holy city was now fully in the hands of Israel. During the years of 1967 and 1968 there was a tetrad of blood moons, falling on the same Jewish Feasts (Passover and Tabernacles) as the 2014/2015 series. Though Pence was born eight years before this event, he was born on the same date. What was even more interesting is that Pence was listed as the 48th Vice President of the United States. Israel officially became a nation again on May 14, 1948. Ruthie wondered what God had in store for Mike Pence. He seemed to be a kind, humble man who had a great respect for God. The name Pence made her think about the story of the 100 sheep in Matthew. Even if one sheep is lost out of the 100, the shepherd (Jesus) will go to great lengths to retrieve it. In a way, Israel was a nation without a shepherd. Even though there were great numbers of Jewish people coming to faith in Jesus, the nation as a whole had not accepted Jesus as Savior. **The Day of Atonement (also known as Yom Kippur) was one of the Lord's Feasts that pointed to the national salvation of Israel. After Rosh Hashanah was fulfilled, Yom Kippur would be next, followed by Tabernacles.** Ruthie wondered how God would time all these things. There were so many signs. But, it seemed most people had their eyes closed.

The year 2017 marked the 100 year anniversary of the Balfour Declaration, which laid the foundation for Israel's land. But, it also marked something else significant. **On June 7, 2017, it would mark the 50 year anniversary of when Israel reclaimed East Jerusalem.** Fifty was an important number in the Bible. It was known as the Jubilee year. In biblical times, every 50th year, slaves and captives were to be set free. In addition, all land had to be returned to its original owner, even if it was lost due to debt. It was called "the year of the Lord's favor." Ruthie could only hope it would be the "year of Israel's favor". She didn't know what was in store, but she had a feeling U.S. leaders would be involved in a big way. She could only pray that U.S. leaders would stand beside Israel, and above all, help her KEEP the land! No negotiations with terrorist nations! No giving in to pressure from the

United Nations. The U.S. needed to embrace Israel like a brother and keep her from harm.

In 2018, it would mark 70 years since Israel became a new nation. At midnight on May 14, 1948, Israel became a nation. The United States was the first nation to recognize Israel's new status. Seventy in the Bible pointed to Jerusalem, and its redemption. Ancient Israel was in captivity for 70 years, after the Babylonians destroyed their Temple and land. But at the end of the 70 years, God put something special on the heart of King Cyrus of Persia. The desire to allow the Jews to rebuild the Temple and city was placed in the thoughts of Cyrus, and he issued a decree for it to be done.

The Book of Daniel showcases two of the most important prophecies of the Bible. Daniel 9, verses 24-27, show the timing of the first and second Advents of Jesus, the Messiah.

"**Seventy weeks** are determined upon thy people and upon thy holy city, to finish the transgression, and to make an end of sins, and to make reconciliation for iniquity, and to bring in everlasting righteousness, and to seal up the vision and prophecy, and to anoint the most Holy. Know therefore and understand, that from the going forth of the commandment *to restore and to build Jerusalem* unto the Messiah the Prince shall be seven weeks, and threescore and two weeks; the street shall be built again, and the wall, even in troublous times. *And after threescore and two weeks shall Messiah be cut off,* but not for himself; and the people of the prince that shall come shall destroy the city and the sanctuary; and the end thereof shall be with a flood, and unto the end of the war desolations are determined. And he shall confirm the covenant with many for one week: and in the midst of the week he shall cause the sacrifice and the oblation to cease, and for the overspreading of abominations he shall make it desolate, even until the consummation, and that determined shall be poured out upon the desolate."

Every time a "week" is mentioned, it actually means "seven". That meant the first line said, "Seventy sevens are determined upon they people...." This would equal 70 times 7, or 490 years. This is referring to the idea that it will be a period of 490 years that will be divided into three periods. Seven weeks (49 years), and Sixty two weeks (threescore and two weeks) which is 434 years, and one week (7 years). After the first two periods, it says the Messiah will be cut off. This is referring to the crucifixion of Jesus. It goes on to say the sanctuary and city will be destroyed, which is referring to the Temple and Jerusalem.

The last part of the prophecy has not yet come. It speaks about a covenant made by a prince for one week (7 years), and in the midst of the week (after 3 ½ years), he will end the worship of the one holy true God, and instead set himself up as a God. This Prince is likely the Antichrist, or the "man of lawlessness." He will first allow the Jews to build their Temple and worship freely through the institution of a "fake peace contract." He would appear as a false Messiah and bring his version of "world peace." After 3 ½ years (42 months) he will break the peace treaty and his vicious, evil nature would spew forth on all of mankind, especially the Jewish people.

Ruthie had studied all these prophecies and she knew 70 was tied to both God, the Law and Jerusalem. God's number for perfection is 7, and 10 points to the 10 Commandments. The Antichrist would set his law upon the land during the 7 year tribulation period, and he would do his best to destroy the Jews and anyone else in his way. He would try to take over Jerusalem. But, God would put an end to it. It was all a matter of timing. All this would occur within the "seventy sevens" timeframe.

It seemed the clock was ticking. Every day the world drew closer to the inevitable return of Jesus. He would first come for his Bride, but then he'd be back for the rest of the world. Who was watching? Who was paying attention to the signs? When it happened, **it would be like a flash of lightning.**

Author's Notes:

Fast facts about lightning: Lightning travels at about 220,000 miles per hour when it travels down from a cloud to the ground. But, there's also a RETURN STROKE, of 220,000,000 miles per hour!

The return stroke is the bright flash we see when observing lightning. **Did you notice how much faster it is <u>on the way up</u>!!!!** The human eye only sees the flash, and most people don't see both the downward <u>and</u> the upward stroke. It's just too fast to catch both, but the fastest part is what we actually see- the return stroke going UP. That is what it will be like when Jesus returns for his Bride- perhaps only flashes of light will be seen, and the swiftness of it all will boggle the minds of anyone who witnesses it. Of course, I'd rather be the one going with the flash, not the one staying behind. Maybe that's why I like the series on Netflix called *The FLASH.*

Other facts: An average bolt of lightning has an electric current of approximately 20,000 amperes- the temperature of lightning is six times hotter than the surface of the sun.

Benjamin Franklin is credited for using a key, kite and lightning to prove the existence of electricity. His image has been on the 100 dollar bill for more than 100 years. The 100th Trump is the last trump and the Bible says Jesus will return at "the last trump." Jesus will return quick like lightning-he's the key!

In **Psalm 29,** it says the "voice of the Lord is like lightning". I don't know about you, but I think there's going to be lightning everywhere when he comes back!

CHAPTER 35
The Field

THERE WERE SO MANY THINGS filling Ruthie's mind these days. Lightning, eclipses, historical facts, planes, birds, and a mixed bag of prophecy clues. Everything was pointing to the rapture of the Church. Maybe she should just start a blog and try to explain all the things she'd learned. Yes, that would do it. Anyone in the world could read a blog on the Internet. She decided she would sleep on it tonight. She wasn't 100 % sure if this is what the Lord wanted her to do, but she would pray about it.

She fell asleep quickly that evening, feeling unsure, but peaceful. She drifted into a dream right away, though the vividness of it all seemed more like real life.

She was standing in a vast golden field. Amber colored stalks swayed to and fro. She could feel the soft swish of a tall, feathery plant. She turned in all directions, finding herself surrounded by it. She realized she must be in a grain field- perhaps a wheat field. She wasn't sure. Whatever grain it was, it was ready to be harvested. The stalks were full and overbearing. She felt lost amongst them. Where should she go? Even if she wanted to leave the field, she wouldn't know which way to turn. There was no end in sight. The field seemed infinite.

She heard voices behind her. Turning, she saw a young woman holding the hand of an older woman. The younger woman pulled the older woman close to her. Though they both embraced, it seemed the younger clung tighter than the older. After the embrace, the two walked on together, hand in hand, slowly disappearing from the field.

A new scene appeared in the same spot where the women had been. An older man stood amongst the grain. He was tall, with an air of prestige, yet kind and humble. He carried large bundles of the grain that was growing in the field. He began walking toward Ruthie. Surprised, she turned around, figuring he must be looking for someone else. But, he stopped right in front of her. He reached out and handed her the stalks of grain from his hands. She gladly accepted, feeling like she didn't quite deserve them.

He looked into her eyes. His stare seemed to penetrate her very soul. "Where you go I go," he said. She felt a wave of everlasting peace wash over her with his words. She wondered what he meant when he said, *"where you go I go."* Suddenly, there was a bright flash, followed by a roaring sound of thunder. The stalks of grain sizzled. Surprisingly, she wasn't afraid.

She opened her eyes. She wasn't it the field anymore. She was in her bedroom. No grain, just furniture. Another puzzle piece. Another puzzle.

Clue number one: the dream took place in a field. Clue two: There were two women and a prominent man.

"Ruthie, are you awake?" Thomas asked, the bedroom door opening just a crack.

She didn't respond. The sound of her own name stirred something in the back of her mind. The wheels were turning…

"Ruthie?" Thomas asked again.

That was it! Her own name! The dream was about……..

"Ruthie! You're awake?" asked Thomas, walking in. "Why wouldn't you answer me?"

She snapped back to the present and said, "I'm sorry Thomas. I'm just feeling groggy."

"Ok, well, I made breakfast. Why don't you get dressed and join me?"

"Of course," she stuttered, still thinking about her own name. "Give me a few minutes."

As soon as Thomas closed the door she grabbed her Bible, turning to the **book of Ruth**. She read the first verse of the book aloud. "Now it came to pass in the days when judges ruled, that there was a famine in the land. And a certain man of Bethlehem Judah went to sojourn in the country of Moab, he and his wife, and his two sons."

She scanned the chapter for something that might give her a clue. After just a few seconds she saw it. Verse 16 read, "But Ruth replied, 'Don't urge me to leave you, or to turn back from you. **Where you go I will go, and where you stay I will stay.**'"

There was the line- **where you go I go**. It's what the man in the field said to her. She knew she was on the right track.

"Ruthie, come on! The food is getting cold," Thomas urged.

This puzzle would have to wait. But, at least she had a head start.

CHAPTER 36
Harvest and Redemption

§

AFTER BREAKFAST RUTHIE KNEW THERE was one thing she had to do. Read the story of Ruth. Surely, there were more clues to the puzzle within that story.

She began by reading all of chapter one. The story begins when a Jewish family leaves their homeland in Bethlehem of Judah. **A great famine has overtaken Bethlehem**, so the family moves to a **foreign land** called Moab. The husband (Elimelek), wife (Naomi) and two sons (Mahlon and Kilion) leave the land of Israel behind, along with relatives, and a life they've always known.

Time passes and Naomi's husband dies, **leaving her a widow**. Her sons marry Moabite women by the names of Orpah and Ruth. Ten years later life takes another bad turn when both of Naomi's sons die. Now, all three women are widows. It seemed life could get no worse.

Time passes and Naomi finds out the famine in Bethlehem is over. She decides she will return to her homeland, **just as the harvest is beginning**. Her two daughters in law begin the journey with her to this new land. But, early in the journey Naomi has second thoughts, and tells the women to go back to Moab.

"Go back each of you, to your mother's home. May the Lord show you kindness as you have shown kindness to your dead husbands and to me. May the Lord grant that each of you will find rest in the home of another husband."

At first this upsets both Ruth and Orpah and they insist on going with Naomi. But Naomi says, "Return home, my daughters. Why would you come with me? Am I going to have any more sons, who could become your husbands? Return home, my daughters; I am too old to have another husband. Even if I thought there was still hope for me- even if I had a husband tonight and then gave birth to sons- would you wait until they grew up? Would you remain unmarried for them? No, my daughters. It is *more bitter for me than for you, because the Lord's hand has turned against me!*"

After this speech, Orpah is convinced it is better for her to go back to Moab. After all, **Bethlehem is a foreign land** for her. She has always known Moab. Going to Bethlehem would be like going into the Lion's Den. **The Moabites and the Israelites had been enemies for generations**. Imagine what it would be like if she were to show up with Naomi. She would never be accepted by the Israelites. What did she have to gain? Would she even be able to find a husband there? Never! Yes, it would be better to go back to Moab.

Ruth, on the other hand, was not convinced by Naomi's speech. Instead she clung to Naomi and said, **"Don't urge me to leave you or turn back from you. Where you go I will go, and where you stay I will stay. Your people will be my people and your God my God. Where you die I will die, and there I will be buried. <u>May the Lord deal with me, be it ever so severely</u>, if even death separates you and me."**

At that moment a thought entered Ruthie's mind. Ruth made a powerful statement. She said she would go wherever Naomi went. She even said she would die with her! This meant Ruth must have really loved her mother in law. She was willing to leave her old life behind to care for a widowed woman who really had nothing to offer her at the time. Just going into Bethlehem would be problematic. After all, in Deuteronomy 23:3, it said, "No Ammonite or Moabite or any of their descendants may enter the assembly of the Lord, not even in the tenth generation." This meant Moabites were not allowed to associate with the Israelites. This went all the way back to Lot. The daughters of Lot had gotten him drunk and then had children by him. The Moabites were the ancestors of Lot's daughters. In addition, the Moabites had sent the prophet Baalam to curse Israel. How would Ruth build a life in Bethlehem when she was a Moabite?

The one thing that kept repeating in Ruthie's mind was the word **foreigner.** Ruth would be a foreigner in Bethlehem. Actually, **Ruth was a foreigner amongst the people of God**. She was from a pagan land, living among people who worshipped pagan Gods. If she wanted, she could simply go back to her own land where she could live comfortably amongst her own people. No one would judge her there. What chance did she have in Bethlehem? Regardless, she will not desert her **widowed mother in law.**

Naomi was a **bitter** woman. In Bethlehem, she had everything- a prominent husband, wealth, two sons and a home. Now, she was coming back to this same land (her homeland), empty handed. No husband. No sons. **Without her husband and sons, she had no way to redeem the land she left behind in Bethlehem, Israel**. Back in those days, a woman could not redeem her own land. It had to be a male relative from her family line. Naomi truly felt she had been cursed by God. Naomi must have felt terribly alone. **But, she still had Ruth.**

Ruthie realized how loyal Ruth must have been to continue on the journey, knowing she had nothing to gain, and everything to lose. Ruthie sighed and read the last verse of chapter one aloud.

"So Naomi returned from Moab accompanied by Ruth the Moabite, her daughter-in-law, arriving in Bethlehem *as the barley harvest was beginning*."

"**The barley harvest**!" Ruthie said to herself. She thought of her dream where she was standing in a vast field among tall golden plants. She thought it was wheat, but it must have been **barley**. Not only that, there were two women in the dream- an older and a younger woman. The younger woman clung to the older woman, not wanting to let her go. Eventually, they walked off together, hand in hand.

She knew there was something significant about barley, but she wasn't quite sure what it was yet. She decided to read chapter two, hoping she'd glean something of significance.

She was encouraged when she read the heading for chapter two. The heading read, "**Ruth Meets Boaz in a Grain Field.**" In her dream she had met a prominent man in a grain field. Surely, this was a great sign.

The chapter began by saying Naomi had a relative on her husband's side named Boaz, and he was from the same family line. In the meantime, Ruth set right to work by asking her mother-in-law if she could go into the fields to pick up leftover grain. In those days, the poor, foreigners or widows, were allowed to pick up any leftover grain along the corners of the field. This goes back to Leviticus 23, verse 22 which said, "When you reap the harvest of your land, do not reap to the very edges of your field or gather the gleanings of your harvest. Leave them for the poor and for the foreigner residing among you. I am the Lord your God."

Even though this was stated in the Old Testament, it was not always followed. **Being a foreigner**, Ruth would need to be especially careful about what field she chose to glean in. Naomi told Ruth to go ahead, not knowing which field she would choose.

Ruth *just happens* to choose the field that is owned by Naomi's relative, Boaz. At the time Ruth does not realize this. She works all day with just a short break. Later on, Boaz arrives in the field and notices Ruth. He asks his overseer about her and finds out she is the "foreigner" who came back with Naomi. The overseer comments on Ruth's hard work and diligence. All this impresses Boaz, so he makes Ruth a generous offer. He tells her to **only glean in his field**. In addition he says he will offer her **protection,** as well as fresh **water.**

Ruth is overcome with joy and asks Boaz how she found favor in his eyes. He replies, "<u>I've been told all about what you have done for your mother-in-law</u> since the death of your husband- how you left your father and mother and your homeland and came to live with a people you did not know before. <u>May the Lord repay you</u>

for what you have been done. May you be richly rewarded by the Lord, the God of Israel, under whose wings you have come to take refuge."

Later on Boaz even gives her bread, wine and roasted grain. As if this weren't enough, he lets Ruth gather more sheaves of barley from the fields. By the end of the day she has an ephah of grain to bring to her mother in law, as well as some roasted grain. When Naomi sees the amount of grain Ruth has gleaned she is astonished. Ruth tells her she was in Boaz's field. Naomi answers, "The Lord bless him! He has not stopped showing his kindness to the living and the dead. That man is our close relative; he is one of our **guardian-redeemers**."

As Ruthie studied the story she could see there was something special about Boaz. Most field owners would not take kindly to foreigners, especially Moabites, on their property. Yet, seeing Ruth's work ethic and humble attitude, he takes notice of her. He extends his generosity by offering her **extra time to harvest,** as well as **bread, wine and water**. He watched over her, and gave her a safe place to work. By the end of the chapter it is clear Boaz is more than just a regular field owner- he is a guardian redeemer.

She looked up the word guardian redeemer in her Bible concordance. It said, "A guardian-redeemer was a close relative of high standing that a family member could call upon in times of need, especially when the family's property, family line or possessions were in jeopardy of being lost." According to Leviticus 25:25, it was the guardian redeemer's job to buy back any family land sold during a financial crisis. He could also buy back enslaved family members (relatives). In addition, he could provide an heir for a dead brother in order to continue the family line.

At that moment something like a spark lit up her brain! Boaz represented something more than just "Naomi's relative" in the story. **He was the one who could save both Naomi and Ruth. Even though Naomi had lost her land and standing in the community, Boaz could reinstate it. He could make things right.**

Ruthie knew the key to fully understanding the story must lie within the last two chapters. The book of Ruth only contained four chapters, but it was clear they spoke volumes, and there was an allegory **hidden** *within the text of the story itself.*

She carefully read through chapter three. It began with Naomi hatching a plan to help Ruth win over Boaz. She says, "My daughter, shall I not seek rest for thee, that it may be well with thee? And now is not Boaz of our kindred, with whose maidens thou wast? Behold, he winnoweth barley to night in the threshing floor. Wash thyself therefore, and anoint thee, and put thy raiment upon thee, and get thee down to the floor; but make not thyself known unto the man, until he shall have done eating and drinking. And it shall be, when he lieth down, that thou shalt mark the place where he shall lie, and thou shalt go in, and **uncover his feet**, and lay thee down; and he will tell thee what thou shalt do."

After Ruthie read this part she felt confused. After all, Naomi gave some strange instructions to Ruth. Why would she tell her to uncover Boaz' feet, and then lay down? **All this would happen at the threshing floor where the barley was being winnowed.** She didn't even know what winnow meant.

She looked these things up to get a better understanding. After a little searching she found out winnowing barley was a technique used *to separate the barley grain from its outer coating.* Generally, the threshing floor would be on top of hard, flat dirt. The grain would be threshed first by beating it with a flail, stomping on it, or perhaps having it trampled by animals. This would separate the inedible outer coating of the grain. *Next, came the winnowing.* The barley grain would be thrown into the air so the wind could blow away the chaff (the light outer coating of the grain/seed), while the heavier part of the grain would fall to the ground. This was the valuable part of the grain that was used for food. **The technique of separating the barley grain was rather easy, as long as you had the right kind of wind.**

Next, she looked up why Ruth would lay at Boaz's feet. She found out **it was customary in the Hebrew culture for a servant to lay at** the feet of their master. It was also a method of proposing marriage to a kinsman redeemer.

Ruthie found it fascinating that Ruth lay at Boaz feet, which is something a servant might do. A servant dedicated their life to their master. Their life centered around putting themselves last, and their master first. Just then Ruthie pictured Jesus in her mind, washing the disciples' feet. She was reminded of the verse from John 13, where Jesus says, "For I have given you an example, that ye should do as I have done to you. Verily, verily, I say unto you, **The servant is not greater than his lord**; neither he that is sent greater than he that sent him." She thought about Ruth, and the symbolism of lying at Boaz' feet. Ruth was saying she would serve Boaz humbly. **In return, if Boaz accepted her proposal, he would take care of her and provide everything she would need.**

Ruthie read the last chapter of Ruth. She knew there was hope when she read the heading of chapter four. It said, "Boaz marries Ruth." She read through the details carefully and found out that Boaz wasn't the only family member who could redeem Naomi's land. There was actually another relative who was closer to Naomi, and therefore would have "first dibs" to the land.

Boaz approached Naomi's relative and offered the land to him. Of course, the relative knew he also inherited Naomi if he chose to buy her land. What he didn't know is that he would also inherit Ruth, a **foreigner and Moabitess**, if he went through with the deal. Once Boaz informed him of this detail, he chose to decline. He did not want to smear his reputation by marrying a foreigner- a non-Israelite. **With that, Boaz stepped in and agreed to marry Ruth the foreigner. He would also be responsible for Naomi and her land.** To make the transaction legal, a shoe was exchanged. The relative who would not buy the land **gave his shoe to Boaz.** Thus, **all the community would now know Naomi, her land, and Ruth would belong to Boaz.**

"A shoe?" Ruthie said to herself. She wondered why **shoes and feet** were so significant. She tried to think of all the instances where feet were mentioned in the Bible. She knew Jesus said **our enemies are under his feet.** He said as Christians we have to ability to trample scorpions and snakes because we have Christ in us, and he is more powerful than any kind of evil. As Christians our feet are equipped with the gospel of peace, and we are to spread this gospel throughout the world. **When Jesus returned his feet would set down on the Mount of Olives**. She could see, even with regards to legal transactions, feet were important.

What was really interesting is when she read verses 11 and 12. Boaz had just announced the transaction to all the elders, and to the people of the community standing at the gate. They responded by saying, *"We are witnesses. May the Lord make the woman who is coming into your home like Rachel and Leah, who together build up the family of Israel. May you have standing in Ephrathah, and be famous in Bethlehem. <u>Through the offspring the Lord gives you by this young woman, may your family be like that of Perez, whom Tamar bore to Judah.</u>"*

Through this one legal transaction, Boaz would build a new family. But, this family would include both the Jew (Naomi) and the Gentile (Ruth). **Both would be redeemed**. Only Boaz could do this. No one else could or would. Ruthie realized Boaz represented more than just a character in this story. He represented Jesus! After all, Jesus, the Jewish Savior, came to this world **to his own people**. He came to save and redeem them. **Though not all accepted, this paved the way to redeem the Gentiles- the foreigners like Ruth.** <u>**Through both groups, salvation and redemption would be brought to the entire world.**</u>

Yet, what about the land? Boaz came to redeem not only his people, but the land as well. Naomi's land was redeemed by Boaz. She closed her eyes to think. "Israel!" she shouted. "Naomi must represent Israel!" Why hadn't she seen it before? Naomi had left Bethlehem with her husband during a famine. Jesus, the savior of the world, was born in Bethlehem. Bethlehem meant house of bread and Jesus is referred to as the bread of life. Naomi and her husband and sons had to travel to a foreign land. **Naomi's husband dies, leaving her a widow**.

Ruthie thought about the people of Israel. When Jesus revealed himself as the Savior to his people, he was rejected. Many did not believe and thus did not receive salvation. In essence, **they encountered a <u>famine</u> in their souls. They did not accept this bread of life.** Not long after Jesus' crucifixion, the Jewish people were scattered to foreign lands. Their Temple was destroyed by the Romans, and they **were sent to live among foreigners. Their land is taken over by their enemies. Like Naomi, the Jewish people must have felt bitter and even abandoned by God when their Temple was destroyed and their people kicked out of their own land. Yet, there was hope. There was a "Boaz" waiting in the wings.** Not only that, there was something else they didn't expect. **There were the foreigners- the Gentiles.** Enter Ruth! In the story Ruth stayed with her Jewish mother in law and followed her to a land where she would be seen as an outcast. In those days, the Gentiles did not fit in with the Jews. Knowing this, Ruth still stood with her mother in law, even finding a way to provide her with food (grain). **However, the only way Ruth is able to provide food is through Boaz. He is the owner of the field, and the provider of the grain. Ruthie realized Ruth must represent the Church.** After all, the Christian Church (including all believers in Christ, both Jew and Gentile) are the followers of Jesus. Their job was to spread the gospel to the world. Of course, one of the most difficult groups to share the gospel with would be the Jewish people who did not know Jesus. Even to this day most Jewish people have a difficult time accepting Jesus as Lord. Yet, regardless of their attitude or belief, **it is the Church's job to "go where they go" and "stay where they stay."**

It is true the Jewish people may have become **bitter** because of severe persecution throughout history. Events such as the Inquisition and the Holocaust left many Jewish people homeless, or dead. **But like Naomi, they have returned to their land. Through the sovereignty of God, and the help of the Gentiles, they now have a nation of their own again.** But, the story isn't finished. All the land has not been redeemed. The nation of Israel has not accepted Jesus as their savior on a national level. **Only part of the story has been fulfilled.**

Ruthie suddenly had an epiphany! **Naomi's land was the key to this whole story. Her land was not fully redeemed** *until* <u>*Boaz married Ruth*</u>. Just as Boaz told Naomi's closest relative, "Ruth the Moabite comes with the land." In the story, the transaction was complete after Boaz and the other relative exchanged a shoe. Then, the deal was sealed. Ruth was married to Boaz, and then Naomi's land was officially redeemed. From there, a new family would begin. A merging of the Jew and Gentile would take place through the grace and love of Boaz- Jesus! When Jesus came to earth to claim his Bride (his Ruth), this would set the stage for Israel's land (Naomi's land) to be redeemed. There would be trials and tribulations, but in the end Jesus would step foot on the Mount of Olives as described in Zechariah 14. It says,

"I will gather all the nations to Jerusalem to fight against it…. Half the city will go into exile, but the rest of the people will not be taken from the city. Then, the Lord will go out and fight against these nations, as he fights on a day of battle. **On that day his feet will stand on the Mount of Olives, east of Jerusalem, and the Mount of Olives will be split in two from east to west, forming a great valley**…. On that day there will be neither sunlight or cold, frosty darkness. It will be a unique day- a day known only to the Lord- with no distinction between day and night. When evening comes, there will be light. On that day **living water will flow out of Jerusalem**, half of it east to the Dead Sea and half of it west to the Mediterranean Sea, in summer and in winter. The lord will be king over the whole earth. **On that day, there will be one Lord, and his name the only name."**

Just like Boaz, who took over possession and sovereignty of Naomi's land, so Jesus will take rightful possession of Israel's land- its guardian-redeemer and protector forever. No more wars. No more fighting. No more bitterness in the land. Now, shalom (peace) would reign. Verse 10 and 11 say, "But Jerusalem will be raised up high……. It will be inhabited; never again will it be destroyed. Jerusalem will be secure."

Ruthie realized the last part of the story of Ruth had not come to pass yet. In fact, right now there was great tension in the Middle East over Jerusalem. The countries surrounding Israel, as well as the United Nations, did not want Israel to keep their land, especially Jerusalem. The latest vote in the UN even stated that Israel had no historical tie to the land. How crazy! The Bible, as well as archaeological evidence, proved it belonged to Israel and their history was engrained there. Truly, Naomi (Israel) needed Boaz (Jesus) now! **When would the feet of Jesus seal the deal for good?**

Ruthie read the last verses of Ruth aloud.

"So, Boaz took Ruth, and she was his wife; and when he went in unto her, the Lord gave her conception, and she bore a son. And the women said unto Naomi, Blessed be the Lord, which hath not left thee this day without a kinsman, **that his name may be famous in Israel**. And he shall be unto thee **a restorer of thy life**, and a nourisher of thine old age; **for thy daughter in law, which loveth thee**, which is better to thee than seven sons, **hath born him**. And Naomi took the child and laid it in her bosom…. And the women her neighbours gave it a name, saying, **There is a son born to Naomi; and they called his name Obed: he is the father of Jesse, the father of David**."

And there it was! Ruth and Boaz have a son together and his name is Obed! Obed becomes the father of Jesse, who is the father of King David!

"<u>**So, the union of the Jew (Boaz) and the Gentile (Ruth) formed the line of King David! And from King David is the line of Jesus Christ**</u>!" Ruthie said aloud.

When Ruth went to the field to glean barley, she was in essence working for Boaz (Jesus). She met him at the threshing floor, among the harvest of the field. Ruth, who represented the Church, is still a servant and worker for Boaz. She is to bring the gospel to the world (the field) so Jesus (Boaz) can harvest a crop of believers. **Working together, the Bride can bring the gospel to everyone, but especially God's ancient people the Jews. This "team" of the Bride**

(Church) and Christ is the key to God's end time plan. There was a reward for everyone who participated. **The Bride would be raptured, and Israel's land would be redeemed. Eventually all of Israel would recognize their Savior- Jesus.**

Ruthie read aloud the last four verses that listed the Genealogy of King David.

"Perez was the father of Hezron, Herzron the father of Ram, Ram the father of Amminadab, Amminadab the father of Nahshon, Nahshon the father of Salmon, Salmon the father of Boaz, Boaz the father of Obed, Obed the father of Jesse, and Jesse the father of David."

She stopped and reread it to herself. One line stood out. "Salmon the father of Boaz." She knew the name Salmon. Where did she know it from? She sat quietly and thought.

"Salmon married Rahab!" she practically screamed. "Rahab of Jericho married Salmon! This is amazing! Rahab and her family were the only ones spared when Jericho was destroyed, and she knew the story foreshadowed the rapture. Now, it all made sense. Rahab, a foreigner, marries a Jewish man named Salmon (one of the spies of Jericho). Rahab and Salmon become the parents of Boaz. Boaz, in turn, becomes the kinsman redeemer of Naomi, and husband to Ruth. From these family lines King David is born, and from that line Jesus is born!

The more Ruthie dug into the Bible, the more she saw how God wove everything together. He had a plan all along. **Through the Jewish people, the world would be blessed with a Savior. That Savior would in turn save even the unrighteous- the foreigner.** But, the job wasn't finished. **Now, the foreigner had to help with God's plan to save his ancient people.** Naomi (Israel) became a widow after she lost her husband. In the Bible God reminds us to take care of orphans and widows. They are in great need both financially and emotionally, as well as spiritually. The Church, like Ruth, should be ever willing to extend a life line to Israel (Naomi). When she does, Jesus takes notice, just like Boaz did with Ruth. Boaz didn't grant favor to Ruth because of her looks or prestige. **<u>He granted her favor because of the kindness</u>**

she showed to her mother in law, Naomi (Israel). Boaz invited Ruth to his table to dine not because she was worthy. **Instead, it was because she was humble, hard-working and willing to extend a life line to his family member Naomi. Jesus, our Jewish savior, has never forgotten his people. Because of the Jewish Savior, we are able to dine with Jesus one day in heaven. The Bride will go to the wedding supper at the rapture.**

Life is like a circle. It all comes back around. Jesus was preparing to once again circle his land. He was getting ready to embrace the Bride, then finally embrace Israel and its land. There would be fire, death and tribulation. But, the end result would be a redeemed world. Until then, the Bride needed to "go where Jesus goes, and stay where he stays." He was surely coming back for the Bride, and then for the world. He most certainly would not forget the Jewish people. A day of redemption was coming, and Jesus would complete the transaction.

Author's Notes about the book of Ruth:

It is the eighth book of the Bible. The number eight represents a new beginning.

It contains **four** chapters. Other fours in scripture: On the **fourth** day, God created the sun, moon and stars (Genesis 1:14-19). The purpose of the sun, moon and stars were for day and night, but also for seasons and years. The Hebrew word for seasons is moed, which means "appointed time", or dress rehearsal. God's feasts, such as Passover, Unleavened Bread, First Fruits, Pentecost, Feast of Trumpets (also known as Rosh Hashanah), Day of Atonement (also known as Yom Kippur) and Sukkoth (also known as Feast of Tabernacles) are all celebrated according to the biblical calendar, which relies on the sun and moon. Also, the fourth of the Ten Commandments is to remember the Sabbath, which is a day of rest. The rapture will be like a day of rest for the Bride, and Rosh Hashanah (Feast of Trumpets) is a foreshadowing of this rest.

In the Bible there are **three harvests**

The first harvest is the <u>barley</u> harvest. In biblical times it was called "the first fruit" because it would come up in the field before the other crops. The barley would be offered as a "first fruit" to the Lord and often a red cord would be tied around the bundle or sheave so everyone would know it was the "first fruit to be offered to the Lord. Keep in mind, **Jesus was resurrected on the Feast of First Fruits**. As his followers, we are considered a "first fruit" of the Lord and at the rapture we will be resurrected or taken up as a first fruit, or offering to God. *Most Christians celebrate the resurrection as Easter.*

As described in the Book of Ruth, after the barley is harvested, it must be threshed. This means it must be stomped on and pressed in order for the seed to be released. As followers of Jesus, we must understand we will be pressed and even stomped on, in order to produce good seed. It is the hard times that will make us into great followers. Just as Christ suffered, so too shall we as his followers. The next step in the barley preparation is the winnow it. This step occurs when the outer coating of the seed is blown away by the wind. This separation occurs easily, and without much effort. That's because the barley seed is fairly soft. Back in ancient times you would put the barley seeds on a sheet and hold it up in the wind. This is an illustration of the Bride of Christ at the harvest. Though we will go through hardships in our earthly life (threshing), it doesn't take much to remove the outer coating of the seed. It comes off easily when the wind hits it. **The rapture is represented by the barley harvest. The Bride will be harvested with ease, just as the wind removes the outer coating easily. Ruth will marry Boaz, and the harvest will be taken in. Barley matured quicker than wheat so it was harvested first.**

1 Corinthians 15:20-23- "But now is **Christ risen from the dead, and become the firstfruits of them that slept.** For since by man came death, by man came also the resurrection of the dead. For as in Adam all die, even so in Christ shall all be made alive. **BUT EVERY MAN IN HIS OWN ORDER; CHRIST IN THE**

FIRSTFRUITS; AFTERWARD THEY THAT ARE CHRIST'S AT HIS COMING."

1 Thessalonians 5:9-10- "For God hath not appointed us to wrath, but to obtain salvation by our Lord Jesus Christ.

The next harvest is the <u>wheat harvest</u>. Wheat ripens later than barley so it is harvested later. In the Bible the wheat harvest often represents judgment. This harvest will come after times of tribulation and suffering. Wheat is not as soft as barley. Back in ancient times a special tool had to be used to separate the wheat seed from its outer coating. This tool was called a **tribulum,** and it was necessary because the seed would not separate from its outer coating by just holding it up to the wind. Pressure and force was needed to get the seed out. The people who are harvested at the wheat harvest will go through the tribulation. This could very well be much of Israel since most of the nation does not recognize Jesus as the Messiah. This can also be people who *claimed to be Christians*, but didn't really know Jesus. Think of the story of the Ten Virgins at Midnight in Matthew. Five were ready for the groom, but the other five were not. The ones who were ready represent the barley, while the other five represent the wheat, or perhaps the grapes (which will be described below). When the rapture happens, the wheat harvest won't be ready yet. Later on, however, there will be a time for the people of the wheat harvest to be saved. Unfortunately, death may be the only way to be saved at this time. People will be martyred for their faith, but they will ultimately receive a reward in heaven.

The last harvest is the <u>grape harvest</u>. This will come from "the four corners of the field". As you probably know, in order to get the juice from grapes you have to crush them. The last half of the Tribulation will be rough. It will be the worst time on Earth. In fact the Bible says there will be no time on Earth that can compare to it. **In biblical times, the harvest of grapes was taken in just prior to the Feast of Tabernacles, which occurred in late autumn.** The Feast of Tabernacles is a festival that foreshadows the reign of Christ on Earth during the Millennial Kingdom. **The grape harvest will be**

taken in just before Christ returns to rule and reign on Earth. In Revelation 14 it says the grapes of the earth will be ripe. These grapes were placed in a giant winepress and blood poured out from it. The amount of blood was so voluminous that it created a river of blood 160-200 miles long.

Note about **SHOES**: In the story of Ruth, a SHOE is exchanged as a "receipt" for the land purchase made by Boaz. This purchase redeems Naomi's land. Naomi represents Israel. After the Holocaust happened, the liberating armies found hundreds of thousands of shoes at the concentration camps. By that point the Jews had been forcefully removed from their homes (land) and taken to camps to die. Their shoes were left behind after their deaths. When Jesus returns he will wipe every tear from their eyes, and redeem their land and lives once and for all. His **feet** will step down on the Mount of Olives.

CHAPTER 37
Magnolia

Learning about the story of Ruth brought great comfort to Ruthie. It offered hope and redemption. In a broken world, everyone needed that. As the world fell apart each day, people needed to know hope was around the corner. Boaz (Jesus) was on his way.

"Hey Ruthie! Did you catch the news yet?" Thomas asked.

"No, I haven't had a chance to….." Thomas cut her off and said, "North Korea is causing a lot of problems. Kim Jung Un is threatening to bomb the United States."

"Isn't he always doing that?" she asked.

"Well, he is crazy and he does make lots of threats, but he seems more belligerent than usual. He's already tested five weapons this year and they said he's making plans to test another one on his grandfather's birthday."

"When is his grandfather's birthday?"

"**April 15**," Thomas stated.

"Ugh, isn't that the anniversary of when the *Titanic* sank? **April 15, 1912 the Titanic sank in the North Atlantic.**"

"If you ask me, if they don't get a handle on this guy, we could be the *Titanic*! North Korea is threatening South Korea, Japan, China and even Hawaii. But they seem to be pretty adamant on hitting the United States. Kim Jung Un doesn't like President Trump. Trump is standing up to him and he doesn't like it one bit. I just hope he doesn't go off the deep end. Even if he doesn't hit us with a weapon, he could start a war just by attacking someone else. He could throw the region into chaos. I guess the Middle East isn't the only hotbed in the world."

Ruthie thought about the prospect of North Korea hitting the U.S. with a nuclear weapon. The West Coast was certainly vulnerable, along with Hawaii. But, was Kim Jung Un really capable of pulling off the launch of an intercontinental ballistic missile? Was he capable of something along the lines of Pearl Harbor? Truthfully, she didn't want to think about it. She hoped the rapture would happen before any kind of nuclear strike by any country would occur. But, who really knew. Lots of crazy things could happen before the rapture, or perhaps even on the day the rapture occurred. During the Tribulation all sorts of chaos would break loose. That was a fact. But, thinking about nuclear war before that time was scary.

"Hey Ruthie, could you do me a favor and go to Publix and pick up some coffee? We're all out."

"Yeah, I guess," she said. She needed some groceries anyway. She headed out in the next few minutes.

After getting everything she needed at Publix, she went through the checkout. The cashier was friendlier than usual and seemed to be in the mood to talk. Out of the blue she asked, "Have you heard about what's going on in North Korea?"

Ruthie looked up and answered, "Yes, it's quite a mess isn't it?"

"I'd say so. That guy is going to start a nuclear war."

"Well, I suppose the best thing we can do is pray," she answered, feeling a bit worried.

"Hope you have a great day," the cashier said, handing her a receipt. She thought that was a strange comment considering the cashier had just said North Korea could start a nuclear war. It was just then when Ruthie noticed her nametag. Her name was **Magnolia**. For some reason the name resonated in her mind. She couldn't put her finger on it, but she knew she should remember it. "Magnolia," she whispered to herself.

"That's my name," the cashier said, overhearing her.

Ruthie smiled and walked out the door.

When she got home she checked the mail. The mailbox only had one piece of mail, which was unusual. Most times there were three to ten pieces. She grabbed it and went inside. She put the letter on the counter, but didn't open it right away. Suddenly, she heard the doorbell. It was her neighbor.

"I brought you some **magnolia** blooms," her neighbor said, handing Ruthie a jar with several blooms inside.

"Thank you," she said. "They smell wonderful." She brought the blooms in and put them on the table.

"*Magnolia blooms*," she thought. The cashier's name was *Magnolia*. She wasn't really sure if it meant anything. She shrugged her shoulders and grabbed the one piece of mail she'd retrieved from the mailbox. When she opened it, her jaw dropped. It was a beautiful card with a picture of a **magnolia** flower on it. It even had the word *Magnolia* etched across the front. "*Magnolia again?*" she wondered. There HAD to be something to this.

Quickly she searched the word magnolia on her phone. She found several entries. The first one said, "The magnolia is often associated with the South, and southern hospitality. It is also often used in weddings in the Bride's bouquet, especially in the southern United States." She looked at the other entry. It said, **"The national flower of North Korea is the** *magnolia sieboldii*. It is a beautiful, delicate white flower, which symbolizes peace in North Korea."

Ruthie took a moment to catch her breath. North Korea? **The magnolia is the national flower of North Korea? She also thought of the solar eclipse.** After all, the eclipse was leaving through the southern part of the United States- Charleston. This city was often called the heart of the south, and the first battle of the Civil War happened there. **Did magnolia point to Civil War or division? Or, did it point to North Korea? Maybe it was both?**

She really didn't know. All she knew is that serious prayer was on her list of important things to do. To be honest, she just wanted to hide.

She wanted to go to the Lord's Hiding Place in heaven. She wanted the rapture to come. Things were heating up in America, and throughout the world. Just like Jesus said in Matthew, the world would be in trouble before he came. But, how much more trouble did we have to endure before he returned for the Bride?

Author's note: The solar eclipse is hitting our land on **August 21, 2017.** On **August 21, 1959,** Hawaii became the 50th US state. Kim Jung Un has repeatedly threatened Hawaii. If North Korea were to be successful in its attempt to create an intercontinental ballistic missile, it could reach Hawaii in approximately twenty minutes. I'm not saying North Korea is going to attack on August 21, or any other time. I'm just saying it may be a good idea to pray for the safety of Hawaii, and any nations near North Korea.

The magnolia is also traditionally used in **southern weddings** here in the United States. The solar eclipse is exiting from Charleston, South Carolina- the heart of the South. And of course, with the word wedding I always think of the wedding supper of the lamb- the marriage of the Bride to the Groom, Jesus.

CHAPTER 38

The Gate

Ruthie heard a knock at the door. She wasn't expecting anyone so she looked through the peephole. It was her neighbor Sam. She opened it.

"Hey there! I was just wondering if you knew your gate is damaged?"

"What do you mean damaged?"

"Actually, the whole gate is on the ground. The hinges were torn off and the gate is just lying flat. It's the one on the **east side** of your yard."

"Oh no! How did this happen?"

"Well, didn't you hear the wind howling last night? I could feel my windows rattling."

"I guess I'm a sound sleeper," she said.

"Let me know if you need some help fixing it. I'd be glad to help."

"Thanks," she said. She decided to take a look at the gate for herself. She walked around the east side of her house and there it was, lying on the ground. Thankfully, the gate itself was still in one piece. Other than having a few hinges torn off, there didn't seem to be any damage to the gate itself. She picked it up and placed it against the house. As she did this, she had a vision. It was so strong she almost lost her balance. She saw a bright light encircling an arched gate. She could see the outline of a figure, but the brightness shrouded the face. She saw a silhouette of doves in the background. A word pervaded her mind and senses- **shalom**, which meant complete and perfect peace.

"Ruthie? Are you ok?"

She could hear a voice speaking to her. She looked up and saw her neighbor Vivian standing in front of her.

"Did you trip on something?" she asked.

Ruthie realized she was on the ground near the propped up gate.

"I don't remember. I propped up the gate and then…"

"Well, maybe you should go inside and rest. Perhaps you're just tired," Vivian said, helping her up.

"Maybe you're right. Thanks Vivian."

Ruthie went inside, still feeling dizzy from the experience. She knew there was something important about the gate. Not only had she seen a glorious gate in her vision, but she was standing by the gate in her own yard- *a gate that had fallen down*. She knew the gate in her yard was located on the **East side** of her house and her neighbor Sam had even mentioned it. *That was it!* She would look up **EASTERN GATE** and see what she found.

She dashed inside to the computer and typed in **EASTERN GATE**. She found many articles. One particular article was titled, **The Eastern Gate and the Return of Jesus**. She decided to read through this one. She wanted to know what the Eastern gate had to do with the return of Jesus.

The article began by explaining the events of Matthew 21. The chapter's title was **Jesus Comes to Jerusalem as King**. It depicted Jesus' Triumphal entry into Jerusalem during Passover. According to Christian theology, it is likely Jesus would have passed through a gate on Palm Sunday. He rode on a humble donkey, while palm branches were laid before him. This would occur just before his crucifixion, where this king would lay down his life for a sinful world- the Savior of both the Jews and the Gentiles. Matthew 21 says Jesus approached Jerusalem by way of the Mount of Olives. **This means Jesus would come from the East.** Since the **eastern gate** would be the closest access to the Temple, **it is likely this would have been the gate he entered through.** Also, each year, on Yom Kippur, the High Priest would make atonement for the sins of the nation of Israel (*this was before*

Jesus). On this one day, the Priest would choose a "scapegoat" to place the sins of Israel upon. A **scarlet cord** would be tied around the scapegoat, and **it would be led through the Eastern Gate** and into the Kidron Valley. Next, it would be led through the Mount of Olives, and finally into the Judean wilderness. When Jesus came to save the world, he literally became the "scapegoat". He took on the sins of the world (and Israel) when he died on the cross. He was even led outside the city to be crucified. The similarities were uncanny.

As Ruthie learned about the **Eastern gate** she was fascinated by the symbolism. **Even the scarlet cord on the scapegoat- it reminded her of the scarlet cord Rahab hung from the window of her home**. This scarlet cord was a sign to spare Rahab's household. Jesus was the only one who could spare us from destruction. His blood, like the scarlet cord, would save us from our sins, and from the destruction that would come upon the world.

Ruthie wondered what became of the Eastern gate. Was it still around? After all, the Romans destroyed the temple back in 70 A.D. Could there be any part of this gate left?

After more research she found out the Eastern gate did exist today, though it had been rebuilt several times since its initial destruction. The Eastern Wall, along with the other city walls, was rebuilt by Suleiman the Magnificent, a ruler of the Ottoman (Turkish) Empire. His wanted to restore the city's architecture, and the current walls that stand today in the Old City of Jerusalem, are the walls he restored. Even though Suleiman restored the gates, for some reason, **he decided to seal the Eastern gate in 1517.** Some sources say he did this because he heard about the Jewish prophecy that the Messiah would enter the Temple through the Eastern gate. By sealing the gate, he thought he would prevent Messiah's entry. In addition, Suleiman had a graveyard built in front of the gate because he knew a Jewish priest would not defile himself by walking through the grounds of a cemetery. **The cemetery and the <u>sealed</u> Eastern wall are still in place today.** However, the walls now standing hold an interesting secret most people are unaware of.

In 1969, an archaeologist named Jim Flemming *accidently* discovered the archway of a gate *lying below the present-day eastern gate.* As Flemming describes it, he was walking along the Eastern gate when all of a sudden the ground gave way and he fell into a large tomb. It had rained the day before, making the ground moist and unstable. When he fell, he was surrounded by bones, but he also saw the top of a gate approximately eight feet below the surface. Though Flemming only saw part of the archway, scholars have said this is **most likely the archway of the original Eastern gate, dating back to Nehemiah's time.** Nehemiah was the prophet who God instructed to rebuild Jerusalem's walls after the Israelites' captivity in Babylon. Nehemiah gathered people together to work on the rebuilding of the walls, so the Temple and city could be fully restored. Other scholars believe the wall could date back to King Herod, who expanded the Second Temple of Jerusalem. No matter which view is followed, it is obvious the gate below predates the gate above. But, the sealed gate above ground holds significance because of some verses from the book of Ezekiel.

In Ezekiel 43 it says, "Afterward he **brought me to the gate, even the gate that looketh toward the east: And, behold, the glory of the God of Israel came from the way of the east**: and his voice was like the noise of many waters: and the earth shined with his glory. And it was according to the appearance of the vision which I saw... and I fell upon my face. And the glory of the Lord came into the house **by the way of the gate whose prospect is toward the east.**"

By reading that passage, it was clear the glory of the Lord entered the Temple *through the* **East gate.** If this was the same Eastern gate Jesus had entered through to get to the Temple, it was surely a sacred gate. Both the glory of the Father and the Son entered through it.

Ruthie read verse 7-9 of Ezekiel 43. "And he said to me, Son of man, **the place of my throne**, and the **place of the soles of my feet, where I will dwell in the midst of the children of Israel forever**, and my holy name, shall the house of Israel no more defile, neither they, nor their kings, by their whoredom, nor by the carcases of their kings in their high places. In their setting of their threshold by my thresholds, and their post by my posts, and the wall between me and them….. Now let them put away their whoredom, and the carcases of their kings, far from me, and I will dwell in the midst of them forever."

There was something startling and awesome about these verses in Ezekiel. **Firstly, God's throne dwelled in Jerusalem. His very feet stood there. Also, God said he would dwell in the midst of the children of Israel forever. Not for a little while. Not for a few thousand years- <u>forever</u>**. From the verses it was clear the nation of Israel had their troubles, but nonetheless, God would remain faithful.

Ruthie immediately pictured Jesus, with his feet planted on the Mount of Olives, which would be near the Eastern gate. This would occur when he came to claim the land for his people- both Jew and Gentile. She pictured Boaz in the story of Ruth, holding the sandal that was exchanged for Naomi's land. Naomi represented Israel and her life foreshadowed the redemption of Israel's land.

Right now the land of Israel was not fully redeemed. **The Eastern gate was still blocked**. The Muslim Dome of the Rock currently stood where the Jewish Temple used to stand. **The only part of the Jewish Temple left was the Western Wall, also known as the Wailing Wall.** This wall was all that remained after the Romans destroyed the Temple. Though Israeli forces had broken through the Lion's Gate on **June 7, 1967** and reclaimed the rest of Jerusalem for Israel, the land was still under dispute. Israel was seen as an "occupier" rather than a nation who owned the deed to the land. According to God, the deed was signed by him, and the use of it belonged to Israel. Genesis 12:7 says, "The Lord appeared to Abram and said, "Unto your descendants will I give this land." In Genesis 13:15 God said, "For all the land which thou seest, to thee will I give it, **and to thy seed <u>forever</u>**." In verse 17, God says, "Get up and walk throughout the land, for I give it to you."

In 1967, when Israel regained **East Jerusalem**, the Jewish people gained access to the Western Wall. On that day the shofar was sounded as Israeli soldiers broke through the Lion's Gate, and entered into the

Old City of Jerusalem. Though the Western Wall wasn't the entire Temple, it was a piece. Since then, millions of Jews have flocked to Jerusalem to pray there. They were denied access to the Temple site because currently a mosque stands in the former location, as well as the Dome of the Rock. The Western Wall is the one sacred space left for the Jews. Many Jewish believers hoped the entire Temple would be rebuilt one day, but to do so right now would start a "holy war" with the Muslims.

Ruthie knew **Jesus would be back to fully redeem the land.** The rapture of the church could take place first. Like the story of Ruth, the Bride (Ruth and Boaz) would be married. Then, a period of time known as the Tribulation would begin. During this time, Israel would be persecuted and tested in ways they never imagined. A peace treaty would occur, but it would be false. After the peace treaty was broken by the Anti-Christ, their very lives would be in jeopardy. Many scholars believed the Anti-Christ would allow the Third Temple to be rebuilt. That would mean the Dome of the Rock would be destroyed in order to make way for the Jewish Temple. **But even if the Temple was rebuilt, Jesus would be the only one to save the nation of Israel, and the world. He is the true temple. He fulfilled the law and the Sabbath when he came to earth the first time. When he returned he would even fulfill the promises tied to the land.** <u>**He is the Boaz the world waits for.**</u>

Would Jesus return through the Eastern Gate? After he stepped foot on the Mount of Olives, would he break through the sealed East gate and enter the Temple? Many Rabbis and Jewish scholars believed the Messiah would do just that. Ezekiel 44 says, "Then he brought me back the way of the gate of the outward sanctuary which looketh **toward the east**; **and it was shut**. Then said the Lord unto me; 'This gate shall be shut, it shall not be opened, and no man shall enter in by it; because the Lord, the God of Israel, hath entered in by it, therefore it shall be shut.'" These verses clearly showed the Eastern gate would be shut. Perhaps the reason the gate was shut is because only Jesus can enter it. The Lord's glory entered through it during the days of the Temple. Jesus may have entered it when he came into Jerusalem at Passover. And when Jesus returned, he could once again enter the gate that **only he could open.** What a fascinating thought. Ezekiel was given a vision of the Millennial Temple thousands of years ago, but someday the world would see the real deal- the Temple in the flesh- Jesus. It was no accident that **East Jerusalem was placed back in Israel's hands on June 7, 1967. This one event allowed Israel access to their holy capital, eastern gate and all.**

CHAPTER 39
Western Wall

◊

Ruthie had researched enough for now so she decided to take some time to relax. She got a cup of coffee and turned on the T.V. As she flipped through the stations something caught her attention. She stopped on UNN news. The words ***Donald Trump makes historic*** visit were scrolling along the bottom of the screen. As she watched she could see **Donald trump was visiting the Western Wall in Jerusalem.** She sat up straight, almost spilling her coffee.

The newscaster said, "**The President of the United States is the first sitting U.S. President to visit the Western Wall since the reunification of Jerusalem during the Six Day War in 1967. The President is wearing a traditional yarmulke, and he is pressing his right hand against the wall.**"

Ruthie felt a jolt of electricity run through her arm. The visit was definitely historic. For a U.S. President to visit the Western Wall was monumental. Even though Israel claimed East Jerusalem in the 1967 war, the world refused to fully recognize it- even the United States. Israel's sovereignty over the land was in dispute. This area of East Jerusalem was prophetic in nature as it would include places such as the Temple Mount, the Mount of Olives and even the Eastern Gate. **All these places were tied to the return of Jesus Christ.**

Interestingly enough, President Trump was visiting the wall a day before the celebration of Jerusalem Day. This year, June 7, 2017, would mark **50 years** since Jerusalem was reunified during the Six Day War in 1967. **Fifty in the Bible marked a Jubilee year, and was tied to the land**. During the Jubilee, the land would be returned to the rightful owner. Israel was certainly the rightful owner according to the Bible, as it was an everlasting covenant. In Genesis 22 Abraham was tested by God. He was sent to Mount Moriah to sacrifice his only son Isaac. Because of Abraham's obedience and faithfulness, he was rewarded. God provided a ram in place of Isaac, and then the Lord said, "I swear by myself, declares the Lord, that because you have done this and have not withheld your son, your only son, **I will surely bless you and make your descendants as numerous as the stars in the sky and as the sand on the seashore. Your descendants will take possession of the cities of their enemies, and through your offspring <u>all nations on earth will surely be blessed</u>**, because you have obeyed me." This promise of God took place at the very spot *now known as the Dome of the Rock*. This area is now under Muslim control, and many areas are off limits to Jewish people. The Dome of the Rock was once the site of the Second Jewish Temple. But, this Temple was destroyed by the Romans in 70 A.D. Since then, the area has been in the hands of many different rulers, but unfortunately even now, with Jerusalem under Israeli control, Jewish believers are not given the freedom to worship at this site. Though Jews and non-Muslims can visit the Temple Mount, prayers there are forbidden. In addition, people are sometimes turned away for reasons such as looking "too Jewish", or wearing a kippah. It is under strict control of the Muslim authorities. Jewish people or non- Muslims are not permitted to enter the Dome of the Rock. **But, the Western Wall was a different story. This one wall, measuring approximately 50 meters long and 20 meters high, is all the Jews have left of their Temple history, and their tie to that part of the land.**

Ruthie hoped the gesture of visiting the Western Wall meant the President would fully support Israel. This didn't mean making any "deals" with regards to the land. In the past, U.S. Presidents had tried to exchange land for peace. There were no deals to be made. **The land**

belonged to Israel period. Truthfully, Israel did not have possession of all the land God gave them. This full land redemption would come to fruition in the future. How it would unfold wasn't completely clear. Would the United States remain faithful to Israel? Or, would pressure result in trying to form some sort of deal with the Palestinians? The President would meet with Mahmoud Abbas, leader of the Palestinian Authority, on Jerusalem Day in Bethlehem. Back in the days of the story of Ruth, Bethlehem belonged to Israel. Boaz lived in Bethlehem, and it was the birthplace of Jesus Christ. Now it was in Palestinian hands- a part of the West Bank territory. How sad was that? The birthplace of Jesus was being controlled and occupied by terrorists, whose main goal was to wipe Jews off the face of the earth. This same land was redeemed for Naomi by Boaz in the book of Ruth. Boaz represented Jesus, and Naomi represented Israel. Had it been redeemed yet? No- but the key player in this story is Ruth. Ruth and Boaz were married and this brought forth the redemption of the land. The Bride- **the rapture**- the marriage supper of the Lamb- **perhaps this was the key to the redemption of the land**. Boaz (Jesus) would take back Bethlehem, and all the areas of Israel that had been lost long ago. They would be restored- <u>**not through a peace deal made by man. The deal would be brokered by God- his terms- his land**</u>! The story continued to unfold, piece by piece. All Ruthie could do was pray for the President and leaders to make the right decision. She needed to pray for God's will to be done.

As Ruthie continued watching footage of the President at the Western Wall, she thought about other walls in history. The book of Nehemiah told the story of how God changed the heart of a King, in order for the walls of Jerusalem to be rebuilt. The King wasn't even Jewish. But, through the supernatural influence of God, this King allowed Nehemiah to rally his people and rebuild the walls of the city.

She couldn't help but think of America. Wall Street in New York City came to mind. It was known as the financial heart of America. **Some say America was built through Wall Street**. Many people didn't realize **Wall Street got its name from the wall that used to stand in that spot**. Built by the Dutch settlers of New York, it was used to prevent invasion. This area later became the street where an Empire began- New York- the Empire State.

During the 9-11 attacks New York City came to a standstill. Thousands were dead. The Twin Towers collapsed, and along with it, the hearts of the nation. **Yet, a wall remained** from the Twin Towers- the World Trade Center. Known as the **"slurry wall"**, it was a 62 by 64 foot section of the World Trade Center's foundation wall. This wall withstood the fire and trauma of that fateful day. If this wall would have collapsed on 9-11, the destruction would have been much more extensive. The subway system would have been flooded, drowning thousands of people. **But, the wall stood**. It now stands in the 9-11 Museum as a reminder of the tragedy, and a symbol of American resolve. Ruthie had studied the history of the World Trade Center Twin Towers and she found it interesting, or perhaps spooky, that **the construction for the Towers began in 1967, the same year Israel unified Jerusalem.** *New ground was being broken in America, while old land was being claimed in Israel.*

Those walls weren't the only ones that came to mind. There was also the idea of building a border wall between the United States and Mexico. President Trump promised the country he would find a way to build it. The wall would protect America and its borders. But, in the long run, would a man -made wall save America? Man-made walls could be torn down, but the protection provided by Jesus was supernatural, and could withstand all attacks. **Perhaps what America really needed was a Savior who could break down walls- just like the ones in Jericho.** When Jesus returned for his Bride a wall would certainly break, and his faithful followers would pass through it into heaven.

Ruthie knew the **Western Wall in Israel represented just a portion of the kingdom God would restore through his son Jesus.** The Apostle Paul wrote in Ephesians 2:14, "For he is our peace, who hath made both one, and hath **broken down the <u>middle wall</u> of partition between us**." Jesus is the one who would break down the barrier- the wall. **We could build a border wall around our country to protect us from foreign invaders. But, in the end, only Jesus would protect us. Only he could save us from ourselves and the world. He is our peace.**

Ruthie turned off the T.V. and decided to pray. This prayer would be for two nations- Israel and the United States. She prayed for a great miracle, much like the wall of water that formed when the Israelites passed through the Jordan River. That's the kind of miracle both nations would need.

Author's note: When the Israelites escaped from Egypt, God showed them a great miracle. He parted the Red Sea and this is considered one of the greatest miracles listed in the Bible. Do you see the **WALL in the verse below?**

"And the children of Israel went into the midst of the sea upon the dry ground: and the waters were a **WALL** unto them on their right hand, and on their left." Exodus 14:22

We don't need a man-made wall in our nation- we need a supernatural one!

What else does the Bible say about **WALLS?**

Ezekiel 38 and 39 describes a time when Israel will be surrounded on all sides by enemies. It describes the war of Gog and Magog. In chapter 38, verse 10 it says, "This is what the sovereign Lord says: On that day thoughts will come into your mind and you will devise an evil scheme. You will say, "I will invade a land of UNWALLED villages; I will attack a peaceful and unsuspecting people- **ALL OF THEM LIVING WITHOUT WALLS AND WITHOUT GATES AND BARS."**

By reading these verses we know that at some point the nation of Israel will be living in peace and safety- *hence, no walls.* But, we also know from reading Bible prophecy that this is a **FALSE PEACE.** That false peace will shatter when the Anti-Christ breaks the peace deal and suddenly decides to invade Israel. The only one who can save Israel will be Jesus Christ himself. He is the one who broke down the dividing wall when he came to Earth the first time. When he returns the second time, ALL WALLS WILL COME TUMBLING DOWN. This is how the WHOLE WORLD, including Israel, will know Jesus is King of Kings. Just like Jericho- the walls will fall and evil will be destroyed.

East **Jerusalem** was claimed and the entire city reunified in **1967**- Jericho was circled one time for **6** days, and then **7** times on the 7th day. Do you see the **6 and 7? 67** Now, think about this- Jesus will redeem Israel's land when he returns to **Jerusalem** one day. The **6 represents man**. The **7 represents God.** When the Israelites circled Jericho 6 times and then 7 it signified man following God's plan. All of Jerusalem was back in Israel's hands on **6-7-67 (June 7, 1967)**. Man achieving victory through God's plan (6,7). Jericho foreshadows God's plan to redeem man in Jerusalem.

CHAPTER 40

Blink

Ruthie knew she couldn't keep everything she'd learned to herself. After all, Jesus wanted everyone to be spared. He was ready and willing to bring all sheep into the fold. The only problem is that many sheep had wandered away. Some didn't even know who the shepherd was. Others had just fallen asleep. It was very likely many would miss the wedding feast with the Groom. Just like the story of the Ten Virgins, some would be ready with their oil, while the others would be caught off guard. Jesus would come like a thief, but only to those who hadn't embraced him.

She decided she would compile all the information she'd learned about the rapture. From lightning and barley, to feasts and trumpets, all of it would be part of the story. She started looking through the notes she'd saved on her phone. There were hundreds of pages to sort through. She didn't realize she'd documented so many bits and pieces of information. She even had pictures of the signs God had shown her, such as the hawk with its prey, and even the street signs that were "signs." It was all there. Surely, she could write a book using all this information.

She grabbed the laptop and started a new document. She wrote the title, **BLINK**. That was the perfect title! The rapture would happen in the blink of an eye. She had her notes and pictures ready to go. What was missing? "Duh!" she said to herself. "My Bible. I need my Bible." How could she forget the single most important piece of information? She ran to her room and grabbed it. This Bible was the one she'd received from her mother a few years ago. It was special because it belonged to her grandmother- Mary Ann McQueen. The Bible was given to her grandmother in 1967. It was dated**, May 27, 1967**. The person who'd given it to her grandmother had just visited the Temple Mount in Jerusalem. A piece of Jerusalem olive wood lay inside the Bible, a souvenir from the trip. The date written in the Bible was significant because in just nine days, the Six Day War would begin on June 5, 1967. Two days later, on June 7, 1967, Israel would claim East Jerusalem, unifying God's capital. Yes, this is the Bible she would use to write her book. Jerusalem was the key to Jesus' return.

    She set the Bible on the table next to her, not realizing it was close to the edge. As it fell from the table she scrambled to grab it. Luckily, she caught it with both hands. It had landed in her hands fully open, with one side in her left hand, and one side in the right. She was about to close it, but felt like she should take a quick look. As she scanned the Bible she saw the pages had landed in the book of Luke. Investigating further, she noticed a heading under Luke 15: ***The Prodigal Son***. She hadn't read the story in a long time. Why not give it a read? Maybe there was a reason the Bible had "fallen" to that exact spot.

    She read through the story, carefully pouring over each word. Each sentence leapt off the page, piercing her emotions as she remembered the lesson of grace and redemption contained in the story. A father has two sons. The youngest son asked the Father to give him his inheritance. The father honored the son's request and gave him the money/valuables of his inheritance. The older son faithfully stayed behind with the father. The younger son journeyed to a far country, leaving his father and brother behind. He squandered his inheritance on sinful pleasures. Soon, a famine hit the land where he lived and he became destitute. It got so bad he had to eat with the pigs. (This meant he was literally at the bottom of the pit because in the Jewish culture pigs were considered unclean.) The son soon realized what a horrible mistake he'd made. He said to himself, "How many hired servants of my father have bread enough to spare, and I perish with hunger."

He decided there was one thing he had to do, though it wouldn't be easy. **He would go back to his father and apologize. He did not expect his father to treat him as his son, but rather a servant. After all he'd done, he did not believe he deserved to be in his father's good graces. He felt like he should be punished.**

He ventured back to his father's land. Though he didn't know this, **his father saw him coming from a long way off. His father was not filled with anger or resentment. Instead his heart swelled with compassion and he grabbed his son and kissed him**. The son couldn't believe it. He said, "Father, I have sinned against heaven, and in thy sight, and am no more worthy to be called thy son." To this the father said, "Bring forth the best robe, and put it on him; and put a ring on his hand, and shoes on his feet: And bring hither the fatted calf, and kill it; and let us eat, and be merry: For this my son was dead, and is alive again; he was lost, and is found. And they began to make merry."

The "lost son" was overjoyed. How could his father show such forgiveness? After everything he'd done, he prepared a feast, and gave him a robe and a ring? How could this be?

The older son soon came in **from the field.** He could hear music and saw people dancing. When he realized all of it was in honor of his sinful brother, he was angry. He wouldn't join the celebration. His father came out and urged him to come inside and be joyful. But the brother said, "Lo, these many years do I serve thee, neither transgressed I at any time thy commandment: and yet thou never gavest me a kid (fatted calf), that I might make merry with my friends: But as soon as this thy son was come, which hath devoured thy living with the harlots, thou hast killed for him the fatted calf." Basically, the eldest son was saying the whole time he served his father and obeyed him, while the other son was off living a despicable, sinful life. Yet all the while, the father never threw a party for him for his faithfulness. But now he was giving the royal treatment to his treacherous son, who squandered his money and life. Resentment began to boil up in the older son.

The father looked at his eldest son and said, "Son, thou art ever with me, and all that I have is thine... we should make merry, and be glad: for this thy brother was dead, and is alive again; and was lost, and is found."

The father reminded the oldest son that what he had always belonged to him, and he always had the privilege to enjoy it. But, **the youngest son was like a dead person**. He was gone forever and they would never have the joy of seeing his face. **But now he had returned alive** and that was something to savor and celebrate. <u>**It was like life from the dead!**</u> It was a miracle- and a second chance at life.

The story ends with the father declaring these simple words: "Thy brother was dead, and is alive again; and was lost, and is found." It doesn't say whether the older brother decides to celebrate, and receive his brother back with open arms. We are not told whether he forgoes his resentment and instead embraces his newly returned brother. But, most hope for that reconciliation and redemption.

The story touched Ruthie's heart. She could see how it could apply to so many situations in life. The father in the story showed mercy, grace and compassion. There was no malice, contempt or anger. **The only thing the father was interested in <u>was the redemption of his son, and his family.</u>**

"Wait," thought Ruthie. "There's something familiar about this." She had to think for a few minutes. Then, she knew. **"Israel,"** she said. **The Prodigal Son was Israel**. It was all too clear. The youngest son represented the nation of Israel, when they became unfaithful to God. Like the youngest son, Israel had strayed far from their father. They were scattered to faraway lands where they often forgot their heritage, and their father's commandments. They became mingled in with a sinful world. Things went from bad to worse when Israel rejected their chosen Messiah, Jesus Christ. Though not all rejected Jesus, the vast majority turned away. The Holy Temple was destroyed in 70 A.D. and the Jewish people were once again scattered throughout the world. They literally had no homeland. Their inheritance had been squandered. The land they'd once possessed was in the hands of their enemies. As the years passed, their fate continued to darken as a vile, cruel regime tried to wipe them from the earth. But, there was hope.

Their inheritance seemed forever lost when their father came to the rescue. Like the father in the prodigal son, God could see his son (Israel) before he ever came back. God was already working on the plan to help his lost son. The nation of Israel entered their land once again and it became official on May 14, 1948. As Israel received her land again (though only part), God the father rejoiced. This left the younger son wondering, "How can this be?"

Ruthie thought about the older son. If the younger son represented Israel, then who did the oldest son represent? "**The Church**!" she said. "But, not everyone in the church -only those who did not understand the father's plan for redemption-only those who didn't understand the prophecies and promises in the Bible. If a Christian studied God's word and had the Holy Spirit, they would know it was always in God's heart (a father's heart) to redeem his child- Israel. Those Christians who tried to replace Israel in some way were not following the heart of Christ, or God. Instead, they were resentful, and could not see past their anger. **The true Church and followers of Christ would love Israel before and after they returned to their father.** They would not bear grudges against their only brother. The Jew and the Gentile were brothers, and on the same branch of the olive tree. Christ had come to save all people, but he came as a Jewish Savior. Yes, it is true the Christians had been with Jesus since his resurrection, for thousands of years. The nation of Israel, like the lost younger brother, had continually rejected Jesus (unless they were Messianic Jews.) The older brother (the Church) had stood by Jesus and proclaimed his name to the world. Yet, it was the Jewish disciples who began this fire in their hearts. Now, it was time to start that fire in Israel's heart. The ember was burning. Had the full fire begun? Not yet. But God was still standing far off, watching his other son- Israel- knowing he was on his way back. The full redemption and celebration had not come yet. But, it was on the horizon. The fatted calf, the robe and ring were ready. The question was, would the Church be ready?

Ruthie had a great love for Israel and she knew she would be overjoyed when THE ENTIRE NATION returned to God by recognizing his son, Jesus Christ, as their savior. How could she be upset by that? She knew one day she, along with the raptured and resurrected Church, would come back with Jesus. He would fight for the nation of Israel. The victory would be swift. The emotions high. The reunion grand.

Zechariah 12, verse 10 says, **"And I will pour upon the house of David, and upon the inhabitants of Jerusalem, the spirit of grace and of supplications: and they shall look upon me, whom they have pierced, and they shall mourn for him, as one mourneth for his only son, and shall be in bitterness for him, as one that is in bitterness for his firstborn."**

When Israel realizes who Jesus is, they will be overcome with emotion, knowing they had rejected him for so long. Like the prodigal son, they will be ever repentant toward their father, feeling unworthy of his forgiveness. But God, the father, will not condemn them and he will not pour out anger upon them- **instead he will pour out grace**. A party will ensue, and the entire family of God will celebrate- Jew and Gentile, as part of God's family.

Even the poignant line spoken by the father is prophetic. He says his son "was dead, but now alive. Lost but now found." Though time is viewed differently in God's eyes, it doesn't mean he does not long for the return of his son- Israel. Here on earth much time has passed and God's people have labored, waiting for the return of God's son- Jesus. Jesus himself was once dead, but alive again after the resurrection. Imagine how God the father felt when his own son was alive again. Now, think about Israel. **How will God feel when the nation of Israel is alive again?** The blood of the son he sent to the earth to save them will now run through the veins of his ancient people. Just as spoken of in Ezekiel 39. **"Neither will I hide my face any more from them: for I** have poured out my spirit upon the house of Israel, saith the Lord God." In Jeremiah 32 God says, **"They will be my people, and I will be their God….. I will make an everlasting covenant with them: I will never stop doing good to them, and I will inspire them to fear me, so that they will never turn away from me. I will rejoice in doing them good and will assuredly plant them in this land with all my heart and soul."** Though Israel went the way of the prodigal son, God has never given up on them. How could you give up on your child? A child is forever in the heart of his father. Why would Israel be any different?

A verse in Malachi popped into Ruthie's mind as she thought about the redemption of Israel, and all of God's people. The spread of the gospel, the rapture, the Tribulation- all these things were needed to bring the family of God to that place of redemption. But this verse seemed so appropriate and prophetic at the moment. **"And he shall turn the heart of the fathers to the children, and the heart of the children to their fathers, lest I come and smite the earth with a curse."** This verse was referring to what Christ would do. **He would turn the heart of the fathers back to their children, and the hearts of the children back to their fathers.** Bible scholars have argued the exact meaning of these verses, written in the book of Malachi, the last prophet sent by God to the Israelites. It would be 400 years before God would speak to the world again after Malachi. He would send his next message through his son Jesus, who would be born in Bethlehem, in a manger.

When Ruthie read the verse she thought of the Jews and the Gentiles- the chosen and the foreigner. Perhaps *the fathers* in the verse were the Patriarchs of the nation of Israel. Abraham, Isaac and Jacob were the ones who were chosen by God to bring forth a great nation- a nation that would be a blessing to the whole world. It would be through this line that Jesus the Savior would come. But, Jesus came to bring **all people together through his blood- both Jew and Gentile**. But, the "fathers" (Jewish spiritual leaders) did not accept this gift. Though the Gentiles accepted Christ, the larger part of the Jewish nation would not, and thus would not accept that the Gentiles were also children of God. The Gentiles were newer of course, having just been grafted in through Christ's death and resurrection. **The dividing wall had been destroyed by the Resurrection of Jesus- the curtain torn- all had access to the Savior.** Now, there were not only Patriarchs, but also children. These new Gentile children were charged with spreading the gospel throughout the world. No longer was God *only the God of the Israelites*. Now even the former pagans (Gentiles) would share in his favor and supernatural calling. Yet, these same Gentiles would now overlook their "fathers". These fathers were the patriarchs who showed the Holy God (Yahweh) to the world. Many Gentile kingdoms would look upon the "fathers" as enemies. Persecutions would ensue and battles would be waged. **All the while, neither group could see they were family- fathers and children**. The Patriarchs' offspring were the Gentiles. These fathers had "adoptive children."

Jesus would be the key. He was the link. At his return, the fathers' eyes would open. They would see all along their children were beside them- the Gentiles who followed Christ. The children who didn't see their parents before would now know their identity. They would realize their parents were the patriarchs. Many people in God's kingdom already knew this secret. It had been revealed to them through scripture and the Holy Spirit. They knew it was coming. The timing was the only mystery left. The last words of God in Malachi are "lest I smite the earth with a curse." God would surely fulfill his word or the earth would be cursed. The only answer in a lost world was reconciliation.

Ruthie had a job in the plan for reconciliation, as well as all Christians. It was all a matter of listening to the Holy Spirit. The plan would move forward with God's will in control. And one day, things would change in the **BLINK** of an eye. She couldn't wait for that day to come.

THE END......................Well, it's the end of this story. There's no end if you stick with Jesus…only eternity!

"Those who trust in the Lord are like Mount Zion, which cannot be shaken but endures forever." *Psalm 125:1*

THE PLEDGE OF ALLEGIANCE

THE PLEDGE OF ALLEGIANCE DIDN'T always have the words UNDER GOD in it. When it was first written by Rear Admiral George Balch, and then revised by Francis Bellamy in 1887, it did not contain the words UNDER GOD yet. Louis Albert Bowman was the first person to begin the process of adding UNDER GOD to the pledge. Mr. Bowman was a lawyer from Illinois, and he was a chaplain of the Illinois Society of the Sons of the American Revolution. On Abraham Lincoln's birthday in 1948, Bowman recited the Pledge of Allegiance, with the words UNDER GOD added to it. He said his inspiration came from Abraham Lincoln's Gettysburg Address. In the transcript of Lincoln's Address he is quoted as saying "the nation shall under God, have a new birth of freedom." After Mr. Bowman's example other organizations began adding the words UNDER GOD to the pledge. By 1952, a letter was sent to President Truman with the suggestion of officially adding UNDER GOD to the pledge. Other requests were made but none succeeded until February 7, 1954 when the idea was brought up to **President Eisenhower.** He was sitting in **Abraham Lincoln's pew** in the New York Avenue Presbyterian Church. Eisenhower heard a very powerful speech where the minister referred to **Lincoln's Gettysburg Address** speech. The minister made it clear that the reason the United States was "set apart" from other nations was because It was UNDER GOD. This made a huge impact on Eisenhower. After this sermon, Eisenhower set to work the next day! He was determined to have

UNDER GOD added to the Pledge officially. At his urging, a bill was eventually introduced to Congress and then signed into law. What date was it? **JUNE 14, 1954.** One of the first groups to adopt this resolution was the **ILLINOIS AMERICAN LEGION.**

Now here is what I find interesting: First of all, I didn't know the UNDER GOD *wasn't added until later*! Secondly, I see that it was initiated by Louis Albert Bowman from ILLINOIS! Do you remember that the intersection of BOTH solar eclipses is in ILLINOIS! Also, the date ***UNDER GOD*** was officially added is JUNE 14. Remember, our first flag was adopted on JUNE 14, 1777, and our President's birthday is JUNE 14 (Donald Trump). Also Anne Frank's first official diary entry was on JUNE 14, 1942.

Here's what I'm thinking. Two solar eclipses are intersecting in **Illinois-** the place where the UNDER GOD addition to the pledge was birthed. Also, note that adding the phrase UNDER GOD to the Pledge came from Abraham Lincoln's Gettysburg Address speech. We know Lincoln made this speech after the bloodiest battle on U.S. soil during the Civil War (November 19, 1863). Lincoln gave a heartfelt speech, where he called out to a nation in crisis. The first solar eclipse hitting U.S. soil enters through Lincoln County, Oregon and hits our land at **10:15** a.m. on August 21, 2017. Abraham Lincoln was shot at **10:15** p.m. on Good Friday, April 14, 1865. The last city the solar eclipse shadow touches is Charleston, South Carolina (not far from Ft. Sumter- this is where the first shot of the Civil War occurred).

We know the Civil War almost ripped our country apart, but we did have leaders like Lincoln who reminded us to stand with God- to pledge our allegiance to God. Lincoln also knew the importance of standing with the Jewish people. In my other book, *What are the Chances*, I go into detail about this. June 14 is Anne Frank's first official diary entry. She is perhaps the most well- known face of the Holocaust. June 14 is our flag day- our allegiance to God day! What better way to stand with God than to stand with his people- the nation of Israel! Our land will be blessed if we stand by God's land- Israel, and **Jerusalem** in particular. Did you know Abraham Lincoln had a wish to visit Jerusalem? Did you know it was Lincoln who wrote the Proclamation for Thanksgiving to become a National Holiday? I know most of us sit around and eat turkey, but did you know it was actually *intended* as a day to give thanks to God???????

And what about President Eisenhower? He's the one who pushed to get UNDER GOD added to the Pledge. Did you know it was Eisenhower who made sure the horrors of the Holocaust were documented? He made sure pictures were taken, and evidence gathered that would be **IRREFUTABLE PROOF** the Holocaust happened. He wrote a letter on **APRIL 15, 1945**, where he addresses the atrocities committed in the concentration camps and stresses the importance of documentation. Eisenhower was also Supreme Commander of the Allied Forces in Europe. He planned the successful invasion of North Africa, France and Germany (on the Western Front). Do you really think this kind of providence just happens?

America needs to wake up and turn back to the Lord. I'm not talking about everyone going to church and going through the motions! I'm talking about making a commitment to the Lord, and to Israel. Israel is demonized in the media for simply defending its land. They are under constant attacks by terrorists and they are surrounded by nations who hate them. They need our support and prayers!

Unfortunately, we are a divided nation right now. The eclipse paths are quite telling. They split the country in half. My question is: which half are you on? God's half, or the other one?

APRIL 15, 1912, TITANIC SANK IN THE NORTH ATLANTIC. ABRAHAM LINCOLN DIED ON APRIL 15, 1865. EISENHOWER WROTE THE LETTER APRIL 15, 1945. Connect the dots America! Stand with God and stand with Israel !!!

THE MYSTERY OF 13

You probably think 13 is an unlucky number don't you? Many people cringe at the prospect of Friday the 13th, or even being born on the 13th. The number has such a bad reputation that many elevators do not have a 13th floor. This superstition goes all the way back to the Last Supper. Jesus was seated will all 12 of his disciples for the Passover meal, making the total number 13. One of those disciples, Judas, would betray Jesus for 30 pieces of silver. This act of betrayal would forever be associated with the number 13. Though technically, we know Jesus planned on going to the cross to die for our sins, which is a very lucky thing for us. He even knew Judas would be the one to betray him.

Here are some other ways to look at **13:**

Let's look at the number 13 closely. Firstly, it is a **PRIME** number. That means its only factors are one and itself. I like to think of prime numbers as God's numbers because God is the great I AM. There is no other God but him. He is, he was and he's the one to come. God divided by one is God! Nothing else could divide into him because he's the only one! God's factors are GOD and ONE- and he is the only one true God! Other numbers that share prime status are three and seven. Three points to the Trinity- God the father, God the Son and the Holy Spirit. Seven points to God, and the days of his creation. Seven is his divine number, and has always been considered a lucky number. The number seven is used over 700 times in the Bible, with three not far behind. Both are prime numbers.

The number **67 is prime**. 1967 is when Israel unified the city of Jerusalem during the Six Days War- this was divinely orchestrated. Only the one true PRIME God could do it. **6+7 =13**

13 times 2 equals 26. 26 is the sum of the Hebrew characters that are the name of YAHWEH- This is the Hebrew name for God. Hebrew letters have numerical values, so this is how the calculation is done.

13 times 3 equals 39- Jesus received 39 lashings while going to the cross. "By his stripes, we are healed." Jesus was placed on the cross at the 3rd hour, and died at the 9th. This may seem unlucky, but how could it be? Jesus overcame death and rose from the dead. He defeated Satan because he went to the cross. Because of this, we are able to inherit eternal life.

13 times 4 is 52- It took Nehemiah, and the Jewish builders, 52 days to rebuild the walls of Jerusalem. This was part of the restoration of the Temple of God, and divinely orchestrated.

13 times 7 is 91- Psalm 91 is one of the most supernatural prayers of protection in the Bible. This one Psalm covers all your bases as far as protection from accidents, sickness, evil plots, and even damage to your dwelling. You name it, it's in there. I have used it myself for protection. This Psalm reminds us that we are under God's **SHADOW,** and wings of protection. Makes me think of the shadow of the solar eclipse- we have nothing to fear if we are under God's shadow of protection to begin with. The judgment is not for those who dwell in the shadow of the Most High, or under his wings.

I have written previously about **13 being the NUMBER OF JERICHO**. The Israelites marched around the city one time for six days, and then 7 times on the seventh day, for a total of 13 circles. When they followed these set instructions, they were victorious and inherited their first piece of the Promised Land. Six is the number of man, and 7 is the number of God. 13= 6 +7. God and man working together= redemption

13 is also tied to the United States because of the **13 colonies**, and **13 stripes on our flag.**

13 is also tied to the Jewish calendar. The Jewish calendar uses a 12 month lunar calendar, with an extra month occasionally added- which would equal 13. A year with 13 months is called a PREGNANT YEAR. If it is a pregnant year, the month of ADAR will now become two months, known as ADAR 1 and ADAR 2. The concept of a pregnant year is known as a LEAP year to most of us since we follow a Gregorian calendar. But, on our calendar we add an extra day in February at a leap year. The Hebrew calendar adds a whole month, and this is done seven times every nineteen years.

So, in this case, **13 refers to a pregnant year.** When Jesus talked about the signs that would come before his return, he said there would be birth pains such as wars, earthquakes and famines (Matthew 24). In pregnancy, labor pains come first. Slowly, then more rapidly as time goes on. Eventually a baby is born.

Revelation 12 speaks about a sign that appears in heaven- A woman is clothed with the sun, with the moon under her feet, and a crown of twelve stars on her head. **She is pregnant** and cries out in pain because she is about to give birth. This pregnant woman represents Israel, and the stars on her head are the 12 tribes of Israel. The woman eventually gives birth, but a dragon (Satan) tries to kill her son after he is born. This refers to the birth of Jesus, who came from one of the 12 tribes of Israel- the tribe of Judah. Satan tried to destroy Jesus. He was unsuccessful because Jesus overcame death, and then he ascended into heaven. Satan continues in his plot to destroy the Jewish people. It says in Revelation 12 that the woman (Israel) eventually has to flee for 1,260 days from the dragon (this is known as the Tribulation). God, however, has a place prepared to shelter his people during this time of Tribulation. Satan (Anti -Christ) are not happy and become enraged at the woman (Israel), and are determined to destroy her. But scripture says God will ultimately protect Israel.

Israel has to flee the Antichrist for 1,260 days, which is 42 months- 7 X 6 = 42, and **7+6= 13**

Revelation 3:10 (3 plus 10 equals 13) it says, "Since you have kept my command to endure patiently, I will also keep you from the hour of trial that is going to come on the whole world to test the inhabitants of the earth." This verse is saying the people of God will be taken to a safe place while the tribulation begins on earth- a hidden place. Like Jericho, the Bride will be spared as Rahab was. (Remember 13 is the number of Jericho)

Revelation 13 describes the BEAST or the Antichrist. Verse 18 says the number of the Beast is 666. Perhaps this one is a bit unlucky! This would happen during the Tribulation. The burning and destruction of Jericho can be visualized in this scenario- the Antichrist is trying to destroy all that God has set up. Lucky for us, Jesus always wins!

In **Genesis 13** the Lord says he is giving Abraham and his descendants **all the land of Israel, and tells him his descendants will be as numerous as the dust. We know Jesus will return and redeem the land, the world and Israel.**

Matthew 25:13 - from the STORY OF THE TEN VIRGINS- **VERSE 13**- "Therefore keep watch, because you do not know the day or the hour." (Describing the return of Christ for the Bride- if you watch, you will be ready!!!!)

AMAZING INFORMATION ABOUT THE 2017, 2024 TOTAL SOLAR ECLIPSES

As mentioned in chapter 32 called **Eclipse,** I list quite a few facts about the eclipses, but here I will talk in depth about the INTERSECTION of the eclipses.

To review, there will be a solar eclipse on **August 21, 2017.** Seven years later, there will be an eclipse on **April 8, 2024.** If the paths are laid out on a map, the two paths will intersect to form an X. The point of intersection lands in a village called **Makanda, Illinois.** Makanda is located in Jackson County, Illinois, and it is part of the Carbondale Micropolitan Area. There is a road in Makanda called Salem Road which is close to the intersection point at Cedar Lake. Salem is short for Jerusalem. In Psalm 76:2 it says, "His tent is in Salem, his dwelling place in Zion." This means the Lord's dwelling place is in Jerusalem. Cedar Lake is within the intersection. (This is about five miles from the Shawnee National Forest.) Cedar comes from the word Qatar which means to smudge. The wood of a cedar tree was used for *purification rituals in many cultures*. Cedar wood was **used to build both Temples in Jerusalem**. The Hebrew word for a cedar tree is erez. This means to be firm. **A cedar has very firm, tenacious roots.** These details make me wonder if the Lord is saying our roots in him *as a nation* need to be firm, and we need to be *firm about supporting Israel's land- especially Jerusalem!*

Makanda is a small place, with a little over 500 residents. A small village will witness a GIGANTIC event twice! Yet, think about tiny

Israel. It's the size of New Jersey, yet it's where the most important event on Earth took place- Jesus' death and resurrection. And one day, tiny Jerusalem is where the next most important event will take place- the return of Jesus Christ to Earth! So maybe little, tiny Makanda is a reminder that it's not the size of the city or town, it's the importance of that place to God that matters! God always uses the small things to show his gigantic glory!

Mount Jefferson- On **March 30, 1806**, Lewis and Clark first laid eyes on this amazing mountain. They named it Mount Jefferson, after the President who funded their expedition to map the new land acquired during the Louisiana Purchase- **the purchase OF LAND that doubled the size of America in one transaction.** THE AUGUST 21, 2017 eclipse shadow **will pass over Mt. Jefferson** at around 10:21 a.m., traveling at 2,245 mph. It will be a prime spot to watch! Why? Because it has a high elevation, and limited light pollution. Quite the historical spot if you ask me!

The intersection of both eclipses happen **in Jackson County**. The county was named after Andrew Jackson, who was the **7th president of the United States**. He was the founder of the Democratic party. He is also known for his part in the relocation of Native Americans, and the Trail of Tears. **He forcibly removed the Indians from their land!** *Little word of advice- America should never encourage the removal of Israeli citizens from their land! The land belongs to Israel.*

The point of greatest duration will be just southeast of Carbondale, Illinois. *(Keep in mind Makanda is part of the Carbondale area)*. It will last for 2 minutes and 42 seconds. What does the name Carbondale mean? Let's see, we have CARBON and DALE. Let's start with CARBON. **Carbon is found in all living things. It is essential to all life.** In science you are familiar with the carbon cycle, and how humans/plants use oxygen and carbon for respiration and photosynthesis. Carbon is unique because of its ability to form very strong bonds. Carbon is part of what's called hydrocarbons- these are extracted naturally as fossil fuels such as oil, coal and natural gas. So, carbon is the building block for fuel. Right now the whole climate change argument is based off the idea of carbon emissions. There's also the use of carbon dating, which scientists use to date fossils and artifacts, etc.

A diamond is CARBON. Diamonds are the hardest known natural mineral, as shown by the Mohs scale for minerals.

Now, how about DALE? **A Dale is a broad valley**. Synonyms are a gorge, basin or ravine.

So, if we put the meanings together (carbon and dale), think of "building block of life" and valley. This makes me wonder if the solar eclipses are a way of getting people to understand that GOD is the building block of life!!! He always has been. Our country is certainly in a valley right now with the division in our land. If we don't get ourselves straight we may stay in the valley, or worse yet, end up in a gorge!!! Diamonds are carbon, and they are precious indeed. One of the world's most precious diamonds, also known as the Koh-i-Noor, is valued at over a billion dollars. Diamonds are also found in wedding rings. But, the most valuable thing in our lives should be Jesus Christ. He is our groom. No diamond in the world can equal what he can give to us. I always think of the end of the movie *Titanic*. Rose has the most valuable diamond in the world (the heart of the ocean) and she throws it into the sea. It's just an earthly possession after all. Eternity is our greatest jewel.

There are two major roadways that intersect Carbondale- Illinois **Route 13** and **U.S. Route 51**. Route 13 is considered the oldest highway in Illinois. Route 13 caught my attention because it makes me think of the United States- 13 stripes on our flag, 13 colonies, etc. I also think of Jericho, with a total of 13 circles made around the city. And guess what Jericho means? Moon! In a solar eclipse the sun's light is blocked by the moon.

Route 51- Let's look what Psalm 51 says- "Have mercy on me, O'God. Blot out my transgressions, wash away my iniquity and cleanse me from my sin………. May it please you to prosper Zion (Israel)- to **build up the WALLS of Jerusalem.** Then you will delight in the sacrifices of the righteous." (verses 1-2 and 18-19)

Carbondale's nickname used to be the "Star of Egypt." This reminds me of the miracle of Passover, when the Israelites left Egypt, escaping captivity and bondage. Maybe these eclipses are a reminder that our redemption is coming soon- one day we will escape the sinful bonds of this earth and go to the hidden place in heaven! Only the Lord knows, but it is important to keep up with the signs here on Earth. But we must repent as a nation, and as individuals, just like it says in Psalm 51- **and we should support Israel. NO LAND DEALS. JERUSALEM BELONGS TO ISRAEL. IT IS GOD'S LAND!**

Passover occurs on **March 30** at sundown in 2018. Abraham Lincoln's Proclamation for a National Day of Fasting and Repentance occurred **on March 30, 1863** (during the Civil War). It's time to fast and repent America. Did you know that Lincoln was shot during Passover? He died on a Saturday- the Jewish Sabbath.

THE LORD'S FEAST KNOWN AS SHAVUOT

There are seven Feasts of the Lord listed in the Bible. Shavuot is the fourth feast. The word itself refers to "seven weeks." God commanded this feast be celebrated every year. It occurred exactly seven weeks after the first barley harvest. The Feast of First Fruits would have occurred seven weeks prior and the first crop of barley would have already been presented. It was waved before the altar as an offering to God. The Feast of First Fruits points to the resurrection of Jesus, as he was the first fruit out of the ground. He actually rose from the dead on the Feast of First Fruits. **Barley ripens <u>before the other crops</u> that have been planted, so this is what would have been presented at First Fruits**.

Seven weeks later, at Shavuot, the other crops would be ready for harvesting. During Shavuot the first fruits of these other crops would be offered. This could include wheat, grapes, figs, pomegranates, olives and dates. As soon as the farmer/caretaker of the field saw one of these crops ripening, **he would tie a red string around an offering of it, and then place this in a silver and gold basket**. If you were poor, you would use a simple wicker basket instead. Once all the "first fruits" were in the basket, you would make your way to Jerusalem. If you lived far away, it could take several days. People from all over would make the commanded journey with their offerings.

Once the people arrived in Jerusalem, it was time to present their offerings. This time, instead of waving barley before the altar, **the first** crop of the wheat harvest was given to the Temple priest. The priests would then bake the wheat into **two loaves of leavened bread**. These loaves would be waved in front of the altar.

Now here's where it gets interesting, and somewhat of a <u>foreshadowing of end times</u>. We know at the end times there will be a seven year tribulation. Many scholars (including myself) believe a rapture of the church will take place just before this seven year tribulation begins. If you look at the pattern of Shavuot, keep in mind **it all has to do with the harvest**. God uses the harvest as a way to illustrate not only how crops are grown and gathered, but also <u>how people are grown and gathered.</u>

We see that **First Fruits occurs before Shavuot**. It coincides with the same exact day Christ rose from the dead to be the First Fruit of the ground. Prior to Christ's resurrection, the Jews had already been "practicing this feast" by bringing the first crop of barley as an offering during this same festival every year. Remember, **the barley ripened first**. Barley is a softer grain, and its grain is easily separated in the wind. At this time the wheat would not have been ready. Knowing this, we can understand a pattern for the rapture. When Christ raptures the Bride, those who are dead will have their physical bodies resurrected (just as Christ was resurrected). Those of us still alive on earth will be "caught up", or snatched away- bodies and all- with Christ. **We are the barley crop. The rapture is the harvest of the soft grain- those who readily accepted Christ and fully received him. Their hearts were ready and freely given to him.**

Now, let's see what happens at Shavuot. This occurs SEVEN WEEKS after FIRST FRUITS (think about "resurrection"). In the Bible we see that WEEKS can stand for years. For instance, in Daniel 9:27 it says, "And he shall confirm the covenant with many for one week". This one week is actually referring to seven years. During Shavuot *the other crops are ready for harvesting*. One crop in particular is brought to the temple to be waved before the altar- it is baked into two loaves of leavened bread. **This is the wheat harvest. The wheat**

crop is very different from the barley crop because the grain is not easily separated. A tribulum is needed to separate the hard outer coating of the wheat. The tribulum was an ancient sledge used for threshing the wheat. It contained teeth of iron or stone. Unlike the barley, which is separated easily in the wind, the grain of the wheat had to be put through lots of pressure and "trauma" to get the grain seed out. After the rapture occurs, the Tribulation will begin. This will be a time of great "trauma" and pressure on the inhabitants of the earth. People still here will be "squeezed" and tested to unimaginable levels. Much of the nation of Israel will go through this terrible time and it is often referred to as *The Time of Jacob's Trouble.* **Jacob is another name for Israel.** It is this time of testing that will bring Israel to their Messiah. Matthew 24: 21 says, "For then there will be great distress, unequaled from the beginning of the world until now- and never to be equaled again. If those days had not been cut short, no one would survive." Jeremiah 30:7 says "Alas! For that day is great, so that none is like it: it is even the time of Jacob's trouble; but he shall be saved out of it."

Once the "wheat" is put through the tribulum, the grain will be released, and then those first fruits will be presented to God as an offering. It's interesting to note that two loaves of leavened bread were presented at the Temple. Once the barley harvest has occurred, and then the wheat, there will be two harvests of people. The two loaves could very well represent the Jews and Gentiles as the "one new man". Two distinct groups converging. The leaven being in the bread points to sin, which is within each group, but they are both saved through Christ's first fruit offering at the cross, and resurrection.

Some scholars think this "wheat" harvest could occur someday on the **Day of Atonement**, also known as Yom Kippur, because this feast has not been fulfilled yet. This is the day when the high priest would make atonement for Israel. Jesus, as we know, became the high priest and atoned for our sins at the cross. *But, the nation of Israel is blinded to this.* So, sometime in the future, during the Tribulation, the nation of

Israel will be made aware of this amazing fact, and they will finally recognize Jesus as their Atonement. Again, it would make sense that this occur on the Day of Atonement- obviously we do not know what year or hour because the Day of Atonement occurs *every year* according to the biblical calendar. But, God has not forgotten his feasts and only he knows which year it would be when and if it happens on Yom Kippur/ Day of Atonement.

Shavuot has been fulfilled by Jesus. The Holy Spirit descended upon his followers, fifty days after he resurrected. The spirit of Jesus would dwell inside his followers on the day we know as **Pentecost** (another name for Shavuot), and they would labor in the fields for him. Jesus himself said his spirit would come to his followers **fifty days after his resurrection**. Once received, they could sow seed by sharing the gospel, and harvest new believers through testimony of the gospel. The Feast of Shavuot had been practiced as a dress rehearsal for years and years. This was all in anticipation of when Jesus would literally **become the feast by sending his holy spirit**. From that point on, a great harvest began for both Gentile and Jewish believers. This harvest will continue up until Christ returns.

Shavuot, though fulfilled, *foreshadows future events*. It is a feast fully understood in the book of Ruth, *where the marriage of Ruth to Boaz foreshadows the marriage of Jesus (Boaz) to his Bride (Ruth).*

Ruth, who represents the Church, works in the fields of Boaz. This illustrates how the Church works the fields (the world) for Jesus. Just as Boaz watched over Ruth in the fields, and gave her grain and water, so Christ does the same for his followers. He is the bread of life, and he is the living water. He offers protection from the enemies of darkness.

Ruth represents the barley harvest, while Naomi represents the wheat harvest. Ruth was not bitter, even though she was a widow. She diligently worked the fields and took care of her mother in law selflessly. She was a true servant. All these things are expected from the Church up until the day of the first harvest (barley)- the rapture.

Once Ruth (the church) marries Boaz (Jesus), then the stage is set for the redemption of Naomi (Israel). This harvest of Israel will only take place after the barley harvest- the Church. Then, after the Tribulation, Boaz (Jesus) will redeem the land, and all of Israel.

Revelation About Psalm 91

The Words Of Psalm 91

He that dwelleth in the **secret place** of the most High shall abide under the **shadow** of the Almighty. I will say of the Lord, **He is my refuge and my fortress**: my God in him I will trust. Surely he shall deliver thee from the snare of the fowler, and from the noisome pestilence. He shall cover thee with his feathers, and **under his wings shalt thou trust**: his truth shall be thy shield and buckler. Thou shalt not be afraid for the terror by night; nor the arrow that flieth by day: Nor the pestilence that walketh in darkness; nor the destruction that wasteth at noonday. A thousand shall fall by their side, and ten thousand at thy right hand; but it shall not come nigh thee. Only with thine eyes shalt thou behold and see the reward of the wicked. Because thou hast made the Lord, which is my refuge, even the most High, thy habitation; there shall be no evil befall thee, neither shall any plague come near thy dwelling. For he shall give his angels charge over thee, to keep thee in all they ways. They shall bear thee up in their hands lest thou dash thy foot against a stone. Thou shall tread upon the lion and adder (snake): the young lion and the dragon shall thou trample under feet. Because he hath set his love upon me, therefore will I deliver him: I will set him on high, because he hath known my name. He shall call upon me, and I will answer him: I will be with him in trouble; I will deliver him, and honor him. With long life will I satisfy him, and show him my salvation."

Psalm 91 is a wonderful prayer of protection. Within the text are promises that God will give his angels charge over us when we are in trouble. He will protect us from disease, and the constant attacks of the enemy (his arrows). He will surround our homes with a hedge of protection- **a wall of protection**. By the authority of our Savior, we can trample the enemy with our feet. God will hear our voice the moment we cry out and he will rescue us from doom and destruction. **Like a shadow covers the ground, the Lord covers us fully.** Like a mama duck guarding her chicks, he places us close to himself, **embracing** us close to his heart.

I love seeing how God uses numbers in the Bible. As I look at Psalm 91- the number 91, there are a few things that come to mind. We see the number 9 and 1. Nine points to redemption and divine completeness. Jesus died on the cross at the **ninth hour**. Also the number nine is made up of three threes and we know three points to the Trinity. On the cross, Jesus of course, was the picture of the Trinity- father, son and Holy spirit (which would be given fifty days later at Pentecost).

Yom Kippur, or the Day of Atonement, is one of God's Holy Feast days. In Israel it was the day the High Priest made atonement for the entire nation of Israel. **Erev Yom Kippur (Eve before Yom Kippur)** begins at sunset on the **9th** day of the Hebrew month of Tishrei. The destruction of God's Holy Temple took place on the **9th** of the Hebrew month of AV. (this happened twice- once with the Babylonians, and then with the Romans) In addition, the first recorded Gentile to convert *to Christianity* was Cornelius. It was the **9th** hour of the day when Cornelius received a vision from an angel regarding Peter. This message was given to Peter, who came and preached the gospel to Cornelius and his followers. Cornelius was the first uncircumcised Gentile to be baptized, thus beginning a new chapter in the kingdom of God.

Now for the One in Psalm 91: The number one points to God- the Alpha and the Omega- the one true and holy God. One also points to the ONE sacrifice made by Jesus Christ on the cross for ALL people. This one sacrifice would give all forgiveness.

When I look at the number 91, and Psalm 91, I see it points to One Holy God who sent his ONE and only son, to be our redemption. Because of this, we are completely protected and free from the curses of Satan and the Law. Psalm 91 lays out the curses we are protected from because of Christ's blood spilled on the cross.

Looking at this Psalm, I see more than what meets the eye. When I see the "secret shelter" of the Most High, I think of the secret place God has prepared for us in heaven. On the day of the rapture, we will be taken to the hidden place on the Father's property, sheltered from the pestilences that will plague the earth during the Tribulation. At that time the earth will be full of darkness and evil. Only the Bride will be spared, and covered under the wings of God/Jesus. I think about Flight 1549 and how every person on that flight was spared death. They rushed to take refuge on the wings of the plane. At the rapture, the **wings** of Jesus will lift us up, and out of the darkness to come. No longer will we be prey to the attacks of the enemy. No longer will disease affect our bodies. Those who truly know the name of Jesus will be lifted up on high, and will be remembered.

On Rosh Hashanah, also known as the ***Feast of Trumpets and the Hidden Day***, the Jewish people believe God will remember them by writing their names in the Book of Life. This is their deliverance and promise. The shofar is a reminder for God to remember them, and for their own souls to remember God. As Christians, we should see this special day as a reminder that one day We WILL BE TAKEN TO THE SHELTER OF THE MOST HIGH. Since we have called upon the name of the Lord, we will be remembered and delivered from the most terrifying time on Earth. Yes, there are arguments about whether the rapture will take place before the Tribulation, or mid-way through it. I personally believe it will be like a Jewish wedding, and the Bride will be sheltered from the 7 years of Tribulation. But, we shall see. Will it happen on Rosh Hashanah? Well, the feast itself does show amazing symbolism that points to the return of Jesus. Also, we know Christ will fulfill all the feasts at some point. What year we do not know. What exact hour we do not know. Rosh Hashanah is also called the **Feast of which the day and the hour was not known,** due to the fact that the moon was "hidden". It was a new moon and it was hard to detect when the first sliver of the moon would be seen. This is why it is a two day feast. So, I do believe God gives us some hints. He's not going to pinpoint **an exact** time and date and hour because it is his plan, and his discretion. He is sovereign and we are not. Also keep in mind that Rosh Hashanah happens every year. Kind of like Christmas- it happens every year. So, even if we said Jesus is returning on Rosh Hashanah, we wouldn't know what year.

So, what do we do? I say **always be ready**! But, why not pay special attention to his feasts. He created them for a reason. Everything God does has purpose and meaning. **The Bible says his feasts are dress rehearsals.** If you are in a play or performance don't you attend the dress rehearsal so you can be ready? The same is true of God and his holy feasts. Why not practice so when the real thing comes you are more than ready? If anything you will be fascinated at how the feasts teach important lessons about Jesus, and the way we should live.

For now I say **LOOK UP**, for your redemption draws near. If you are a prodigal son, LOOK UP. If you were always with Jesus, LOOK UP. There's hope found in one name –JESUS CHRIST!

Interesting numerical pattern of 91: 9 pointing to redemption/divine completion, and one pointing to Yahweh, the one Holy God who is sovereign

Looking at 91, I see 19 as well, which is 91 backwards. I think about Exodus **19:4** which says, "You yourself have seen what I did to Egypt, and how I carried you on eagles' wings and brought you to myself." This refers to when God delivered the Israelites from slavery. The plague of the firstborn struck all those households without the blood of the lamb on their doorposts. This foreshadowed the idea that we would be saved by the blood of Jesus on the cross. Just like the Israelites would be brought out on eagles' wings, the people of God (referred to as eagles), would be delivered from spiritual bondage by Jesus. When the rapture occurs, the people of God will again be like eagles, and brought to God.

Then, there's Revelation **19:11** (See the 19, and also 91, as well as 911). This verse says, "I saw heaven standing open and there before me was a white horse, whose rider is called Faithful and True. With justice he judges and wages war." This verse comes to fruition when Jesus returns to redeem the earth. He comes back with the people of God and wipes out all evil. The land and people are redeemed. He is the only one who could do it. The Jew and Gentile are the "one new man."

Additionally, I see Romans- chapters **9 through 11**. These chapters lay out the plan of salvation for the Jew and Gentile. Chapter 11 in particular describes how the Jew and Gentile are on the same branch of the olive tree.

Other 91's or 19 (the reverse order of 91)

In 1948, after Israel's war of independence, the Western Wall became occupied by Jordan. From that point on, Jews could no longer visit or pray there. They were barred from the site. But, **19 years later**, on June 7, 1967, Israel claimed East Jerusalem, and thus the Western Wall became their possession once more. In addition, the Western Wall is believed to be founded in **19 BCE-** part of Herod the Great's Temple Extension project.

Psalm 91 talks about dwelling in the shadow of God. When we are under his shadow, we are protected. A shadow can be likened to shade. When we are in the shade, we are protected from the heat of the Sun. Back when there was no air conditioning, having shade was very important, and even a luxury.

A solar eclipse occurs when the shadow of the moon blocks the Sun's light. A shadow will fall upon the land as the eclipse travels along its path. In the Bible, and in most cultures, solar eclipses (shadows) falling upon the land have never been considered "good." They are usually interpreted as God's judgment. But, think of it like this- if we dwell in the shadow of God to begin with, we need not be concerned with the shadow crossing our land. The shadow is a reminder to *turn back* to the one who created it- God!

In the Greek (according to Strong's Concordance) the word eclipse is translated as **ekleipo**. It means to leave out, leave off or to cease. It can also mean to fail, pass by, die off or come to an end. It can mean to fall short. For example, it can mean for the Sun's light to fail, or cease.

So, essentially we can say that a solar eclipse (like the ones coming in 2017 and 2024) can possibly mean that the Lord is inviting us into his shadow. But, there are certain things that must cease, or stop. Certain national sins must end, and the nation must turn back to the One Holy God who is in charge of the universe. The nation is called to stand on the promises of God, and with his plan for the world, and for Israel. Those places in the shadow's path (the eclipse's shadow) are a reminder that God is sovereign, and he is the only one who can shelter us from what's to come. We can repent and turn to him- or we can fail. We can fall short. It's up to us. If the nation does not turn as a whole, God does not forsake his followers. We are still in his shadow, and under his wings. And we will be called to be the light to the nations. The light in the darkness. The light amongst the shadow.

NOTES ABOUT TRUMPETS

Take a look at Numbers 10, also given the heading: **The Silver Trumpets**

"And the Lord spake to Moses saying, Make thee two trumpets of silver; of a whole piece shalt you make them: that thou mayest use them for <u>the calling of the assembly,</u> and for the <u>journeying of the camps</u>. And when they shall blow with them, all the assembly shall assemble themselves to thee at the door of the tabernacle of the congregation. And when they shall blow but with one trumpet, then the <u>princes</u>, which are heads of the thousands of Israel, shall <u>gather themselves unto thee</u>. When ye blow an alarm, then the camps that lie on the east parts shall go forward. When ye <u>blow an alarm</u> the second time, then the camps that lie on the south side shall take their journey: they shall <u>blow an alarm</u> for their journeys. But when the congregation <u>is to be gathered together</u>, ye shall blow, but ye shall not sound an alarm. And the sons of Aaron, the priests, shall blow with the trumpets; **and they shall be to you for an ordinance forever throughout your generations. And if ye go to war in your land against the enemy that oppresseth you, then ye shall blow an alarm with the trumpets; and ye shall be remembered before the Lord your God, and ye shall be saved from your enemies.** Also, in the day of your gladness, and in your solemn days, and in the beginnings of your months, ye shall blow with the trumpets over your burnt offerings, and over the sacrifice of your peace offerings; that they may be to you a memorial before your God: I am the Lord your God." NUMBERS 10, VERSES 1-10

As you read the verses it is clear the trumpets had a wide array of purposes. They were used **to sound alarms and gather the assembly.** They were used when offerings were given, and when the people needed supernatural deliverance from their enemies. Notice in the verses it says the trumpets would be a **FOREVER ORDIANCE**. <u>It also says the priests shall blow the trumpets, as well as the princes.</u>

Here's something fascinating and thought-provoking. As believers in Christ we are called a "kingdom of priests" and a "holy nation". Jesus tore down the dividing wall that separated us from the father in heaven. We no longer needed a priest to make atonement for us. Jesus became our priest and we have full access to him any time. **In the verses above it says the priests and princes are to keep the trumpets (shofars) a <u>forever</u> ordinance. That means even Christians are to remember the trumpet call.** Why? Well, we know from reading scripture that Jesus will return at the sound of the last trump. In 1 Thessalonians 4:16, it says, "For the Lord himself shall descend from heaven with a shout, with the voice of the archangel, and with the trump of God: and the dead in Christ shall rise first." We know his return will be preceded by the sound of the trumpet!

Let's go back to the title of the passage: the silver trumpets. What does silver represent? **Redemption!** When Jesus returns at the sound of the "Last Trump"- at the trumpet's call, we can be assured he is here to redeem. Not only that, we know he will also redeem the land of Israel. In Numbers 10 it says to blow the trumpet and we will be saved from our enemies. One day Jesus will step foot on the Mount of Olives and the enemies of Israel will be defeated. In Zachariah 14, it says the enemies of Israel will be struck by a horrible fate- their flesh and eyes will rot, along with their tongues (perhaps nuclear warfare or great fire). This may happen on the Day of the Lord. This is a day where the Lord will fight for Israel. Ezekiel 38 and 39 attest to this as well. Revelation 19 further backs this up.

As far as the trumpet sounding, keep in mind the trumpet's use is multi-faceted. The trumpet will be sounded at the rapture, but it will also be sounded at events after the rapture. During the seven year tribulation, the Bride of Christ, who was raptured, will be in "the hidden place" in heaven. Like Rahab who was spared in Jericho, the Bride will be spared the tribulation. Some scholars think the Bride will go through some of the tribulation- at least three and a half years of it. They believe in a mid-trib rapture. I personally think it will be more like the **Jewish wedding**, since Jesus is Jewish. I believe the seven years will be spent in Jesus' hidden place on his father's property in heaven (see John 14:2). Rosh Hashanah is called *the Hidden Day*- the day when no one knew the day or hour- except the Bride. **The Bride was ready and waiting for the call of the trumpet**. Even though the Groom came like a thief in the night, she was awake at the sound of the trumpet. That's why the blast of the trumpet is a **FOREVER ORDINANCE**.

After the seven years are over **another trumpet will be sounded**. This is the one where the BRIDE RETURNS WITH JESUS. We return with him, but he does all the fighting. Did you know the name **BOAZ** means man of standing, or gibbor hayil. This actually means **"war hero"**. The story of Ruth highlights Boaz, the man who would redeem a foreigner named Ruth, and an Israelite widow named Naomi. This man would create a family line from a foreigner and from the nation of Israel- *the Jew and Gentile would be merged into the family of God*. When Jesus returns, like Boaz, **he will be a true war hero.** He will have his Bride (both Jewish and Gentile believers) with him. He will step foot on planet earth and it will FINALLY BE FINISHED! The land will be fully redeemed and a new age will begin.

Did you know something amazing was discovered in 1968 that backs up the use of the trumpet in the Holy Temple? Not long after the Six Day War in 1967, when Israel gained control over all of Jerusalem, Benjamin Mazar was conducting an excavation of the southwest corner of the Temple Mount in Jerusalem when he found something quite astonishing. While digging, large portions of the huge walls built by

King Herod were revealed. When Rome destroyed the Temple in 70 AD they also destroyed its walls. Just as Jesus said in Matthew 24, verses 1 and 2, "And Jesus went out, and departed from the temple: and his disciples came to him for to shew him the buildings of the temple. And Jesus said to them, 'See ye not all these things? Verily I say unto you, **There shall not be left here one stone upon another, that shall not be thrown down'**."

In accordance with Jesus' words, stones were certainly thrown down. During this particular excavation an important stone (one that had been "thrown down"), was found. The excavators discovered a stone that had fallen when the Romans pillaged and destroyed the Temple, along with its surroundings. The stone found contained an inscription which read **"of the place of trumpeting"**. The stone bearing the inscription is thought to be a sign to direct priests who would blow the trumpets to announce the beginning and end of the Sabbath, or to announce the holy feasts/festivals. The Jewish historian Josephus made note of this in his records by saying there was a particular spot where the priests would stand to give "notice" by use of the trumpet to mark the beginning and end of the "seventh day". (*Josephus: The Jewish War*). Josephus described various areas of the Temple and he makes note of a designated place for the priests to blow the trumpets.

The stone can now be found in the Israel Museum in Jerusalem. The words on the stone- ***the place of trumpeting***- may seem historical, and nothing more. Yet, in the hearts of all believers, it should be a reminder of a promise. The promise is that our kinsman redeemer- Jesus (Boaz) will restore things here on Earth. The physical temple has been destroyed, but not the spiritual one. That temple lives within the Bride of Jesus, awaiting the day when he will return at the blast of the trumpet. The trumpet will call forth an assembly of believers, and take them to the *true place of the Sabbath rest.*

The Bible is more than just laws and stories. Within its pages are layers of mysteries, waiting to be unraveled. If we ask God for guidance he will open our eyes to the deep levels of meaning within. We can look on the surface and I suppose we will get the facts. But, we will leave behind the best parts- we leave behind the very fingerprints of God. God will give us as much as we ask for. But, once we ask, be prepared to follow God on a journey. Just like Ruth, who journeyed to a foreign land, be prepared to go on a journey into new territory. Be prepared to glean new revelations. But, above all, be prepared to receive the awesomeness of God. Then, the Bible will be more than rules, stories and parables. It will be your LIFE.

Blessings to everyone. I hope to see you someday "in the air" at the trumpet call.

HEBREW MONTHS CORRESPONDING WITH WESTERN (GREGORIAN) CALENDAR MONTHS

HEBREW MONTH	WESTERN CALENDAR MONTHS	FEASTS OF THE LORD OCCURING DURING THE MONTH
NISAN	March/April	Passover, Feast of Unleavened Bread, First Fruits
IYYAR	April/May	
SIVAN	May/June	Shavuot/Pentecost
TAMMUZ	June/July	
AV	July/Aug	Tisha B AV
ELUL	Aug/Sept	month of repentance
TISHREI	Sept/Oct	Rosh Hashanah, Yom Kippur, Feast of Tabernacles
HESHVAN	Oct/Nov	
KISLEV	Nov/Dec	Hanukkah

TEVET	Dec/Jan	
SHEVAT	Jan/Feb	
ADAR	Feb/March	Purim

The Feast/holiday dates will occur at different dates each year *on the Western calendar.* Refer to a Hebrew/Jewish calendar for specific dates each year. A table is provided on the following page for Rosh Hashanah and Yom Kippur for the next eight years. The date remains the same on a Hebrew calendar, but most people still have to align their schedule with the Western calendar for purposes of work and school schedules.

DATES FOR ROSH HASHANAH (FEAST OF TRUMPETS) AND YOM KIPPUR (DAY OF ATONEMENT) FOR THE NEXT EIGHT YEARS 2017-2024

Keep in mind the dates vary each year (on the Western Gregorian calendar) because the Hebrew calendar follows the cycles of the Moon and the Sun, unlike the traditional Gregorian calendar, which only follows the Sun.

2017

ROSH HASHANAH- Begins at sundown on September 20 and ends the evening (sundown) of Friday, September 22

YOM KIPPUR- Begins at sundown on September 29 and ends at sundown on September 30

This is the year a solar eclipse will touch United States land exclusively- bisecting the nation- August 21, 2017 (the first day of Elul- one month before Rosh Hashanah)

2018

ROSH HASHANAH- Begins at sundown on September 9, and ends at sundown on September 11

YOM KIPPUR- Begins at sundown on September 18 and ends at sundown on September 19

2019

ROSH HASHANAH- Begins at sundown on September 29, and ends at sundown on October 1

YOM KIPPUR- Begins at sundown on October 8 and ends at sundown on October 9

2020
ROSH HASHANAH- Begins at sundown on September 18, and ends at sundown on September 20
YOM KIPPUR- Begins at sundown on September 27 and ends at sundown on September 28

2021
ROSH HASHANAH- Begins at sundown on September 6 and ends at sundown on September 8
YOM KIPPUR- Begins at sundown on September 15 and ends at sundown on September 16

2022
ROSH HASHANAH- Begins at sundown on September 25, and ends at sundown on September 27
YOM KIPPUR- Begins at sundown on October 4 and ends at sundown on October 5

2023
ROSH HASHANAH – Begins at sundown on September 15 and ends at sundown on September 17
YOM KIPPUR- Begins at sundown on September 24 and ends at sundown on September 25

2024
ROSH HASHANAH- Begins at sundown on October 2 and ends at sundown on October 4
YOM KIPPUR- Begins at sundown on October 11 and ends at sundown on October 12

This is the year of the second total solar eclipse to touch the United States (also passes through Mexico and Canada)- April 8, 2024

On a Hebrew calendar Rosh Hashanah always occurs on Tishrei 1 and is usually celebrated up through Tishrei 2.
Yom Kippur always occurs on the 10th day of Tishrei.

MORE ECLIPSE FACTS

States Within The Shadow Of The August 21, 2017 Total Solar Eclipse:

Oregon, Idaho, Montana, Wyoming, Nebraska, Kansas, Missouri, Iowa, Illinois, Kentucky, Tennessee, Georgia, North Carolina and South Carolina. *Montana has very limited visibility- only the southwestern tip of Montana sees totality. Iowa has limited visibility as well- only about 450 acres of the southwestern tip is in the path. You will get a better view in one of the other states listed above.*

States Within The Shadow Of The April 8, 2024 Solar Eclipse

Texas, Arkansas, Missouri, Illinois, Kentucky, Indiana, Michigan, Ohio, Pennsylvania, New York state, Vermont and New Hampshire
STATES OF OVERLAP (WITHIN PATH OF BOTH ECLIPSES): <u>ILLINOIS, MISSOURI, KENTUCKY</u>

Historical Dates That Line Up With Solar Eclipse Dates

AUGUST 21, 2017 – TOTAL SOLAR ECLIPSE ON U.S. SOIL

August 21, 1858- First Lincoln-Douglas debate in Illinois (In November of 1860, Lincoln beats Douglas for the Presidency)- *Lincoln is considered the first Republican*

August 21, 1942- A Nazi flag is installed on top of Mount Elbrus, the highest mountain in Europe. A sure sign of evil..........

August 21, 1959- Hawaii becomes the 50th state (the **last** U.S. state- **our nation's most recent piece of acquired LAND**). It is the only U.S. state located outside North America. It is awfully close to North Korea.

APRIL 8, 2024 TOTAL SOLAR ECLIPSE ON U.S. SOIL AND MEXICO, CANADA

On April 8, 1864- the U.S. Senate approves the 13th Amendment and sends it to the states to be ratified- (Emancipation of slaves)

On April 8, 1865- (Civil War) General George A Custer's Union cavalry captured a supply train and drove off its Confederate defenders. General Custer was able to capture and burn three trains which were full of supplies and provisions for the Confederate Army under General Robert E Lee. **On April 8**, Phillip Sheridan attacks a rail depot near Appomattox Court House. The rebel forces were driven back and important supplies/provisions were captured. On April 9, the Battle of Appomattox Court House was fought and is considered the last **major** battle of the Civil War. This was the last battle for Robert E Lee's Army (in northern Virginia) before surrendering to the Union. **So, this date lines up with the surrender and ultimate ending of the Civil War.**

BIBLIOGRAPHY:

The following are resources I used in my research for this book

Aish.com

Annefrank.org

Answers in Genesis: **The Walls of Jericho**, 1999 online article : **answersingenesis.org**

Audubon Society: **www.audubon.org**

Battle Hymn of the Republic (Public Domain), first written by Julia Ward Howe in November, 1861- published in February 1862

Beth Moore: **Embracing Jesus** (Two Day workshop presentation, Orlando, Florida), April 2017

Chosen People Ministries: **www.chosenpeople.com**

Eisenhower.archives.gov

Hebrew for Christians: **www.hebrew4christians.com**

History.com

How the States Got Their Shapes, by Mark Stein, MJF books (Fine Communications), 2008

In God We Trust, by Richard G. Lee, published by Thomas Nelson, 1982

Lion and the Lamb Ministries website: **lionandlambministries.org**

Mark Biltz, El Shaddai Ministries- *online resources*- Feasts of the Lord - **www.elshaddaiministries.us**

My Jewish Learning: **www.myjewishlearning.com**

National Archives: Abraham Lincoln, **archives.gov**

National Geographic- **nationalgeographic.com**

Pray for Zion: **www.pray4zion.org**

The Great American Eclipse website: **www.greatamericaneclipse.com**

The Diary of Anne Frank- Translated from Dutch by B.M. Mooyaart-Doubleday, published by Bantam Books, 1952 by Otto Frank and 1967 by Doubleday (Randomhouse)

The Hiding Place, by Corrie ten Boom, 35th Anniversary Edition with Elizabeth and John Sherrill (2006), by Chosen Books, 1971, 1984

Ruth: The Living Room Series, by Kelly Minter, Adult Ministry Publishing, Lifeway Church Resources, 2009

Shofar call international: **www.shofarcall.com/teaching**

Strong's Concordance: NAS Exhaustive Concordance of the Bible with Hebrew-Aramaic and Greek Dictionaries, 1981, 1998 by the Lockman Foundation. Lockman.org

Wikipedia: for general facts

Scriptures taken from the Holy Bible, King James Version, and New International Version (full citing on copyright page)

PHOTOS

This is a picture of the hawk I describe in the story. He is eating the squirrel carcass. *Photo credit: Jennifer NeSmith*

This is one of the neighborhood stone markers I mention in the story. There are markers at both entrances of my neighborhood. They both look like this. The hawk pictured above was sitting on one. This is also where the lightning strike occurred. *Photo credit: Angela Rodriguez*

This is the Kingfisher Drive street sign- notice it is near the neighborhood stone marker. I was almost struck by lightning in between the Kingfisher sign and the marker. *Photo credit: Angela Rodriguez*

This is the eagle picture I mention in the story (sitting on electrical pole 13- *the picture that was pulled up on Facebook.* The eagle was spotted and photographed by my neighbor. *Photo credit: Shannon Cloud*

Here's a picture of the street signs near the spot where the eagle above was photographed. Dawley means **gathering.** Verse reference: "For wheresoever the carcase is, there will the eagles be gathered together"- the Rapture. Interestingly enough, the book/movie *Left Behind* stars a main character who is left behind- his name is Rayford Steele. Different spelling than Raeford above, but the same name. *Photo credit: Angela Rodriguez*

One day I was visiting a cemetery with my son Jonah. As I looked at the graves I made the comment, "When the **rapture** happens, the bodies of believers will be resurrected to be with Jesus." In a flash, this owl flew over our heads and landed in a nearby tree. He sat quietly and posed for over half an hour. Owls are **raptors**, which means they snatch their prey from the air, or off the ground. *Photo credit: Angela Rodriguez*

This is my sweet little cat Mango. A few months before I knew where the solar eclipses were intersecting, I kept feeling like the word Mango was important. I didn't know why. Eventually I found out the eclipses intersect in Makanda, Illinois. *Makanda means Mango. Photo credit: Angela Rodriguez*

This is a picture of the inside cover of the Bible that belonged to my grandmother- Mary Ann McQueen. Note up top where it says: *Given by Mrs. W.B. Mount on May 27, 1967. Mrs. Mount had just returned from the Holy Land.* There is a piece of Jerusalem Olive Wood under the inscription. I found the Bible at my mother's house in Tennessee, located on Highway 67. 1967 is the year Israel reclaimed East Jerusalem and unified God's holy capital.

This is the picture I took at the doctor's office after I'd just finished reading *The Hiding Place*, by Corrie ten Boom. The "hole in the wall" reminded me of the hiding place from the story. You may be able to see the reflection of my phone and hand in the picture. *Photo credit: Angela Rodriguez*

www.ingramcontent.com/pod-product-compliance
Lightning Source LLC
LaVergne TN
LVHW051038080426
835508LV00019B/1581